P229 ~ 252

Example

Writing Academic English

A WRITING AND SENTENCE STRUCTURE HANDBOOK

SECOND EDITION

Alice Oshima • *City College of San Francisco*
Ann Hogue • *College of Marin*

Editorial: Kathleen Sands Boehmer
Manufacturing/Production: James W. Gibbons
Editorial/Production Services: Jeanine Ardourel & Associates
Text Design: Al Burkhardt
Cover Design: John F. Kelly

Acknowledgments:

p. 30, Culture, Logic, and Rhetoric: Adapted with permission of *Language Learning* and Robert B. Kaplan.
p. 67, World Refugees: Adapted from *Newsweek*, April 28, 1980. © Newsweek, Inc. All rights reserved.
p. 69, Nonverbal Communication: Adaptation reprinted with permission of Macmillan Publishing Company from *An Introduction to Intercultural Communication* by John C. Condon and Fathi Yousef © 1975 by Macmillan Publishing Company.
p. 71, Chart and Global Distribution of CO_2 Emissions: © *National Geographic.*
p. 72, Global Temperatures. World Watch/NASA
p. 72, Carbon Dioxide in the Atmosphere: *Sierra* Vol. 74, No. 4, July/August 1989, "Turning Down the Heat" by James R. Udall.
pp. 96–97, How a Solar Hot Water System Works: Daystar Corporation.
p. 101, Native American Influences on Modern American Culture: Adapted from *Writing English: A Composition Text in English as a Foreign Language* by Janet Ross and Gladys Doty. Copyright © 1975 by Harper & Row, Publishers, Inc. Reprinted by permission of Harper Collins Publishers.
p. 132, Job-Hopping Suddenly Becomes Rage in Japan: Adapted from Michael Berger, *San Francisco Chronicle*, March 19, 1990 © *San Francisco Chronicle.* Reprinted by permission.
pp. 134, 136, 137: Artificial Languages: Excerpts from *All About Language* by Mario A. Pei. Copyright 1954 by Mario A. Pei. Reprinted by permission of Harper & Row, Publishers, Inc.
p. 136, Our Growing Deserts: Reprinted by permission of the *Bulletin of the Atomic Scientists.* Copyright © 1978 by the Educational Foundation for Nuclear Science, 6042 South Kimbark Avenue, Chicago, IL 60637, USA.
pp. 139–40, Convenience Goods: Jerry B. Poe, *An Introduction to the American Business Enterprise*, 7th Ed., pp. 383–384. © 1989. Richard B. Irwin, Inc., Homewood, IL.
p. 149: *Readers' Guide to Periodical Literature*, 1990. Copyright © 1990 by the H.W. Wilson Company. Material reproduced with permission of the publisher.

Printed in the United States of America.

ISBN 0-201-51409-5

18 19 20-WC-99 98

Contents

Preface ix

To the Student xiii

PART ONE ***Writing a Paragraph*** 1

1 **What Is Academic Writing?** 2

Audience, Tone, and Purpose 2
The Writing Process, Stage 1: Prewriting 3
Prewriting Step 1: Choosing and Narrowing a Topic 4
Prewriting Step 2: Brainstorming 4
The Writing Process, Stage II: Planning (Outlining) 9
Step 1: Brainstorming by Listing 9
Step 2: Grouping 10
Step 3: Writing the Topic Sentence 11
Step 4: Simple Outlining 11
The Writing Process, Stage III: Writing and Revising Drafts 12
Step 1: Writing the First Rough Draft 12
Step 2: Revising Content and Organization 12
Step 3: Proofreading the Second Draft for Grammar and Mechanics 13
Step 4: Writing the Final Copy 13
Review 15

2 What Is a Paragraph? An Overview **16**

Paragraph Structure 16

The Three Parts of a Paragraph 17

Unity and Coherence 17

The Assignment Format 18

How to Write a Title 19

The Topic Sentence 19

Position of Topic Sentences 20

The Two Parts of a Topic Sentence 22

Writing Topic Sentences: Two Reminders 23

The Concluding Sentence 25

Review 27

3 Unity and Simple Outlining **29**

Unity 29

Simple Paragraph Outlining 33

The "Parallel Form" Rule 34

The "Equivalent Value" Rule 35

Review 37

4 Coherence **39**

Repetition of Key Nouns 39

Use of Consistent Pronouns 41

Transition Signals 41

Types of Transition Signals 42

Logical Order 48

Review 50

5 Kinds of Logical Order **53**

Chronological Order 53

Topic Sentences 55

Transition Signals 56

Writing a Chronological Paragraph 57

Logical Division of Ideas 58

Transition Signals for Logical Division 59

Order of Importance 60

Transition Signals for Order of Importance 60

Two Topic Sentence Tips 62

Review 63

6 Concrete Support **65**

Facts Versus Opinions 65

Concrete Supporting Details 67

Examples and Illustrative Incidents 68

Figures and Statistics 70

Review 73

PART TWO **Writing an Essay** 75

7 The Essay 76

Writing an Essay 76
The Introductory Paragraph 78
The Concluding Paragraph 82
Essay Outlining 83
Transition Signals Between Paragraphs 86
The Writing Process (Continued): Writing and Revising the Essay 89
The Final Copy 92
Review 93

8 Patterns of Essay Organization 95

Chronological Order 95
Organization 98
Thesis Statements for Chronological Order 99
Logical Division 100
Transition Signals and Thesis Statements 102
Cause and Effect 104
Organization 104
Transition Paragraphs 104
Chain Organization 106
Cause and Effect Structure Words 108
Comparison and Contrast 113
Comparison Structure Vocabulary 115
Contrast Structure Vocabulary 119
Organization 122
Review 125

PART THREE **Using Outside References** 127

9 Quotations, Paraphrases, and Summaries 128

Quotations 128
Reporting Verbs and Phrases 130
Paraphrasing 133
Writing a Paraphrase 135
Summarizing 137
Writing a Summary 137
Documenting Sources 140
Citations Within the Text 141
Preparing a List of Works Cited 141
Review 144

10 Using the Library **145**

The Card Catalog 145

Reading the Cards 146

Periodical Indexes 147

Other Sources of Information 150

Reference Books 150

Microfilm 150

Computer Data Banks 150

Review 152

PART FOUR **Sentence Structure** **153**

11 Types of Sentences **154**

Clauses 154

Independent Clauses 154

Dependent Clauses 155

Clause Connectors 155

Kinds of Sentences 156

Simple Sentences 156

Compound Sentences 157

Complex Sentences 161

Compound-Complex Sentences 164

Coordination vs. Subordination 165

Review 167

Parallelism 168

Conjunctions—And, Or, But 168

Correlative Conjunctions 169

Review 171

Sentence Problems 171

Sentence Fragments 171

Choppy Sentences 173

Run-On Sentences and Comma Splices 175

Stringy Sentences 177

Review 179

12 Noun Clauses **180**

Types of Noun Clauses 180

Sequence of Tenses 182

That-Clauses 182

Subjunctive Noun Clauses 184

Wh-Question Clauses 186

Subject Pattern 186

Object Pattern 188

Yes/No Question Clauses 190

Review 193

13 Adverbial Clauses 195

Types of Adverbial Clauses 195
Time Clauses 196
Place Clauses 197
Manner, Distance, and Frequency Clauses 198
Reason Clauses 200
Result Clauses 201
Purpose Clauses 202
Concession Clauses 203
Strong Contrast Adverbial Clauses 204
Review 205

14 Relative Clauses 208

Relative Pronouns and Adverbs 208
Position of Relative Clauses 209
Punctuation of Relative Clauses 209
Relative Pronouns as Subjects 211
Relative Pronouns as Objects 213
Possessive Relative Clauses 215
Possessive—Subject Pattern 215
Possessive—Object Pattern 216
Relative Pronouns as Objects of Prepositions 218
Relative Pronouns in Phrases of Quantity 220
Relative Pronouns in Phrases of Quality 222
Relative Adverbial Clauses 224
Review of Relative Clause Patterns 225
Relative Adverbs 226
The Relative Clause 226

15 Participles and Gerunds 229

Participles 229
Participial Phrases 230
Participial Phrases from Relative Clauses 230
General Forms in the Active Voice 231
General Forms in the Passive Voice 232
The Continuous Form 232
Perfect Forms 233
Punctuating Participial Phrases 234
Participial Phrases from Adverbial Clauses 238
Participial Phrases from Time Clauses 238
Participial Phrases from Reason Clauses 242
Participial Phrases from Simple Sentences 245
Gerunds 248
Gerunds Used as Subjects 248
Gerunds Used as Objects 249
Gerunds as Objects of Prepositions 250
Review 251
Participles 251
Gerunds 252

APPENDIXES

A Punctuation **253**

Commas 253

Introducers 254

Coordinators 254

Inserters 255

Linkers 255

Semicolons 256

Between Sentences 256

Before Connectors 257

Between Items in a Series 257

Colons 259

Lists 259

Long Quotations 259

Subtitles 259

Time 259

Formal Salutations 260

Quotation Marks 260

Direct Quote 260

Unusual Words 261

Titles 261

B Chart of Transition Signals **262**

C Summary of Verb Forms **264**

The Present Tenses 265

The Past Tenses 266

The Future Tenses 267

INDEX **271**

Preface

Writing Academic English is a comprehensive rhetoric and sentence structure textbook/workbook for intermediate to advanced college or college-bound international students and English as a second language students. It can also be used for native speakers of English who must develop the basic skills of paragraph and essay organization or who need to brush up on sentence structure and specific mechanics of English.

The textbook teaches the steps in the writing process, the parts of a paragraph and the important elements contained therein, the parts of the basic essay, and several important patterns of organization. In addition, the text teaches how to use outside references, reviews basic sentence structures, with special emphasis on subordinated structures, and gives practice in other important academic writing skills such as writing under time pressure, summarizing, and paraphrasing.

The book demystifies the process of composition by using a step-by-step method of teaching paragraph and essay writing. The paragraph and essay forms are broken down into small, learnable parts. The students learn and work on each part before going on to the next one. After each part is presented, it is repeated again in subsequent lessons until, finally, the parts grow to become the whole—the paragraph or the essay. Through this method, we hope that students will develop confidence in their ability to write the academic English necessary for all college work.

Because most academic writing is expository in nature, we have purposely limited the rhetorical components to exposition. The material in the book is based on current and general topics of interest and provides practice exercises with technical, scientific, and business contexts.

The book is divided into four main parts: Writing a Paragraph, Writing an Essay, Using Outside References, and Sentence Structure. The parts are further divided into chapters. Each chapter provides model paragraphs, clear explanations, and exercises, and ends with a review of the important points of the chapter. The appendixes provide a review of punctuation rules, a chart of transition signals, and a summary of verb forms.

Additional features of the book include charts of various structure words and glossing of scientific and technical terms and other potentially unfamiliar vocabulary. Part I includes Writing Under Pressure assignments, giving students the opportunity to practice the skills they have learned in a particular chapter in a mock test-taking situation, forcing them to think, organize, and write under the pressure of time. This part also includes at the end of each chapter a cumulative Paragraph Checklist for students to refer to when completing their writing assignments. Part II includes for easy reference Essay Checklists as well as structure vocabulary charts for various forms of essay organization.

As the first edition, this second edition of *Writing Academic English* retains the same major focus of paragraph and essay organization and development and emphasis on improvement of sentence structure. This new edition also maintains the step-by-step approach to teaching writing. However, Chapter 1, which explains the steps of the writing process, is new, and Chapter 4, Coherence, has been expanded to include sections on repetition of key nouns and the use of consistent pronouns. Part III, Using Outside References, has been extensively revised to provide more detailed and clearer explanations. The chapters on passive and conditional sentences have been deleted, and a section on gerunds has been added. New models on current topics of general interest have also been added. Finally, numerous other deletions, additions, and revisions have been made to help the students understand and learn the process of writing more easily.

Suggestions for Using the Text

Writing Academic English is intended to be covered in one 15-week semester, for classes meeting five days a week. This requires a fairly rapid pace, however, and may not permit thorough treatment of each and every chapter in Part III, Using Outside References, and Part IV, Sentence Structure. If the class meets three days a week, it will take two semesters to complete the book.

Here are some teaching suggestions that you might consider:

Brainstorming

For class brainstorming, choose a familiar topic and write it on the chalkboard. Encourage the students to brainstorm the topic while you write their responses on the chalkboard. Extend the list by asking students questions relevant to the topic to generate more ideas.

As often as possible, have students break up into small groups. One student in each group should be the recorder. You may allow each group to agree upon a topic, or you may assign one.

Topic Suggestions

The topics given for each writing assignment are only suggestions. Keep an eye out for interesting and challenging topics from current events. Weekly news magazines are a good source of graphs and charts, which can be used as the basis of many good paragraphs.

Practice Exercises

The final practice exercises of the grammar chapters usually ask students to produce six or eight sentences (or occasionally a paragraph) of their own. Because these are the most important practices of the entire chapter since they show whether the students can produce the structure correctly on their own, we hope that you are not tempted to skip these practices.

Order of Lesson Presentation

The separation of sentence structure from rhetoric allows each instructor flexibility in order of lesson presentation; however, we have some suggestions. Only the chapters in Part I (Writing a Paragraph), must be taught in sequence, although we recommend that the first chapters of Parts II (Writing an Essay) and IV (Sentence Structure), which serve as introductory overviews, be taught before the succeeding chapters. It is a good idea to teach parallelism (in Part IV, Sentence Structure) and use of the colon (Appendix A, Punctuation) before teaching the thesis statement. Also, if you teach adverbial time clauses before chronological order, the students will not only learn to write these clauses correctly but will also recognize their importance in this form of organization.

Verb Forms

The Summary of Verb Forms (Appendix C) is a handy reference for all students and is a review for those students who have problems with a particular tense. Any student having problems could review the rules for a specific tense on his/her own, and, if necessary, you can provide supplementary exercises for the student to complete. As a final step, the student would be asked to hand in several original sentences (or better yet, a paragraph) using a particular verb tense. You can assign topics that naturally elicit a particular tense.

In-Class Writing

In-class writing assignments are especially helpful in the early stages because you are available for immediate consultation. Also, you can work your way around the room checking to make sure that everyone is on the right track. We feel, however, that even with in-class assignments, each student should make the initial effort independently. The pair and group work can involve brainstorming, writing, and editing.

Acknowledgments

We dedicate this book to our students, who were the intellectual stimulus for our writing the book in the first place. Our special thanks go to the reviewers; Jeanine Ardourel, our editor; and finally to our colleagues, whose invaluable suggestions and encouragement have been helpful in the development of the second edition: Warren D. Anderson, Southern Illinois University; Deborah S. Hardwick, Houston Community College; Mary Anne Saunders, George Washington University; Cynthia Weber, Berkeley Adult School; Thomas Tragardh, Joan Meehan, and Kathleen Moriwaki, City College of San Francisco; and Barbara Bonander, Margaret Smith, and Liz Terplan, College of Marin. Finally, we wish to thank our families, without whose support and patience this book would not have become a reality. To everyone, we are truly grateful.

A.O., A.H.

To the Student

Many people have the mistaken notion* that being able to write well is a talent that one either has or doesn't have. This is not necessarily true. You can learn to write effectively if you are willing to learn some strategies and practice them.

Writing is a skill that people in all walks of life* must perform almost daily. A department manager for any kind of company, for example, may write a report to his/her boss requesting more money or more personnel. The boss, in turn, writes reports to the company's stockholders and corresponds with the company's customers, banks, insurers, and so on.

Even as an ordinary citizen, you occasionally have to write business letters. If you are dissatisfied with something you have bought and want a replacement or a refund, you must write a letter. If you break your new desk lamp, you might have to write to the manufacturer to get a new part. Knowing how to write effectively will get results faster.

As a student, you are facing and will face many writing tasks in order to complete your education successfully. Then, after graduating, you will write letters to businesses when you look for a job. Whether or not you are invited for interviews will depend on the impression your letters make.

Now is the time to learn some strategies so that the activity of writing will become a challenging and even enjoyable task.

Good writing in English requires good grammar and good organization. In this book, you will study both. You will learn selected* grammatical structures in order to perfect your grammar and improve your style. You will also learn to organize your thoughts in writing. At the end of the semester, you will know how to organize your

---

notion: idea **walks of life:** occupations **selected:** chosen

ideas quickly and write about them clearly, and you will be able to write in the sophisticated,* mature style required in academic courses.

The first part of this book presents the basic principles* of English rhetoric.* Rhetoric has two aspects*: organization and style. English rhetoric is very different from the rhetoric of your native language. Good style in Chinese or Japanese is very different from good style in English; good organization in Arabic, Persian, and Spanish is very different from good organization in English. Therefore, in order to write well in English, you must learn not only the rules of English grammar, but also the principles of English rhetoric. Learning the principles of rheotric is just like learning the rules of grammar: first you must study them, then you must practice them.

If you read carefully and do all of the practices thoughtfully, we guarantee* that your writing will improve. We also guarantee that you will find the task* of writing much, much easier.

---

sophisticated: complex
principles: rules
rhetoric: the art of writing
aspects: parts
guarantee: promise
task: job, work

PART

Writing a Paragraph

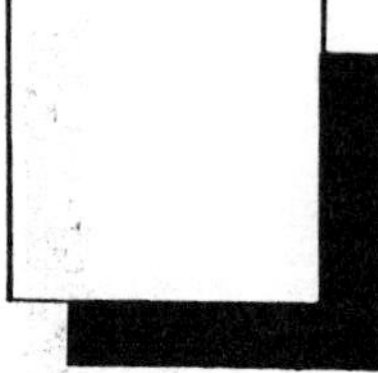

CHAPTER 1

What Is Academic Writing?

Academic writing, as the name implies, is the kind of writing that you are required to do in college or university. It differs from other kinds of writing (personal, literary, journalistic, business, etc.) in several ways. Its differences can be explained in part by its special audience, tone, and purpose.

Audience, Tone, and Purpose

Whenever you write, consider your audience, that is, the people who will read what you have written. Knowing your audience will help you reach your goal of communicating clearly and effectively. For example, you may write letters to friends to tell them what a great time you are having socializing in school while neglecting* your studies. You may have to write an essay for a history, political science, psychology, or English exam. Later, you may have to write a letter to a prospective* employer. Each of these letters has a specific audience, and what you say and how you say it will affect your audience's understanding of your message. In academic writing, your audience is primarily your professors.

Not only should you be concerned with your audience, but you should also be concerned with the tone of your writing. Tone reveals your attitude towards your subject by your choice of words, by your choice of grammatical structures, and even by the length of your sentences. A letter to a friend, for example, would have a friendly, personal tone; it would probably contain some "slang" expressions and many active verb forms. A technical or scientific paper, by contrast, would contain more passive verb forms and technical vocabulary; it would have a highly formal, impersonal tone.

---

neglecting: not paying attention to **prospective:** possible or future

The tone of a piece of writing is determined more by its intended audience than by its subject matter. For example, the latest medical research in the United States is reported in *The American Journal of Medicine*. These scientific articles are written for a very special audience of scientists and doctors who understand medical and technical vocabulary. However, if the same articles were written for newspapers or popular magazines, they would be written in general English with technical words explained in everyday vocabulary because the intended audience, the general public, might not understand highly technical terminology. Academic writing is always formal in tone.

No matter what kind of writing you do, you should have a specific and clear purpose. In literary writing, the purpose is often to entertain, whereas journalistic writing usually seeks to inform or to persuade. In academic writing, your purpose will most often be to explain. It may also be to persuade or to convince your audience of the correctness of your point of view on a particular issue.

The purpose of a piece of writing will determine the rhetorical form* chosen for it. For example, an article that tries to persuade readers that nuclear power plants are unsafe has a different purpose from an article that explains how a nuclear power plant operates. The persuasive article will be organized in one way, and the expository* article in another way. In this book, you will learn the basic rhetorical forms of academic writing, starting with single paragraphs and building multiparagraph essays.

As you write each assignment in this course, and later in your life, whenever you need to communicate in writing, keep in mind your audience, tone, and purpose so that the message your reader receives is the message you intend to convey.*

The Writing Process, Stage I: Prewriting

Writing, particularly academic writing, is not easy. It takes study and practice to develop this skill. For both native speakers and new learners of English, it is important to note that writing is a *process*, not a "product." This means that a piece of writing, whether it is a composition for your English class or a Hemingway short story, is never complete; that is, it is always possible to review and revise, and review and revise again. The famous American writer Ernest Hemingway once said that if he wrote one good page a day, he was working well. Since Hemingway spent several hours each day writing, you can imagine how many times this great writer revised his work!

There are four main stages in the writing process: prewriting, planning, writing and revising drafts, and writing the final copy to hand in. Each stage will be explained and practiced in Part I of this book. In this chapter, you will concentrate on prewriting techniques, which are activities to help you generate* ideas for your writing assignments.

When you are faced with a writing assignment, you may sometimes suffer from "writer's block"; that is, ideas will not easily come into your head, and you sit staring at your blank paper. Writer's block can happen to anyone, even professional writers. Before you begin your study of academic writing, you should learn some techniques for overcoming writer's block and for getting started quickly.

---

rhetorical form: organizational form and style
expository: explanatory
convey: express
generate: produce

Prewriting Step 1: Choosing and Narrowing a Topic

If you are given a specific writing assignment (such as an essay question on an examination), then, of course, what you can write about is limited. On the other hand, when you are given a free choice of subjects and can write about something you are interested in, then you must narrow the subject to a particular aspect of that general subject. Suppose you are interested in the environment. It would be impossible to cover such a big topic in a paragraph. You would have to narrow the subject to perhaps environmental pollution, if that is your interest. Environmental pollution, however, is still too broad a topic for a paragraph, so you might even further narrow the topic to a type of environmental pollution, such as pollution of the oceans. However, writing about ocean pollution is still too broad because it would include pollution by oil, chemicals, sewage, and garbage. Therefore, you might decide to write about oil as a source of ocean pollution. Finally, you might make this topic even narrower by writing only about the massive oil spill in Alaska in 1989. The point is, you must narrow the subject of your paragraph to a specific focus so that you can write about it clearly, completely, and effectively.

The diagram below illustrates the process of narrowing a general topic to a specific one.

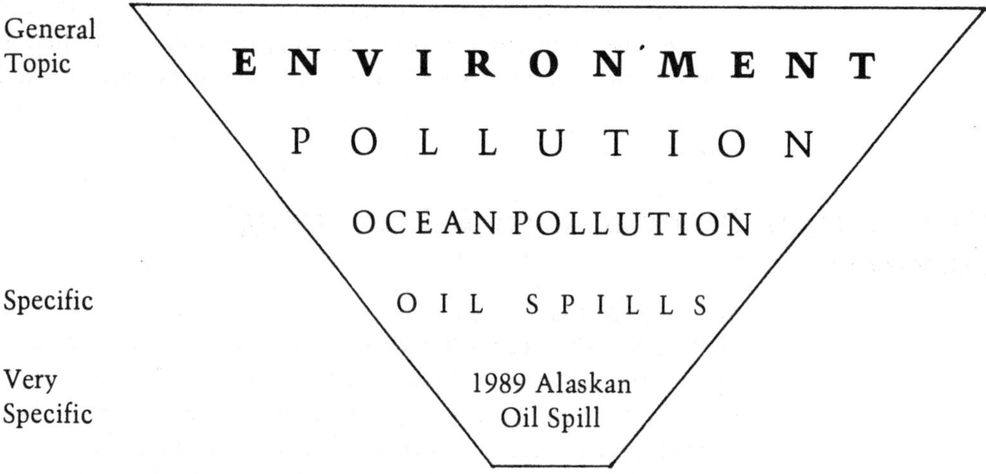

PRACTICE 1: ***Choosing and Narrowing a Topic***

Individually, in a small group, or with your whole class, narrow each of the following general topics to one specific aspect that could be written about in one paragraph.

School
Television
Sports
Entertainment
Food

Prewriting Step 2: Brainstorming

After you have chosen a topic and narrowed it to a specific focus, the next prewriting step is to generate ideas. This is done by a process called brainstorming. Although these brainstorming activities may seem unnecessary at first, after doing them a few times, you will realize their usefulness. Brainstorming for ideas can get you started writing more quickly and save you time in the later stages of the writing process.

Three useful brainstorming techniques are *listing, freewriting,* and *clustering.* Learn how to do each of them and then decide which is the most productive for you.

Listing

Listing is a brainstorming technique in which you think about your topic and quickly make a list of whatever words or phrases come into your head. Your purpose is to produce as many ideas as possible in a short time; your goal is to find a specific focus for your topic.

Follow this procedure:

1. Write down the general topic at the top of your paper.
2. Then, make a list of every word or phrase that comes into your mind about the topic. Don't stop the free flow of ideas by judging or editing them before you write them down. Keep the ideas flowing. The harder you think, the more ideas will flow. Of course, try to stay on the general topic. If, however, you write down information that is completely off the subject, don't worry about it—you can cross it out later.
3. Use words, phrases, or sentences. Don't worry about spelling or grammar. Remember, your primary goal is to jot* down ideas as quickly as they come to you without worrying about whether an idea is important, interesting, or related to your subject. (Try to focus on the topic, however.)

Here is an example of the listing technique on the topic of fitness.

MODEL: *Listing*

Getting Fit*

eating right
junk food
good diet
lots of fresh fruits/vegetables
3 meals a day
regular exercise
lose weight
join health club*
swim every day
regular homework schedule
weightlifting
work hard
play hard
jog before breakfast
feel and look younger
watch less TV
don't eat snacks
lose weight
drive carefully
no red meat
aerobics*
walk to do errands*
drink less coffee
sleep 8 hours
cut out* desserts
no candy, soda
no junk food
relax more on weekends
enjoy friends, family
crash diet*

---

jot: write down quickly **fit:** healthy **health club:** a place where people pay to exercise
aerobics: exercises which help your heart increase the supply of oxygen to your blood
errands: short trips to carry out various tasks (shopping, laundry, post office, bank, etc.)
cut out: stop (doing something)
crash diet: eating less to lose weight quickly

4. Now rewrite your list and group similar ideas together. Cross out ideas which don't fit or are duplications.

eating right
~~junk food~~
A (good diet)
lots of fresh fruits/vegetables
3 meals a day
don't eat snacks
~~lose weight~~
no red meat
drink less coffee
cut out desserts
no candy, soda
no junk food
~~crash diet~~

~~sleep 8 hours~~
~~relax more—weekends~~
~~enjoy friends, family~~

~~drive carefully~~

B (regular exercise)
~~lose weight~~
join health club
swim every day
weightlifting
jog before breakfast
aerobics
walk to do errands

~~regular homework schedule~~
~~watch less TV~~

~~work hard~~
~~play hard~~

feel and look younger

From this new list, it is clear that "good diet" and "regular exercise" have the most ideas, so these are circled. The writer can choose either one as a specific focus for his/her paragraph.

PRACTICE 2: *Brainstorming by Listing*

Brainstorm by listing ideas on one or two of the following topics. Follow the three steps outlined above on page 5.

How to be a good student
Tourist attractions in your country or city
Problems of working students
Problems of foreign students
(one of the topics from Practice 1: Choosing and Narrowing a Topic on page 4)

Freewriting

Freewriting is a brainstorming activity in which you write freely about a topic because you are looking for a specific focus. While you are writing, one idea will spark* another idea. As with listing, the purpose of freewriting is to generate as many ideas as possible and to write them down without worrying about appropriateness, grammar, spelling, logic, or organization.

Follow this procedure:

1. Write the topic at the top of your paper.
2. Write as much as you can about the topic until you run out of ideas. Include information, facts, details, examples, etc., that come into your mind about the subject.

spark: cause to start coming to mind

3. After you have run out of ideas, reread your paper and circle the main idea(s) that you would be interested in developing.
4. Take that main idea and freewrite again.

The purpose of freewriting is to write as much as possible, whether you are looking for a narrow (specific) topic to write about or whether you already have a narrow topic and want to write down ideas about it. Remember, the more you freewrite, the more ideas you will have. Don't despair* if your mind seems to "run dry." Just keep your pencil moving.

Remember that freewriting is a "practice" writing process to generate ideas. It is not the finished copy that you hand to the teacher. You may do several freewriting papers before you decide on a narrow topic to develop for your assignment.

In the following model, the student is supposed to write a paragraph about one major problem at his college. The student doesn't have any idea of what to write about, so he starts freewriting about some of the problems that come to mind. Notice that he has written the purpose of his freewriting activity at the top of the paper as a reminder of what his paragraph focus is.

MODEL: *Freewriting*

Problems at Evergreen College

Audience: My English instructor and classmates

Purpose: To describe a major problem at Evergreen College

What is the biggest problem at Evergreen College? Well, I really don't know. In fact, I can't think of one particular problem although I know there are many problems. For one thing, the classrooms are usually overcrowded. At the beginning of this semester, Science Hall 211 had 45 students although there were only 31 desks. A few of the seats attached to the desks were broken, so about 20 students had to sit on the floor. Besides, the classrooms are poorly maintained. In several of my classes, there are broken chairs and litter on the floor. Students even leave their dirty cups and other garbage on the desks. So the rooms are messy. The library is too small and always crowded with students. Not all students really study in the library. Sometimes they talk a lot and this is really quite distracting to me and other serious students who want and need a quiet place to study. So the present library should be expanded or a new library should be built. Oh yes, I think that another problem is parking near the campus. The college has a big parking lot across the west side of campus, but it is always full. So, many times students have to park their cars in the residential areas, which could be so far away from the campus that they have to run to class to make it. Yes, parking is a big problem that many students face everyday. I have a car, and many of my friends have one. We really have a problem. So, I think the biggest problem at Evergreen College is not enough parking spaces near the college campus . . .

The student kept on freewriting until he found a major problem in his college that sparked his interest: the parking problem at Evergreen College. Notice that after he finished freewriting, the student reread his paper and circled the main ideas, one of which he will consider as the major problem at Evergreen College.

Let's say that the student has decided to choose parking as a major problem at Evergreen College. Now that the student knows the topic that he wants to write about, he will again brainstorm by freewriting; only this time, the specific topic will be on the parking problem only. His freewriting paper might look like this.

---

despair: be discouraged

MODEL: *Freewriting*

The Parking Problem at Evergreen College

Audience: My English instructor and my classmates

Purpose: To describe the biggest problem at Evergreen College

I think finding a parking space close to the campus at Evergreen College is a major problem. There are not enough parking lots for students to park their cars. Therefore, students have to come early to get a parking space, and even then, sometimes they are unlucky and can't get a good parking space. Once I couldn't find a space in the west side parking lot, and I had to drive in the streets for a half hour before I found one. So, I was late for class. Some students are late to class almost every time the English class meets. Some even drop the class, not because they can't handle it, but because they can't find a place to park close to the campus. The teacher warns them time and time again not to be late, but they can't help it.... What is the solution to the parking problem? Maybe the college should spend some funds to construct a multilevel parking lot that will accommodate three times as many cars as the present parking lot holds....

The student can continue freewriting as long as he can generate ideas related to the topic. Then, after completing that task, he can reread it and develop certain points, add some more ideas or even delete others. The student can do this freewriting activity several times until he is satisfied with what he has written.

PRACTICE 3: *Brainstorming by Freewriting*

Clustering is another brainstorming activity that you can use to generate ideas. Here's how to use this technique: In the center of your paper, write your topic and draw a "balloon" around it. This is your center or core balloon. Then write whatever ideas come to you in balloons around the core. Think about each of these ideas and make more balloons around them. Your richest idea will produce a cluster of balloons.

For example, suppose you had to describe a person who is close to you in some way. Using the clustering technique to get ideas, you might end up with a paper such as the following:

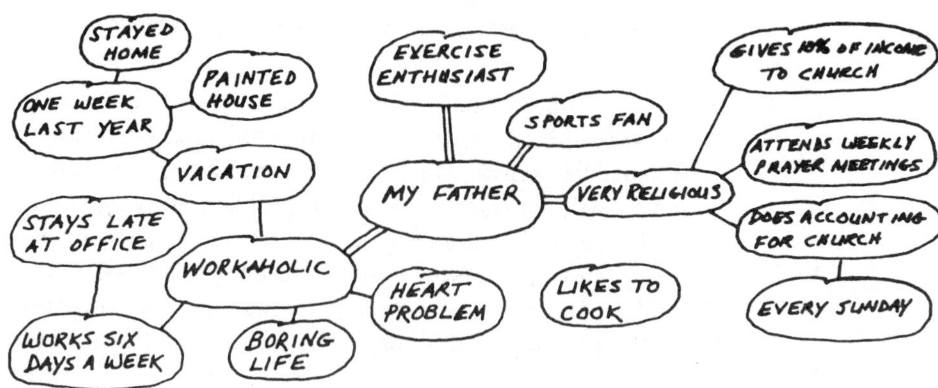

The largest cluster of balloons was generated from the "workaholic" balloon, so this would be a good focus for this student's paragraph about his father.

PRACTICE 4: ***Brainstorming by Clustering***

Use the clustering technique for ten minutes to generate ideas about a person who is close to you.

The Writing Process, Stage II: Planning (Outlining)

In Stage I, you chose topics and narrowed them, and you generated ideas by brainstorming. Now you are ready for Stage II in the process of writing, which is the planning stage.

In the planning stage, you organize the ideas you generated by brainstorming. The most efficient way to do this is to make an outline.

Step 1: Brainstorming by Listing

The following model shows how to develop an outline from a brainstorming list.

MODEL: ***Listing***

Metropolitan City's Problems

buses and streetcars
dirty bus interiors
late bus arrivals
housing is expensive
high property values
need affordable rentals
expensive apartments
impossible to buy property
traffic jams
heavy downtown traffic
late arrivals
arrive in bunches*
missed appointments
commuter traffic
accidents
daily schedules
commuter traffic
passengers are victims
no parking
high rents
shortage of rental units
congested* streets
increasing crime
too many cars
no rent control
unsafe streets
extra waiting time

bunches: groups **congested:** crowded

Step 2: Grouping

The next step is to go over the list and mark all points that relate to the same ideas with the same capital letter: A, B, C, etc.

MODEL: ***Grouping***

Metropolitan City's Problems

A buses and streetcars
A dirty bus interiors
A late bus arrivals
B housing is expensive
B high property values
B need affordable rentals
B expensive apartments
B impossible to buy property
C traffic jams
C heavy downtown traffic
A late arrivals
A arrive in bunches
A missed appointments
C commuter traffic
C accidents
A daily schedules
C commuter traffic
A passengers are victims
C no parking
B high rents
B shortage of rental units
C congested streets
D increasing crime
C too many cars
B no rent control
D unsafe streets
A extra waiting time

Now you can list all the A's, B's, C's, etc. in sublists, as follows. Cross out points which are duplicates or which you don't want to use.

Group A

buses and streetcars
~~dirty bus interiors~~
~~late bus arrivals~~
late arrivals
arrive in bunches
missed appointments
daily schedules
passengers are victims
extra waiting time

"Dirty bus interiors" was crossed out because it is irrelevant.* "Late bus arrivals" was crossed out because it is a duplication. The remaining points are related to either schedule problems or passenger inconvenience, so they can be grouped into two subgroups as follows:

1. Daily schedules
2. Passengers are victims

Now list all of the points which are about the daily schedules:

1. Daily schedules are unreliable.*
   —Late arrivals
   —Arrive in bunches

Do the same for the "passengers are victims" idea:

---

irrelevant: not important to the topic **unreliable:** not dependable, not trustworthy

2. Passengers are victims.
   —Missed appointments
   —Extra waiting time

When you have grouped all of the points into their appropriate subgroup, you have created an outline, or plan, for a paragraph.

Step 3: Writing the Topic Sentence

Finally, develop a topic sentence to cover the points listed under Group A. The topic of Group A is obviously public transportation. Moreover, most of the points are about the unreliability of public transportation. Unreliability is the controlling idea, and a topic sentence might be:

> One problem is the city's unreliable public transportation.

or

> One of the city's biggest problems is the unreliability of its public transportation system.

Step 4: Simple Outlining

An outline is a plan for a paragraph. In an outline, you write down the main points and subpoints in the order in which you plan to write about them. The following is an example of a simple outline of the ideas about the unreliable public transportation in Metropolitan City.

MODEL: *Simple Outline*

Topic sentence	One problem is the city's unreliable public transportation.
Supporting point	1. Daily schedules are unreliable.
Supporting detail	—Late arrivals
Supporting detail	—Arrive in bunches
Supporting point	2. Passengers are victims.
Supporting detail	—Are late to appointments, work, classes
Supporting detail	—Must allow extra time to wait for buses

With this outline in front of you, it should be relatively easy to write a paragraph about the problems of public transportation in Metropolitan City. There is a topic sentence, two main supporting points, and two supporting details for each main point. You could, of course, add some examples and a concluding sentence if you wanted to, but the main planning has been completed.

PRACTICE 5: *Simple Outlining*

Develop a simple outline for Groups B and C of the model on page 10. Use the outline done for Group A (page 11) as your model. Feel free to cross out points that you don't need and add new ideas that are appropriate. Each outline should contain a topic sentence, one or two main supporting points, and one or two supporting details for each main supporting point. You may begin each topic sentence with the words, "Another problem is . . . ."

The Writing Process, Stage III: Writing and Revising Drafts

Stage III in the writing process, after brainstorming and outlining, is to write and revise several drafts until you have produced a final copy to hand in. Remember that no piece of writing is ever perfect the first time. Each time you write a new draft, you will refine and improve your writing.

Step 1: Writing the First Rough Draft

The first step in the revision process is to write a rough draft from your outline. This is how to proceed:

- At the top of your paper, write down your audience and your purpose.
- Write down the topic sentence and underline it. Doing this will remind you of the focus of your paragraph.
- Skip one or two lines per line of writing and leave margins of one inch on both sides of the paper. These blank spaces will allow you to add more details, information, examples, etc., in order for you to fully develop your points. Also, you can add comments in the margins for your attention later on, such as "define ________," "check spelling," "add an example," and so on.
- Write your paragraph, following your outline as closely as possible. Try writing steadily. Don't add ideas which aren't in your outline unless you are certain they are relevant.
- Don't worry about grammar, punctuation, or spelling. This first rough draft does not have to be "perfect"; in fact, it won't be because your main goal is to write down as much information as you can, following the points in your outline.

While you are writing, you may not be able to think of a word or phrase, or you may be unable to complete a thought. Don't worry—just leave a space or a line; it can be filled in later. Also, while you are writing about one major point, you might come up with an idea for another major point. Don't risk forgetting it! Jot it down in the margin of your paper near where it belongs.

Above all, remember that writing is a continuous process of discovery. Therefore, as you are writing, you will think of new ideas that may not be on your brainstorming list or in your outline. You can add new ideas or delete original ones at any time in the writing process. Just be sure that any new ideas are relevant!

Step 2: Revising Content and Organization

After you write the rough draft, the next step is to revise it. When you revise, you change what you have written in order to improve it. You check it over for content and organization, including unity, coherence, and logic[1]. You can change, rearrange, add, or delete, all for the goal of communicating your thoughts more clearly, more effectively, and more interestingly.

During the first revision, do not try to correct grammar, sentence structure, spelling, or punctuation; this is proofreading, which you will do later. During the first revision, be concerned mainly with content and organization.

[1]These terms are explained in later chapters.

This is how to proceed:

- Read over your paragraph carefully for a general overview. Focus on the *general* aspects of the paper and make notations in the margins so that you can rewrite parts that need to be improved.
- Check to see that you have achieved your stated purpose.
- Check for general logic and coherence. Your audience should be able to follow your ideas easily and understand what you have written.
- Check to make sure that your paragraph has a topic sentence and that the topic sentence has a controlling idea.
- Check for unity. Cross out any sentence that does not support the topic sentence.
- Check to make sure that the controlling idea is developed with sufficient supporting details. Be certain that each paragraph gives the reader enough information to understand the main idea. If the main point lacks sufficient information, make a notation in the margin such as: "Add more details" or "add an example." Make sure that you haven't used general statements for support. (Note: Using concrete supporting details will be taken up in Chapter 6.)
- Check your use of transition signals.
- Finally, does your paragraph have or need a concluding sentence? If you wrote a final comment, is it on the topic?

Now, rewrite your paragraph, incorporating all of the necessary revisions. This is your second draft.

Step 3: Proofreading the Second Draft for Grammar and Mechanics

The next step is to proofread your paper to check for grammar, sentence structure, spelling, and punctuation.

- Check over each sentence for correctness and completeness: no fragments or choppy or run-on sentences.
- Check over each sentence for a subject and a verb, subject-verb agreement, correct verb tenses, etc.
- Check the mechanics: punctuation, spelling, capitalization, typing errors, etc.
- Change vocabulary words as necessary.

Step 4: Writing the Final Copy

Now you are ready to write the final copy to hand in. Your instructor will expect it to be written neatly and legibly in ink or typed. Be sure that you make all the corrections that you noted on your second draft. After rereading the final copy, don't be surprised if you decide to make a few minor or even major changes. Remember that writing is a continuous process of writing and rewriting until you are satisfied with the final product.

The following model shows you how one student worked through the process of writing and revising drafts before arriving at the final copy.

MODEL: *The First Rough Draft*

Public Transportation in Metropolitan City

A big problem is Metropolitan's inadequate public transportation system. Thousands of residents rely on the city's buses and streetcars to travel throughout the city. Some people must transfer to other lines more than once before they finally arrive at their destinations. Metro Transportation System's daily scheduels are totally unreliable. A bus or streetcar that is supposed to arrive at 7:45 am. It may not arrive eight o'clock or even later. Unfortunately passengers become unhappy victims of the waiting game. This causes them to be late for work or to miss important appointments. Once I waited so long in incredibly bad weather. I caught a bad cold and ended up in bed for a week. Then, on the day of my psychology exam, the streetcar was thirty minutes late. In order to get to their destinations on time, people must leave home earlier to allow for waiting time at the bus and streetcar stops.

The writer checked the paragraph for unity and decided that the third sentence was off the topic, so she crossed it out. She decided to add the transition expression "for example" in front of the example of unreliability, and she made a note to add more details to support the idea of unreliability. Also, she made a note to add a transition expression before the sentence beginning "I caught . . ." and to check the spelling of "scheduel." Finally, she added a brief concluding sentence. She then wrote the second draft.

MODEL: *The Second Draft*

Public Transportation in Metropolitan City

A big problem is Metropolitan's inadequate public transportation system. Thousands of residents rely on the city's buses and streetcars to travel throughout the city. Metro Transportation System's daily schedules are totally unreliable. For example, a bus or streetcar ~~that is supposed to~~ arrive at 7:45 am. It may not arrive eight o'clock or even later. Sometimes three buses or streetcars will arrive in bunches, one after another. Moreover, it is not unusual for a bus driver or a streetcar conductor to pass up groups of people anxiously waiting in the snow in freezing weather because he is behind schedule and wants to make up for lost time. Unfortunately passengers become unhappy victims of the waiting game. ~~This~~ causes them to be late for work or to miss important appointments. For instance, once I waited so long in ~~incredibly bad~~ weather. I caught a bad cold and ended up in bed for a week. Then, on the day of my psychology exam, the streetcar was thirty minutes late. In order to get to their destinations on time, people must leave home earlier to allow for waiting time at the bus and streetcar stops. [In conclusion,] ~~W~~[w]ith such inadequate public transportation in the city, it is not ~~wonder~~ [surprising] that increasing numbers of people are ~~driving their cars in the city, which increases traffic congestion~~ [turning to private automobiles].

Next, the writer proofread the paragraph for grammar, sentence structure, punctuation, capitalization, etc. She improved the sentence structure by joining the second and third sentences with a comma and "but," and she corrected the faulty sentence structure of the sentence which begins with "For instance." She checked the form of the abbreviation "A.M.," and she corrected the punctuation in two places. She improved her choice of words in several places. She checked over the new concluding sentence she had written and made some changes. Then, she wrote the final copy to hand in.

MODEL: *The Final Copy*

Public Transportation in Metropolitan City

A major problem is Metropolitan's inadequate public transportation system. Thousands of residents rely on the city's buses and streetcars to travel throughout this large city, but Metro Transportation System's daily schedules are totally unreliable. For example, a bus or streetcar that should arrive at 7:45 A.M. may not arrive until eight o'clock or even later. Sometimes three buses or streetcars will arrive in bunches, one after another. Moreover, it is not unusual for a bus driver or a streetcar conductor to pass up groups of people anxiously waiting in the snow in freezing weather because he is behind schedule and wants to make up for lost time. Unfortunately, passengers become unhappy victims of the waiting game, which causes them to be late for work or to miss important appointments. For instance, once I waited so long in below zero weather that I caught a bad cold and ended up in bed for a week. Then, on the day of my psychology exam, the streetcar was thirty minutes late. In order to get to their destinations on time, people must leave home earlier to allow for waiting time at the bus and streetcar stops. In conclusion, with such inadequate public transportation in the city, it is not surprising that increasing numbers of people are turning to private automobiles.

Review

These are the important points you should have learned from this chapter:

1. Academic writing is a special kind of writing for college and university work. It is intended for a specific audience (primarily your instructors and professors).
2. Academic writing is formal in tone.
3. The purpose of academic writing is usually to explain or to persuade. The purpose of a piece of writing will determine its rhetorical form.
4. Prewriting activities are useful for narrowing a topic and generating ideas.
5. Three useful brainstorming techniques are listing, freewriting, and clustering.
6. Revision is an essential part of the writing process. Your first effort is called the rough draft. After checking it for content and organization (using the Paragraph Checklists at the ends of most chapters), write your second draft. Check your second draft for grammar and mechanics, and then write a final copy to hand in.

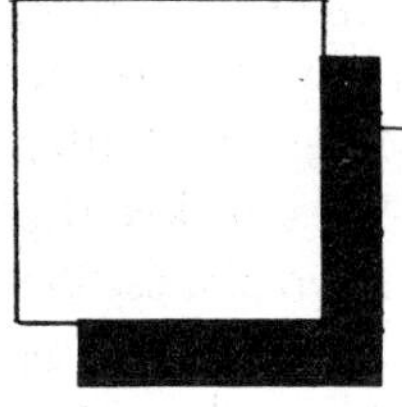

CHAPTER 2

What Is a Paragraph? An Overview

A **paragraph** is a basic unit of organization in writing in which a group of related sentences develops one main idea. A paragraph can be as short as one sentence or as long as ten sentences. The number of sentences is unimportant; however, the paragraph should be long enough to develop the main idea clearly.

A paragraph may stand by itself. In academic writing, a paragraph is often used to answer a test question such as the following: "Define management by objectives, and give one example of it from the reading you have done for this class."

A paragraph may also be one part of a longer piece of writing such as a chapter of a book or an essay. You will first learn how to write good paragraphs, and then you will learn how to combine and expand paragraphs to build essays.

Paragraph Structure

The following model contains all the elements of a good paragraph. Read it carefully two or three times and try to analyze its structure.

MODEL: *Paragraph Structure*

Gold

1 Gold, a precious metal, is prized for two important characteristics. First of all, gold has a lustrous* beauty that is resistant to corrosion.* Therefore, it is suitable for jewelry, coins, and ornamental purposes. Gold never needs to be polished and will remain beautiful forever. For

lustrous: glowing
corrosion: chemical damage

example, a Macedonian* coin remains as untarnished* today as the day it was minted* twenty-three centuries ago. Another important characteristic of gold is its usefulness to industry and science. For many years, it has been used in hundreds of industrial applications. The most recent use of gold is in astronauts' suits. Astronauts wear gold-plated heat shields for protection outside the spaceship. In conclusion, gold is treasured not only for its beauty but also for its utility.

The Three Parts of a Paragraph

A paragraph has three major structural parts: a topic sentence, supporting sentences, and a concluding sentence.

The **topic sentence** states the main idea of the paragraph. It not only names the topic of the paragraph, but it also limits the topic to one or two areas that can be discussed completely in the space of a single paragraph. The specific area is called the controlling idea. Notice how the topic sentence of the model states both the topic and the controlling idea:

(*Topic*) (*Controlling Idea*)

- Gold, a precious metal, is prized for two important characteristics.

Supporting sentences develop the topic sentence. That is, they explain the topic sentence by giving reasons, examples, facts, statistics, and quotations. Some of the supporting sentences that explain the topic sentence about gold are

- First of all, gold has a lustrous beauty that is resistant to corrosion.
- For example, a Macedonian coin remains as untarnished today as the day it was minted twenty-three centuries ago.
- Another important characteristic of gold is its utility in industry and science.
- The most recent application of gold is in astronauts' suits.

The **concluding sentence** signals the end of the paragraph and leaves the reader with important points to remember:

- In conclusion, gold is treasured not only for its beauty but also for its utility.

Unity and Coherence

In addition to the three structural parts of a paragraph, a good paragraph also has the elements of unity and coherence.

Unity means that you discuss only *one* main idea in a paragraph. The main idea is stated in the topic sentence, and then each and every supporting sentence develops that idea. If, for example, you announce in your topic sentence that you are going to discuss two important characteristics of gold, discuss only those. Do not discuss anything else such as the price of gold, the history of gold, or gold mining.

Coherence means that your paragraph is easy to read and understand because (1) your supporting sentences are in some kind of logical order and (2) your ideas are connected by the use of appropriate transition signals. For example, in the paragraph about gold, there are two supporting ideas: gold is beautiful and gold is useful. Each of these supporting ideas is discussed, one after the other, and an example is given for each one. This is one kind of logical order. Furthermore, the relationship between the ideas is clearly shown by using appropriate transition words and phrases such as "first of all," "the second important characteristic," "for example," and "in conclusion."

Macedonian: from an ancient Mediterranean culture
untarnished: unchanged in color
minted: made, manufactured

In summary, a well-written paragraph contains five elements: a topic sentence, supporting sentences, a concluding sentence, unity, and coherence. In Part I of this book, you will study and practice each of these elements.

The Assignment Format

Below are instructions and a model of one possible format for the assignments you will prepare for this class. Your instructor may ask you to use this format, or he/she may have other requirements.

1. Use lined paper.
2. Write a title in the center of the top line.
3. Write the practice number, page number, and practice name in the upper left-hand corner.
4. Write your name, the course number, and date in the upper right-hand corner.
5. Leave one-inch margins on both sides of the page.
6. Indent the first line of every paragraph. When typing, indent the first line 5 spaces. When writing by hand, indent the first line about one inch from the margin.
7. Write on every other line.
8. Number your pages.

M O D E L : ***Assignment Format***

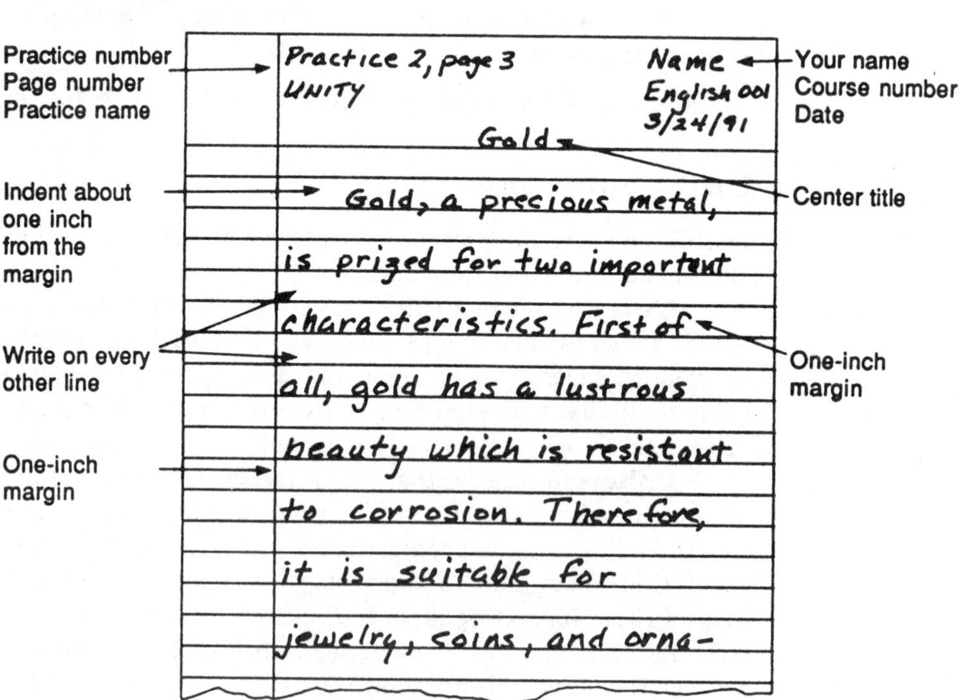

Notice that the first line in the paragraph is indented—moved to the right. While the practice of indenting is changing, particularly in business letter writing, it is still the accepted practice in academic writing.

How to Write a Title

Single paragraphs do not usually have titles. Giving your practice paragraphs titles, however, may help you to organize and limit your thoughts. For longer essays or reports, though, the use of titles will become more necessary.

A title tells the reader what the topic of the paragraph is. It is usually a word or phrase, not a sentence. It should be brief, but not so brief that it doesn't tell the reader what to expect.

Remember these points when writing a title:

1. The first, last, and all important words in a title are capitalized. Prepositions and articles are not considered important words in a title. Prepositions of more than five letters, however, may be capitalized. Articles that begin the title, of course, are capitalized.
2. The title of a paragraph or essay is not underlined.
3. The title is not enclosed in quotation marks, nor is it ended with a period.

- My Greatest Culture Shock
- How to Choose a Good Used Car
- Inflation Affects Everybody
- Backpacking in the Mountains
- Riding the Subway in New York

The Topic Sentence

Every good paragraph has a topic sentence, which clearly states the topic and the controlling idea of the paragraph. It is a complete sentence. It is usually (but not always) the first sentence in the paragraph.

A topic sentence is the most important sentence in a paragraph. It briefly indicates what the paragraph is going to discuss. For this reason, the topic sentence is a helpful guide to both the writer and the reader. The writer can see what information to include (and what information to exclude). The reader can see what the paragraph is going to be about and is therefore better prepared to understand it.

There are three important points to remember about the topic sentence:

1. A topic sentence is a *complete sentence*; that is, it contains a subject, a verb, and (usually) a complement. The following are *not* complete sentences.
   - Driving on freeways.
   - The importance of gold.
   - How to register for college classes.
2. A topic sentence contains both a *topic* and a *controlling idea*. It names the topic and then limits the topic to a specific area to be discussed in the space of a single paragraph. The following examples show how a topic sentence states both the topic and the controlling idea in a complete sentence.
   - Driving on freeways requires skill and alertness.
   - Gold, a precious metal, is prized for two important characteristics.
   - Registering for college classes can be a frustrating experience for new students.

3. A topic sentence is the most general statement in the paragraph because it gives only the main idea. It does not give any specific details.

   The following is an example of a general statement that could serve as a topic sentence:

   The Arabic origin of many English words is not always obvious.

   This sentence, on the other hand, is too specific to serve as a topic sentence:

   The slang expression "so long" (meaning goodbye) is probably a corruption of the Arabic "salaam."

   Some sentences may be too general to be good topic sentences:

   English is a difficult language to learn.

Position of Topic Sentences

The topic sentence may be the first or last sentence in a paragraph. The topic sentence may also be the first *and* last sentence of the paragraph—"sandwich-style." A "sandwich-style" paragraph is especially helpful to your reader if the paragraph is very long. The second topic sentence in the "sandwich-style" paragraph also serves as a concluding sentence.

Study the following three paragraphs. Notice the different positions for the topic sentence in each. The topic sentences are underlined.

MODEL: *Position of Topic Sentences*

Hurricanes

Hurricanes, which are also called cyclones, exert tremendous power. These violent storms are often a hundred miles in diameter, and their winds can reach velocities* of seventy-five miles per hour or more. Furthermore, the strong winds and heavy rainfall that accompany them can completely destroy a small town in a couple of hours. The energy that is released by a hurricane in one day exceeds the total energy consumed by humankind throughout the world in one year.

Famous School "Failures"

Albert Einstein, one of the world's geniuses, failed his university entrance examinations on his first attempt. William Faulkner, one of America's noted writers, never finished college because he could not pass his English courses. Sir Winston Churchill, who is considered one of the masters of the English language, had to have special tutoring in English during elementary school. These few examples show that failure in school does not always predict failure in life.

Synonyms

Synonyms, words that have the same basic meaning, do not always have the same emotional meaning. For example, the words "stingy" and "frugal" both mean "careful with money." However, to call a person stingy is an insult, while the word frugal has a much more positive connotation.* Similarly, a person wants to be slender but not skinny, and aggressive but not pushy. Therefore, you should be careful in choosing words because many so-called synonyms are not really synonymous at all.

---

velocities: speeds **connotation:** positive or negative meaning

PRACTICE 6: *Recognizing Topic Sentences*

Remember, the topic sentence indicates the main idea of a paragraph and is the most general statement in the paragraph.

STEP 1 Decide which of the following sentences is the topic sentence of the paragraph.

STEP 2 Write TS on the line next to that sentence.

STEP 3 Decide the order of the supporting sentences and number them SS1, SS2, SS3, and so on.

Paragraph 1

_____ **a.** Next, add antifreeze to your windshield washer fluid; otherwise, the fluid will freeze and possibly break the container.

_____ **b.** First, put on snow tires if you plan to drive on snowy, icy roads very often.

_____ **c.** Driving in winter, especially on snowy, icy roads, can be less troublesome if you take a few simple precautions.*

_____ **d.** Finally, it is also a good idea to carry tire chains, a can of spray to unfreeze door locks, and a windshield scraper in your car when driving in winter weather.

_____ **e.** Second, check the amount of antifreeze in your radiator and add more if necessary.

Paragraph 2

_____ **a.** Furthermore, researchers are continuing to work on the development of an efficient, electrically powered automobile.

_____ **b.** Researchers in the automobile industry are experimenting with different types of engines and fuels as alternatives to the conventional gasoline engines.

_____ **c.** One new type of engine, which burns diesel oil instead of gasoline, has been available for several years.

_____ **d.** Finally, several automobile manufacturers are experimenting with methanol, which is a mixture of gasoline and methyl alcohol, as an automobile fuel.

_____ **e.** A second type is the gas turbine engine, which can use fuels made from gasoline, diesel oil, kerosene, other petroleum distillates,* or methanol.

Paragraph 3

_____ **a.** Later on, people began to write on pieces of leather, which were rolled into scrolls.

_____ **b.** In the earliest times, people carved or painted messages on rocks.

_____ **c.** In the Middle Ages, heavy paper called parchment was used for writing, and books were laboriously copied by hand.

---

precaution: advance action to prevent something

distillate: a substance obtained from another substance

_____ **d.** With the invention of the printing press in the middle of the fifteenth century, the modern printing industry was born.

_____ **e.** Some form of written communication has been used throughout the centuries.

Paragraph 4

_____ **a.** If there had been a big storm on the day of a baby's birth, the baby might have been named Thunder Cloud.

_____ **b.** American Indian names are very descriptive, for Indians were usually named for a physical attribute, for an occurrence in nature, or for an animal.

_____ **c.** Grey Eagle, Red Dog, Big Bear, and Spotted Wolf are examples of Indians named after animals.

_____ **d.** Indians with distinctive physical characteristics might be given names such as Big Foot or Crooked Leg.

Paragraph 5

_____ **a.** After an attack by a great white, 462 stitches were required to sew up an Australian scuba diver.

_____ **b.** With their razor-sharp teeth and strong jaws, great white sharks are very dangerous.

_____ **c.** Nevertheless, one did just that near a public beach in Australia in 1985.

_____ **d.** Even when they attack humans, however, great whites do not usually eat them.

_____ **e.** It bit in half and totally devoured* a young woman swimmer.

_____ **f.** Great whites do not usually attack humans, but when they do, they always cause serious injury.

The Two Parts of a Topic Sentence

A topic sentence has two essential parts: the topic and the controlling idea. The *topic* names the subject or main idea of the paragraph. The *controlling idea* makes a specific comment about the topic, which indicates what the rest of the paragraph will say about the topic. It limits or controls the topic to a specific aspect of the topic to be discussed in the space of a single paragraph.

TOPIC — CONTROLLING IDEA

(Convenience foods) are <u>easy to prepare</u>.

In this example, the topic is named: convenience foods. A specific comment is then made about the topic: they are easy to prepare. From this sentence, the reader immediately knows that the supporting sentences in the remainder of the paragraph will explain or prove how quick and easy it is to prepare convenience foods and perhaps give some examples (frozen dinners, canned soups, etc.).

---

devoured: ate

CONTROLLING IDEA TOPIC

The native foods of America's immigrant population are reflected in American cooking.

In this example, the topic is American food. The controlling idea of this topic sentence is that Americans eat many foods from other countries. Therefore, the reader should expect the paragraph to give examples of popular "foreign" foods such as fried rice (Chinese), tacos (Mexican), sauerbraten (German), sukiyaki (Japanese), spaghetti (Italian), and so on.

TOPIC CONTROLLING IDEA

The average American teenager consumes enormous quantities of junk food.

In this example, the topic is the average American teenager. The controlling idea about the topic states that the American teenager eats junk food. Thus, the rest of the paragraph should discuss the quantities and types of junk food that American teenagers eat (soft drinks, potato chips, candy bars, etc.).

PRACTICE 7: *Identifying the Parts of a Topic Sentence*

Circle the topic and underline the controlling idea in each of the following sentences.

Example: Driving on freeways requires skill and alertness.

1. Driving on freeways requires nerves of steel.*
2. Driving on freeways requires an aggressive attitude.
3. The Caribbean island of Trinidad attracts tourists because of its calypso music.
4. Spectacular beaches make Puerto Rico a tourist paradise.
5. Living in an American college dormitory can be a stressful experience for newly arrived foreign students.
6. Many religious rules developed from the health needs of ancient times.
7. The spread of AIDS can be slowed by educating the public.
8. A major problem for foreign students is taking essay examinations.
9. Participating in class discussions in English is a problem for foreign students.
10. In my opinion, many television commercials for cosmetics lie to women.
11. Owning an automobile is a necessity for me.
12. It is an expensive luxury to own an automobile in a large city.

Writing Topic Sentences: Two Reminders

1. A topic sentence should be neither too general nor too specific. If it is too general, the reader cannot tell exactly what the paragraph is going to discuss. If it is too specific, the writer may not have anything left to write about in the rest of the paragraph.

   Think of a topic sentence like the name of a particular course on a restaurant menu. When you order food in a restaurant, you want to know more about a particular course than just "meat" or "soup" or "salad." You want to

nerves of steel: very strong nerves (idiom)

know *generally* what kind of salad it is. Potato salad? Mixed green salad? Fruit salad? However, you do not necessarily want to know all of its ingredients.

Similarly, the reader of a paragraph wants to know *generally* what to expect in a paragraph, but he/she does not want to learn all of the specific details in the first sentence.

Too general: American food is terrible.

Too specific: American food is tasteless and greasy because Americans use too many canned, frozen, and prepackaged foods and because everything is fried in oil or butter.

Good: American food is tasteless and greasy.

2. Do not include too many unrelated ideas in your topic sentence; if you do, your paragraph will not be unified.

Too many ideas: San Francisco is famous for its temperate climate, its many tourist attractions, and its cosmopolitan* atmosphere.

The three parts of this controlling idea are too unrelated for a single paragraph. They would require three separate paragraphs.

Good: San Francisco is famous for its cosmopolitan atmosphere.

PRACTICE 8: *Writing Topic Sentences*

A. Write good topic sentences for the following paragraphs in the space provided. Remember to include both a topic and a controlling idea.

Paragraph 1

____

____.

Americans relaxing at home, for example, may put on **kimonos,*** which is a Japanese word. Americans who live in a warm climate may take an afternoon **siesta*** on an outdoor **patio*** without even realizing that these are Spanish words. In their gardens, they may enjoy the fragrance of **jasmine** flowers, a word that came into English from Persian. They may even relax on a **chaise longue*** while sipping a drink made with **vodka**, words of French and Russian origin, respectively.

Paragraph 2

____

____.

In European universities, students are not required to attend classes. In fact, professors in Germany generally do not know the names of the students enrolled in their courses. In the United States, however, students are required to attend all classes and may be penalized* if they don't. Furthermore, in the European system, there is usually just one comprehensive examination at the end of the students' entire four or five years of study. In the American system, on the other hand, there are usually numerous quizzes, tests, and homework assignments, and there is almost always a final examination in each course at the end of the semester.

---

cosmopolitan: international
kimono: lounging robe
siesta: afternoon nap
patio: courtyard
chaise longue: lounge chair
penalized: punished

Paragraph 3

____

____.

House construction in various parts of the world depends mainly on the availability of building materials. For example, the Eskimos, living in a treeless region of snow and ice, sometimes build temporary homes out of thick blocks of ice. People who live in deserts, on the other hand, use the most available material, mud or clay, which provides good insulation* from the heat. In Northern Europe, Russia, and other areas of the world where forests are plentiful, people usually construct their homes out of wood. In the islands of the South Pacific, where there is a plentiful supply of bamboo and palm, people use these tough, fibrous* plants to build their homes.

B. Write two or three topic sentences for each of the following topics. In other words, give two or three controlling ideas for the same topic.

Example:

Topic: Television's effects on children

Topic sentences: (1) Television is harmful to children because it teaches them violence as a way of solving problems.

(2) Television retards* a child's reading ability.

1. Smoking cigarettes
2. Foreign travel
3. Space exploration
4. Rock music or rock musicians
5. Your country's/city's tourist attractions.

C. With your classmates, choose three topics that interest you as a group. Write a topic sentence for each topic. Be sure to include a controlling idea.

The Concluding Sentence

Now that you know how to write a good topic sentence for a paragraph, you should also learn how to write a good concluding sentence. A concluding sentence is not absolutely necessary; in fact, a concluding sentence is not customary for every paragraph in a multiparagraph essay. However, for single paragraphs, especially long ones, a concluding sentence is helpful to the reader because it signals the end of the paragraph and because it is a reminder of the important points.

A concluding sentence serves three purposes:

1. It signals the end of the paragraph.
2. It summarizes the main points of the paragraph.
3. It gives a final comment on your topic and leaves the reader with the most important ideas to think about.

---

insulation: protection
fibrous: containing fiber
retards: slows down

Use one of the following end-of-paragraph signals to introduce your concluding sentence:

(These are followed by a comma.)

Finally,
In conclusion,
In summary,
Therefore,
Thus,
As a result,
Indeed,

(These are *not* followed by a comma.)

We can see that . . .
It is clear that . . .

The examples below demonstrate two different types of concluding sentences. The first one paraphrases the topic sentence; i.e.,* the concluding sentence repeats the main idea of the topic sentence in different words. The second example summarizes the two main points of the paragraph, which were not specifically stated in the topic sentence.

MODEL: *Concluding Sentences*

Synonyms

Synonyms, words that have the same basic meaning, do not always have the same emotional meaning. For example, the words "stingy" and "frugal" both mean "careful with money." However, to call a person stingy is an insult, while the word frugal has a much more positive connotation. Similarly, a person wants to be slender but not skinny, and aggressive but not pushy. Therefore, you should be careful in choosing words because many so-called synonyms are not really synonymous at all.

Gold

Gold, a precious metal, is prized for two important characteristics. First of all, gold has a lustrous beauty that is resistant to corrosion. Therefore, it is suitable for jewelry, coins, and ornamental purposes. Gold never needs to be polished and will remain beautiful forever. For example, a Macedonian coin remains as untarnished today as the day it was minted twenty-three centuries ago. Another important characteristic of gold is its usefulness to industry and science. For many years, it has been used in hundreds of industrial applications. The most recent use of gold is in astronauts' suits. Astronauts wear gold-plated heat shields for protection outside the spaceship. In conclusion, gold is treasured not only for its beauty but also for its utility.

---

i.e.: that is (abbreviation of the Latin phrase *id est*)

PRACTICE 9: *Writing Concluding Sentences*

STEP 1 Underline the topic sentence in each paragraph.
STEP 2 Determine the main idea of each paragraph.
STEP 3 Add a good concluding sentence to each. You may either paraphrase the topic sentence or summarize the main points.
STEP 4 Begin each concluding sentence with an end-of-paragraph signal.

Paragraph 1

You can reduce gas consumption in your car by careful driving and good maintenance. Don't speed. Gas consumption is about 10 percent higher at 60 miles per hour than at 50 miles per hour and even greater at higher speeds. Avoid fast stops and starts because they wear your tires out in addition to using a lot of gas. Check your tire pressure often because underinflated tires reduce gas mileage considerably. Get your car tuned up regularly because an inefficiently operating engine results in inefficient fuel consumption. ____________________

Paragraph 2

Alternative energy sources are becoming increasingly attractive as the energy crisis becomes more severe. Solar heating systems, which use the sun's radiation as a source of energy, are a promising alternative energy source. Nuclear power plants are already in operation in several parts of the country. Government and private industry are even investigating the possibility of capturing the power of ocean waves and tides for conversion* into usable energy. Coal is once again becoming an acceptable fuel as the nation searches for solutions to the energy shortage. Even garbage is seen as a potential source of energy. In some communities, garbage is burned to heat buildings and light city streets. ____________________

Review

These are the important points you should have learned from this chapter:

1. A good topic sentence:
   - is a complete sentence with a subject, a verb, and a controlling idea.
   - is neither too general nor too specific. It states clearly what the main idea of the paragraph is but does not include specific details.
   - is usually the first sentence in the paragraph.
2. A good concluding sentence:
   - signals the end of the paragraph.
   - summarizes the important points briefly or restates the topic sentence in different words.

---

conversion: change

WRITING PRACTICE

Choose one of your topics from the three brainstorming practices in Chapter 1 (pages 4, 6, or 8) and write a paragraph approximately ten sentences in length about it.

Follow these steps to success:

STEP 1 Develop an outline from the ideas you generated by brainstorming. Include a topic sentence and a concluding sentence. Underline them.

STEP 2 Write a rough draft from your outline, and check it against the Paragraph Checklist below for organization. Make sure your topic sentence has a controlling idea.

STEP 3 Write a second draft, and check it for grammar and mechanics.

STEP 4 Write a final copy to hand in.

Paragraph Checklist

Form:	______ Does your paragraph have a title?
	______ Did you write on the correct side of the paper?
	______ Did you indent?
	______ Did you write on every other line?
	(Refer to the Assignment Format on page 18 for complete instructions.)
Topic Sentence:	______ Does your topic sentence contain a controlling idea?
Concluding Sentence:	______ Does your paragraph have a concluding sentence?

WRITING UNDER PRESSURE

1. Choose one of the topic sentences you wrote for Practice 8B or 8C on page 25. Brainstorm by listing, freewriting, or clustering to develop supporting ideas.
2. Write a paragraph from your brainstorming.

   Suggested time limits:

Brainstorming:	8 minutes
Writing the paragraph:	10 minutes
Checking	2 minutes
	20 minutes

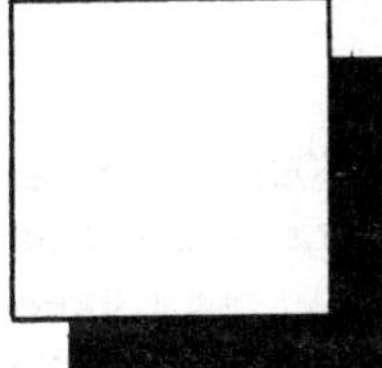

CHAPTER 3

Unity and Simple Outlining

Unity

Another important element of a good paragraph is **unity**. Every good paragraph has unity, which means that in each paragraph, only *one* main idea is discussed. If you start to discuss a new idea, begin a new paragraph. Furthermore, every supporting sentence in the paragraph must be directly related to the main idea. Do not include any information that does not directly support the topic sentence.

Uni- is a Latin prefix meaning "one." When we talk about paragraph unity, we mean that you should discuss only *one* main idea in each paragraph. For example, if your paragraph is about the advantages of a college education, discuss only that. Do not discuss the disadvantages of getting a college education. To make it even easier, discuss only *one* advantage in each paragraph, such as the ability to get a better job. However, sometimes it is possible to discuss two or even three aspects of the same idea in one paragraph *if they are closely related to each other.* For example, it is possible to discuss both "better job" and "better salary" in the same paragraph because they are closely related, but it is not a good idea to discuss both "better job" and "better general knowledge about the world" in the same paragraph because they are not so closely related.

The second part of unity is that every supporting sentence must *directly* explain or prove the main idea, which is stated in the topic sentence. Sometimes students write supporting sentences that are "off the topic." For example, if you are writing a paragraph about the high cost of college tuition, you could mention inflation as a factor. But if you write several sentences about inflation, you are getting "off the topic," and your paragraph will not have unity.

Study the two paragraphs below. Both paragraphs discuss the same topic. In your opinion, which paragraph has unity and which one doesn't? Explain how individual sentences break the unity either by introducing a new idea or by being "off the topic."

MODEL: *Unity*

Paragraph 1: Surviving Cancer

Progress is gradually being made in the fight against cancer. In the early 1900s, few cancer patients had any hope of long-term survival. In the 1930s, less than one in five cancer victims lived more than five years. In the 1950s, the ratio was one in four, and in the 1960s, it was one in three. Currently, four of ten patients who get cancer this year will be alive five years from now. The gain from one in four to four in ten represents about 69,000 lives saved each year.

Paragraph 2: Surviving Cancer

Progress is gradually being made in the fight against cancer. In the early 1900s, few cancer patients had any hope of long-term survival. But because of advances in medical technology, progress has been made so that currently four in ten cancer patients survive. It has been proven that smoking is a direct cause of lung cancer. However, the battle has not yet been won. Although cures for some forms of cancer have been discovered, other forms of cancer are still increasing. Heart disease is also increasing.

PRACTICE 10: *Unity*

A. The following short essay has not been divided into paragraphs, but it should contain six: an introductory paragraph, four "body" paragraphs, and a concluding paragraph.

STEP 1 Read the entire essay once or twice.

STEP 2 Decide where each new paragraph should begin. (Where does the author begin to discuss a different topic?)

STEP 3 Underline the first sentence of each paragraph.

Culture, Logic, and Rhetoric

Logic,* which is the basis of rhetoric, comes from culture; it is not universal. Rhetoric, therefore, is not universal either but varies from culture to culture. The rhetorical system of one language is neither better nor worse than the rhetorical system of another language, but it is different. English logic and English rhetoric, which are based on Anglo-European cultural patterns, are linear*—that is, a good English paragraph begins with a general statement of its content and then carefully develops that statement with a series of specific illustrations. A good English paragraph may also use just the reverse sequence: it may state a whole series of examples and then summarize those examples in a single statement at the end of the paragraph. In either case, however, the flow of ideas occurs in a straight line from the opening sentence to the last sentence. Furthermore, a well-structured English paragraph is never digressive.* There is nothing that does not belong to the paragraph and nothing that does not support the topic sentence. A type of

---

logic: way of thinking or reasoning
linear: in a straight line
digressive: wandering away from the main topic

construction found in Arabic and Persian writing is very different. Whereas English writers use a linear sequence, Arabic and Persian writers tend to construct a paragraph in a parallel sequence using many coordinators* such as **and** and **but**. In English, maturity of style is often judged by the degree of subordination* rather than by the degree of coordination. Therefore, the Arabic and Persian styles of writing, with their emphasis on coordination, seem awkward and immature to an English reader. Some Asian writers, on the other hand, use an indirect approach. In this kind of writing, the topic is viewed from a variety of angles. The topic is never analyzed directly; it is referred to only indirectly. Again, such a development in an English paragraph is awkward and unnecessarily vague* to an English reader. Spanish rhetoric differs from English rhetoric in still another way. While the rules of English rhetoric require that every sentence in a paragraph relates directly to the central idea, a Spanish-speaking writer loves to fill a paragraph with interesting digressions. Although a Spanish paragraph may begin and end on the same topic, the writer often digresses into areas that are not directly related to the topic. Spanish rhetoric, therefore, does not follow the English rule of paragraph unity. In summary, a student who has mastered the grammar of English may still write poor papers unless he/she has also mastered the rhetoric of English. Also, the student may have difficulty reading an essay written by the rules of English rhetoric unless he/she understands the "logical" differences from those of his/her own native tongue.

B. Divide this essay into paragraphs as you did the preceding one. There is more than one possible answer.

The Confusing English Spelling System

One of the most difficult and confusing aspects of the English language is its spelling system. There is often a discrepancy* between the pronunciation of a word and its spelling. One cannot always know how to spell a word by its pronunciation nor how to pronounce it by its spelling. For example, there are twelve different ways to spell the sound **sh** in English: **sh**oe, na**ti**on, **sch**ist,* o**ce**an, **s**ure, mi**ss**ion, ma**ch**ine, spe**ci**al, man**si**on, nau**se**ous, con**sci**ous, and an**xi**ous. To give an opposite example, the vowel combination **ou** can be pronounced in at least five different ways, as in the words **through, although, thought, tough,** and **out.** In order to understand the discrepancies in the English spelling system, it is good to know something about the history of the language. First, it is helpful to realize that English was originally the spoken language of people in England who could neither read nor write. While the uneducated people spoke English, the educated upper classes spoke in French and wrote in Latin. Later, when English became a written language, there was no system for spelling English words. Moreover, the first writers of English were French-speaking scribes* who knew English only slightly; therefore, they carried many French spelling habits into English. In addition, these scribes, who were used to writing in Latin, often inserted letters into words even when they were not pronounced because the corresponding word in Latin was spelled that way. The **b** in **debt** and **doubt,** for example, came from Latin **debitum** and **dubitare.** Finally, the confusion increased when the pronunciation of certain words changed while the spelling remained the same. This is the case with the words **light** and **night,** where the **gh** originally represented a distinct sound. In conclusion, although it may not improve your spelling, it may soothe your feeling of frustration to know that English spelling is just as troublesome for native speakers as it is for foreign learners.

---

coordinators: words that join equal elements
subordination: the joining of two unequal elements
vague: unclear
discrepancy: difference
schist: a crystalline rock
scribes: writers, copiers

PRACTICE 11: *Unity*

A. Each of the following paragraphs breaks the rule of unity because it contains one or more sentences that do not directly support the topic sentence.

STEP 1 Locate and underline the topic sentence of each paragraph.

STEP 2 Find the sentence(s) that do not support the topic sentence and cross them out.

Paragraph 1

Tourism is the state of Hawaii's leading industry. Every year, some six million tourists visit the islands. During the popular winter months, a planeload or shipload of tourists arrives every fifteen minutes. New hotels, new resorts, and new restaurants are being built every year to accommodate the increasing numbers of visitors. Sugar cane and pineapples are also important industries in Hawaii.

Paragraph 2

The rapid increase in crime in Chicago is causing a great deal of concern to the city's citizens. People are afraid to go out into the streets at night because they are afraid of being robbed or even killed. More and more families are moving out of the city into the suburbs* because of the high crime rate. The chief of police was fired last month because of his inability to reduce crime. People are buying strong locks for their doors and installing heavy iron bars across their windows to prevent burglaries. Some citizens are even purchasing guns to protect themselves and their property. Indeed, it seems that the increase in crime is turning the average home in Chicago into a prison for its inhabitants.

Paragraph 3

The convenience and economy of small cars account for their popularity. They are easy to park quickly and take smaller parking spaces. Small cars are also a means of conserving energy because they use less gas than big cars. Small cars are inconvenient and uncomfortable on long trips, however, because of their limited passenger and trunk space. They are also more economical to operate and maintain, and they cost less. Because of all these advantages, the demand for small cars remains high.

B. Each of the following paragraphs has not only two or more topic sentences but also irrelevant sentences.

STEP 1 Decide where each paragraph should be divided into two or more paragraphs. Underline the topic sentence of each.

STEP 2 Find the irrelevant sentence(s) and cross them out.

Paragraph 1

The recent water shortage in California forced changes in Californians' lifestyles. When water was rationed,* Californians learned to conserve water. They didn't water their lawns and gardens or wash their automobiles. Also, they took fewer showers and baths. The water shortage lasted two years. Californians also learned to recycle* water. For example, they used the rinse water from their

---

suburbs: small communities surrounding a large city
rationed: limited in amount
recycle: use again

washing machines to water their houseplants and gardens. California's agricultural industry was also severely affected by the water shortage. Because their water was also rationed, farmers planted fewer acres* and had to plan their crops more carefully. Many farmers planted crops that required less water and reduced the number of crops that needed a lot of water. This eventually caused an increase in the price of food in supermarkets all over the country.

Paragraph 2

The United States and Canada will someday join the 95 percent of the world that uses the metric rather than the English system of measurement. No longer will North American schoolchildren have to memorize that there are 12 inches in a foot, 3 feet in a yard, $5\frac{1}{2}$ yards in a rod, 40 rods in a furlong, and 8 furlongs in a mile. Inches will become centimeters, pounds will become kilograms, quarts will become liters, and degrees Fahrenheit will become degrees centigrade (also called Celsius). The English system of measurement has been used in English-speaking countries since about the year 1200. The conversion to the metric system will not be easy, however, and will require enormous amounts of money and time. Proponents* of the change argue that it is necessary in order for North American products to compete in world markets with metric products. For example, every piece of machinery in every factory and every office will have to be replaced. Furthermore, every machine and tool that makes, repairs, or supplies another piece of equipment will have to be changed. Not only every nut, bolt, and screw but also every wrench, drill, and screwdriver will have to be replaced, as any auto mechanic who has tried to fix an imported car with a set of American tools realizes. Therefore, although the United States and Canada are committed to "going metric," it will not happen next week or even next year. Because of the magnitude* of the problems that metric conversion will involve, the change will have to be gradual and, above all, carefully planned.

Simple Paragraph Outlining

An outline is like an architect's plan for a house. An architect plans a house before it is built to make sure that all the parts will fit. Like an architect, you should plan a paragraph before you write it to make sure that all of your ideas will fit.

Learning to outline will improve your writing for three reasons. First of all, it will help you organize your ideas. Specifically, an outline will ensure that you won't include any irrelevant ideas, that you won't leave out any important points, and that your supporting sentences will be in logical order. Second, learning to outline will help you write more quickly. It may take some practice at first, but once you become used to outlining your ideas before you start to write, you will be surprised at how fast you will actually be able to write. Preparing an outline is 75 percent of the work. The actual writing becomes easier because you don't have to worry about what you are going to say; you already have a well-organized plan to follow. Finally, your grammar will improve because you will be able to concentrate on it, not on your thoughts or organization. Improved organization, speed, and grammar make learning to outline well worth the effort.

There are several different outline forms that can be used. The form used in this book is particularly helpful for students who have never practiced outlining before. However, your instructor may recommend a different form.

---

acre: unit of area (1 acre = 4.047 square meters)
proponents: people in favor of something
magnitude: great size

A simple outline for a short paragraph might look like this:

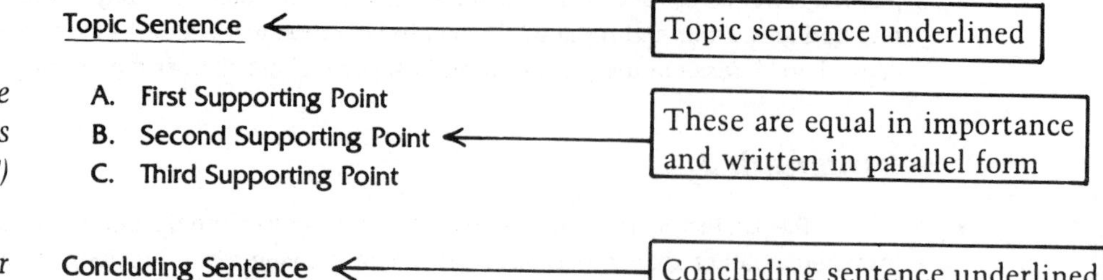

Indent and use capital letters (A, B, C)

No number or letter

Of course, the number of main supporting points (A, B, C) will vary widely from paragraph to paragraph. This particular paragraph has three main supporting points; others may have only two or as many as ten or even twenty. Also, some paragraphs may not have a concluding sentence, and in others, the topic sentence may not be the first sentence.

Study the simple outline below for the second paragraph above. Then reread the paragraph to see how the writer used this plan to write a well-organized paragraph that is easy to understand.

MODEL: ***Simple Paragraph Outlining***

Learning to outline will improve your writing for three reasons.

A. It will help you organize your ideas.
B. It will help you write more quickly.
C. It will help you improve your grammar.

Improved organization, speed, and grammar make learning to outline well worth the effort.

The "Parallel Form" Rule

Equal parts of an outline should be written in parallel form. This means that all ideas with the same kind of letter or number should have the same grammatical form; that is, they all should be complete sentences, or all nouns, or all adjectives, or all prepositional phrases, etc. In the following example, points A, B, and C are all different grammatical structures. Point A is a noun phrase. What is B? C?

Wrong

Fish make excellent pets.

A. Small appetites.
B. Quiet.
C. They are well-behaved.

Because of these three qualities alone, fish make outstanding pets.

Right

Fish make excellent pets.

A. They don't eat much.
B. They are quiet.
C. They are well-behaved.

Because of these three qualities alone, fish make outstanding pets.

Now, points A, B, and C are all complete sentences. You could also make them all single adjectives:

Right

Fish make excellent pets.
- A. Economical to feed
- B. Quiet
- C. Well-behaved

Because of these three qualities alone, fish make outstanding pets.

PRACTICE 12: *Making Outlines Parallel*

Rewrite each of these outlines to make the support part parallel in form.

1. San Francisco is famous for its tourist attractions.
- A. Golden Gate Park is very famous.
- B. Chinatown.
- C. Fisherman's Wharf attracts hundreds of tourists.
- D. Riding the cable cars.

For these four attractions alone, San Francisco is well worth a visit.

2. Gold, a precious metal, is prized for two important characteristics.
- A. It is beautiful
- B. Useful to science and industry.

In conclusion, gold is treasured not only for its beauty but also for its utility.

3. Some of the world's most successful men had trouble in school.
- A. Albert Einstein failed his university entrance exams on his first attempt.
- B. William Faulkner's F's in English.
- C. Special tutoring necessary for Winston Churchill.

These few examples show that failure in school does not always predict failure in life.

The "Equivalent Value" Rule

In an outline, ideas that have the same kind of letter or number must have equal value. This means that every main supporting point must have the same kind of letter or number (capital letters, for instance) and that every idea given a small letter, Arabic numeral, or Roman numeral must be equal. If, for example, your outline contains examples, you should give your examples a different kind of letter or number than you give the point(s) they are illustrating.

Wrong

One problem is the city's unreliable public transportation system.
- A. Daily schedules are unreliable.
- B. Buses arrive late.
- C. Buses come in bunches.
- D. Passengers are victims.
- E. They are late to appointments, work, classes.
- F. They must allow extra time to wait for buses.

<u>One problem is the city's unreliable public transportation system.</u>

A. Daily schedules are unreliable.
   1. Buses arrive late.
   2. Buses arrive in bunches.

Right

B. Passengers are victims.
   1. They are late to appointments, work, classes.
   2. They must allow extra time to wait for buses.

PRACTICE 13: *Outlining (Equivalent Value)*

A. Organize the items in the lists below into a logical outline. Remember to give the items with equal importance the same kind of letter or number.

surfing
skin diving
windsurfing
basketball
team sports
soccer
football
skiing
ice skating
individual sports
tennis
hiking

B. The sentences below are in scrambled order. Arrange them into a logical outline.

American high schools are facing problems on four fronts.
Vandalism* in the schools is increasing.
Teachers who have had to take teacher certification examinations show very low scores.
In 1990, according to an N.E.A.* report, acts of vandalism and theft cost the schools $200 million.
Colleges report that some new freshmen read and write at the sixth-grade level.
Students aren't learning anything.
Taxpayers are protesting the increasing costs by voting against tax increases to pay for schools.
During the last ten years, there have been numerous strikes by teachers demanding higher pay and less work.
On the national Scholastic Aptitude Test (SAT), a national test for high school seniors, the average scores in verbal ability have fallen by ten percent.
Teachers are also creating problems for the schools.
A large school in Chicago, Illinois, reported that one window is broken and two typewriters are stolen every week.
Math scores on the SAT have declined by six percent since 1982.
Traditional methods of financing the schools are breaking down.
The schools in Cleveland, Ohio, were closed for three months last winter because they simply ran out of money.

---

vandalism: willful destruction of property
NEA: National Education Association

Review

These are the important points you should have learned from this chapter:

1. Every good paragraph has unity. Discuss only one idea in each paragraph. All supporting sentences must directly support the topic sentence.
2. An outline is useful as a plan for a paragraph. It organizes the ideas.

WRITING PRACTICE

Choose one of the suggested topics below and write a paragraph that is ten to fifteen sentences in length.

STEP 1 Brainstorm your topic for ideas, using the listing, freewriting, or clustering technique from Chapter 1.

STEP 2 Develop an outline, including a topic sentence and a concluding sentence (if necessary). Underline them.

STEP 3 Write a rough draft, and then check it against the Paragraph Checklist below for organization. Make sure your paragraph has unity.

STEP 4 Write a second draft and check this for grammar and mechanics.

STEP 5 Write a final copy to hand in.

Topic Suggestions

One important problem in your city or country
One way technology has changed our lives
One important quality of a doctor, veterinarian, scientist, teacher, architect, engineer, or any other occupation
One type of pollution

Paragraph Checklist

Form:	_______ Does your paragraph have a title?
	_______ Did you write on the correct side of the paper?
	_______ Did you indent?
	_______ Did you write on every other line?
	(Refer to the Assignment Format on page 18 for complete instructions.)
Topic Sentence:	_______ Does your topic sentence contain a controlling idea?
Supporting Sentences: Unity:	_______ Do all of your sentences directly support your topic sentence?
Concluding Sentence:	_______ Does your paragraph have a concluding sentence?

WRITING UNDER PRESSURE

Write a rough draft for a paragraph on one of the topics listed below. First, brainstorm for ideas and make a simple outline before you begin to write. Check your paragraph over twice, once for content and organization and once for grammar and mechanics. Make any necessary corrections before you hand it in.

Your instructor will give you a time limit.

Suggested time limits:

Brainstorming:	5 minutes
Outlining:	3 minutes
Writing:	10 minutes
Checking:	2 minutes
	20 minutes

Topic Suggestions

One problem you have
One problem of foreign students
A perfect student/teacher/friend
A perfect job
A perfect wife/husband/parent

C H A P T E R 4

Coherence

Another element of a good paragraph is **coherence.** *Co-* is a Latin prefix that means "together" or "with." The verb *cohere* means "hold together." In order to have coherence in writing, the movement from one sentence to the next (and in longer essays, from one paragraph to the next) must be logical and smooth. There must be no sudden jumps. Each sentence should flow smoothly into the next one.

There are four ways to achieve coherence. The first two ways involve *repeating key nouns* and *using pronouns* which refer back to key nouns. The third way is to use *transition signals* to show how one idea is related to the next. The fourth way to achieve coherence is to arrange your sentences in *logical order.* Three of the common "logical orders," which you will learn to use in the next two chapters, are chronological order (order by time), logical division, and order of importance.

Repetition of Key Nouns

The most natural and, therefore, the easiest way to achieve coherence is to repeat key nouns frequently in your paragraph.

Let's look at the model paragraph about gold to see how it uses this technique to achieve coherence. The key noun in this paragraph is *gold.* Circle the word *gold* and all pronouns that refer to it.

Gold

Gold, a precious metal, is prized for two important characteristics. First of all, gold has a lustrous beauty that is resistant to corrosion. Therefore, it is suitable for jewelry, coins, and ornamental purposes. Gold never needs to be polished and will remain beautiful forever. For example, a Macedonian coin remains as untarnished today as the day it was minted twenty-three centuries ago. Another important characteristic of gold is its usefulness to industry and science. For many years, it has been used in hundreds of industrial applications. The most recent use of gold is in astronauts' suits. Astronauts wear gold-plated heat shields for protection outside the spaceship. In conclusion, gold is treasured not only for its beauty but also for its utility.

You should have circled the noun *gold* seven times, the pronoun *it* twice, and the pronoun *its* three times. (The word *it* in line 4 refers to *coin,* not *gold,* so you should not have circled it.)

There is no fixed rule about how often to repeat key nouns or when to substitute pronouns. At the very least, you need to repeat a key noun instead of using a pronoun when the meaning is not clear.

Throughout the following paragraph, the word *gold* has been replaced by pronouns, making the paragraph much less coherent.

Gold

Gold, a precious metal, is prized for two important characteristics. First of all, it has a lustrous beauty that is resistant to corrosion. Therefore, it is suitable for jewelry, coins, and ornamental purposes. It never needs to be polished and will remain beautiful forever. For example, a Macedonian coin remains as untarnished today as the day it was minted twenty-three centuries ago. Another of its important characteristics is its usefulness to industry and science. For many years, it has been used in hundreds of industrial applications. Its most recent use is in astronauts' suits. Astronauts wear heat shields made from it for protection outside the spaceship. In conclusion, it is treasured not only for its beauty but also for its utility.

PRACTICE 14: *Repetition of Key Nouns*

A. In the following paragraph, the key noun is never repeated. Replace the pronoun *it* with the key noun *English* wherever you think doing so would make the paragraph more coherent.

English

English has almost become an international language. Except for Chinese, more people speak it than any other language. Spanish is the official language of more countries in the world, but more countries have it as their official or unofficial second language. More than seventy percent of the world's mail is written in it. In international business, it is used more than any other language, and it is the language of airline pilots and air traffic controllers all over the world. Moreover, although French used to be the language of diplomacy, it has displaced it throughout the world. Therefore, unless you plan to spend your life alone on a desert island in the middle of the Pacific Ocean, it is a useful language to know.

B. In the following passage about dolphins, replace some of the pronouns with appropriate singular or plural nouns.

Dolphins

Interest in dolphins has increased in the past few years. They are interesting because they display almost human-like behavior at times. For example, they help each other when they are in trouble. If one is sick, it sends out a message. Others in the area swim to help it. They push it to the surface of the water so it can breathe. They stay with it for days or weeks—until it recovers or dies. They have also helped trapped or lost whales navigate their way safely out to the open sea. They are so intelligent and helpful, in fact, that the U.S. Navy is training them to become underwater bomb disposal experts.

Use of Consistent Pronouns

When you use pronouns instead of key nouns, make sure that you use the same person and number throughout your paragraph. Don't change from *you* to *he* or *she* (change of person), or from *he* to *they* (change of number).

PRACTICE 15: *Using Consistent Pronouns*

In the following paragraph, the pronouns are not consistent. Correct them to make this paragraph more coherent.

Olympic Athletes

An Olympic athlete must be strong both physically and mentally. First of all, if you hope to compete in an Olympic sport, you must be physically strong. Furthermore, an aspiring* Olympian must train rigorously* for many years. For the most demanding sports, they train several hours a day, five or six days a week, for ten or more years. In addition to being physically strong, he or she must also be mentally tough. This means that you have to be totally dedicated to your sport, often giving up a normal school, family, and social life. Being mentally strong also means that he or she must be able to withstand the intense pressure of international competition with its attendant* media* coverage. Finally, not everyone can win a medal, so they must possess the inner strength to live with defeat.

Transition Signals

Transition signals are words such as *first, second, next, finally, therefore,* and *however,* or phrases such as *in conclusion, on the other hand,* and *as a result.*

Think of transition signals as traffic signs that tell your reader when to go forward, turn, slow down, and stop. In other words, tell the reader when you are giving a similar idea (*similarly, moreover, furthermore, in addition*), an opposite idea (*on the other hand, however, in contrast*), an example (*for example*), a result (*as a result*), or a conclusion (*in conclusion*).

Using transition words to guide your reader makes it easier to follow your ideas. Transition words give your paragraph coherence.

PRACTICE 16: *Using Transition Signals*

Compare paragraphs 1 and 2 below. Both paragraphs give the same information, yet one paragraph is easier to understand than the other because it contains transition signals to lead the reader from one idea to the next.

Which paragraph contains transition signals and is more coherent? Circle all of the transition signals that you can identify.

Paragraph 1

A difference among the world's seas and oceans is that the salinity* varies in different climate zones. The Baltic Sea in Northern Europe is only one-fourth as saline* as the Red Sea in the

---

aspiring: hopeful
rigorously: strictly, without weakness
attendant: accompanying
media: radio, television, newspapers, and magazines
salinity: salt content
saline: salty

Middle East. There are reasons for this. In warm climates, water evaporates* rapidly. The concentration* of salt is greater. The surrounding land is dry and does not contribute much fresh water to dilute* the salty sea water. In cold climate zones, water evaporates slowly. The runoff created by melting snow adds a considerable amount of fresh water to dilute the saline sea water.

Paragraph 2

Another difference among the world's seas and oceans is that the salinity varies in different climate zones. For example, the Baltic Sea in Northern Europe is only one fourth as saline as the Red Sea in the Middle East. There are two reasons for this. First of all, in warm climate zones, water evaporates rapidly; therefore, the concentration of salt is greater. Second, the surrounding land is dry and, consequently, does not contribute much fresh water to dilute the salty sea water. In cold climate zones, on the other hand, water evaporates slowly. Furthermore, the runoff created by melting snow adds a considerable amount of fresh water to dilute the saline sea water.

Paragraph 2 is more coherent because it contains these transition signals:

Another tells you that this paragraph is part of a longer essay.
For example tells you that an example of the preceding idea is coming.
Two tells you to look for two different reasons.
First of all tells you that this is the first reason.
Second and *furthermore* indicate that additional ideas are coming.
Therefore and *consequently* indicate that the second statement is a result of the first statement.
On the other hand tells you that an opposite idea is coming.

Each transition signal has a special meaning. Each one shows how the following sentence relates to the preceding one. Of course, you should not use a transition signal in front of *every* sentence in a paragraph. Using too many transition signals can be just as confusing as using too few. However, good writing requires that you use enough transition signals to make the relationships among your ideas clear.

Below is a chart showing some of the most common transition signals. You should learn to use all of them, for they can be used with all kinds of writing. Later on, you will learn about special transition signals that are used with certain types of writing, such as chronological order, comparison, and contrast.

Types of Transition Signals

Transition signals can be categorized into four groups by grammatical function. In the chart below, the four groups are *sentence connectors,* (including *transition phrases* and *conjunctive adverbs*), *coordinating conjunctions, subordinating conjunctions,* and a mixed group called *others*. As you study the chart and the examples that follow it, pay particular attention to the punctuation used with each group.

---

evaporates: dries up
concentration: amount
dilute: reduce the concentration of

Transition Signals for General Use

Meaning/ Function	Sentence Connectors		Clause Connectors		Others
	Transition Phrases	Conjunctive Adverbs	Coordinating Conjunctions	Subordinating Conjunctions	
To introduce an **additional** idea	in addition	furthermore moreover besides also too	and		**another (+ noun)** **an additional (+ noun)**
To introduce an **opposite** idea	on the other hand in contrast	however nevertheless instead still	but yet	although though even though whereas while	**in spite of (+ noun)** **despite (+ noun)**
To introduce a **choice** or **alternative**		otherwise	or	if unless	
To introduce a **restatement** or **explanation**					**i.e.** **that is**
To introduce an **example**	for example for instance				**an example of (+ noun)** **such as (+ noun)** **e.g.**
To introduce a **conclusion** or **summary**	in conclusion in summary to conclude to summarize				
To introduce a **result**		therefore consequently hence thus	so		

Sentence Connectors

Transition Phrases

The phrases in this group usually appear at the beginning of sentences. They may also appear in the middle (normally following the subject) or at the end of sentences. They are *always* separated from the rest of the sentence by commas. Hence, these three patterns are possible:

- For example, the Baltic Sea in Northern Europe is only one fourth as saline as the Red Sea in the Middle East.
- The Baltic Sea in Northern Europe, for example, is only one fourth as saline as the Red Sea in the Middle East.
- The Baltic Sea in Northern Europe is only one fourth as saline as the Red Sea in the Middle East, for example.

Conjunctive Adverbs

Conjunctive adverbs (except *too*) may also appear at the beginning, in the middle, or at the end of sentences, and are separated by commas.

- Furthermore, the runoff created by melting snow adds a considerable amount of fresh water to dilute the saline sea water.
- The runoff created by melting snow, furthermore, adds a considerable amount of fresh water to dilute the saline sea water.
- My parents want me to become an engineer, however.

Conjunctive adverbs are also often used with a semicolon and a comma to join two independent clauses* to form a compound sentence.

- In warm climate zones, water evaporates rapidly; therefore, the concentration of salt is greater.
- The company's sales increased last year; nevertheless, its net profit declined.

The transition expressions *that is* and its abbreviation *i.e.* (from Latin *id est*) and the abbreviation *e.g.* (from Latin *exempli gratia*, for example) may also follow this pattern.

- Many societies in the world are matriarchal; that is, the mother is head of the family.
- Many societies in the world are matriarchal; i.e., the mother is head of the family.
- Some English words do not have exact equivalents in other languages; e.g., there is no German word for the adjective *fair*, as in fair play.

Clause Connectors

Coordinating Conjunctions

The five coordinating conjunctions in the chart (plus two additional ones, *for* and *nor*) are used with a comma to join two independent clauses to form a compound sentence.

- In a matriarchy, the mother is the head of the family, and all of the children belong to her clan.*
- In warm climate zones, water evaporates rapidly, so the concentration of salt is greater.
- The company's sales increased last year, yet its net profit declined.

Yet and *but* have similar meanings: they both signal that an opposite idea is coming. *Yet* is preferred when the second clause is an unexpected or surprising contrast to the first clause. When the two clauses are direct opposites, *but* is preferred.

- Thomas Edison dropped out of school at age 12, yet he became a famous inventor.
- I want to study art, but my parents want me to become an engineer.

Yet is roughly equivalent in meaning to *nevertheless*, and *but* is roughly equivalent to *however*.

---

independent clause: subject + verb + complement that express a complete thought
clan: extended family group

Subordinating Conjunctions

These words (and many others including *because, when,* and *so that*) introduce a dependent clause,* which is joined to an independent clause to form a complex sentence. There are two possible positions for the dependent clause:

1. If the dependent clause comes before the independent clause, use a comma after it.

- Although the company's sales increased last year, its net profit declined.

2. If the independent clause comes first, do not use a comma.

- The company's net profit declined last year although its sales increased.

Others

The transition signals in this group include adjectives such as *additional,* prepositions such as *in spite of,* and nouns such as *example.* There are no special punctuation rules for this group (except for *that is, i.e.,* and *e.g.,* which were discussed under conjunctive adverbs).

- The company's net profit declined last year in spite of increased sales.
- Despite increased sales, the company's net profit declined last year. (The comma is necessary because the prepositional phrase comes before the subject of the sentence.)
- An additional reason for the company's bankruptcy was the lack of competent management.
- Examples of vocabulary differences between British and American English include bonnet/hood, petrol/gasoline, windscreen/windshield, and lorry/truck.

PRACTICE 17: *Recognizing Transition Signals*

STEP 1 Circle all of the transition signals in the following paragraphs.

STEP 2 Punctuate the transition signals if necessary.

Genetic Engineering

Genetic* research has produced both exciting and frightening possibilities. Scientists are now able to create new forms of life in the laboratory due to the development of gene splicing.* On the one hand the ability to create life in the laboratory could greatly benefit mankind. For example because insulin* is very expensive to obtain from natural sources, scientists have developed a method to manufacture it inexpensively in the laboratory. Another beneficial application of gene splicing is in agriculture. Scientists foresee the day when new plants will be developed using nitrogen from the air instead of from fertilizer* therefore food production could be increased. In addition entirely new plants could be developed to feed the world's hungry people.

---

dependent clause: subordinating conjunction + subject + verb + complement that express an incomplete thought
genetic: from *gene,* the unit of heredity
gene splicing: gene joining
insulin: a substance needed by people who have diabetes
fertilizer: food for plants

Not everyone is excited about gene splicing however. Some people feel that it could have terrible consequences. A laboratory accident for example might cause an epidemic* of an unknown disease that could wipe out humanity. As a result of this controversy,* the government has made rules to control genetic experiments. Still many people feel that these rules are not strict enough even though the scientific community may feel that they are too strict.

Women's Liberation and English

The "women's lib"* movement toward greater equality for women has produced some permanent changes in the vocabulary of English. The first change is that new words have been added. The words **feminist**, **sexist**, and **male chauvinist** for example became common during the past ten years or so. Another new word is the title **Ms.**, which is often used in place of both **Miss** and **Mrs.** A second change is that sexist titles of many job occupations have been neutralized. A chairman is now a "chairperson," a businessman is a "businessperson," and a salesman is a "salesperson." Moreover a mailman is now a "mail carrier" and an airline stewardess is now a "flight attendant." Finally attempts to give equal treatment to masculine and feminine pronouns in English have led to the search for a new pronoun form to replace **he** (as **he/she** or **s/he**) when referring to neutral nouns such as **the student.** In conclusion some of the new words such as **Ms.** are quite useful; you can use **Ms.** to address a woman when you don't know if she is married. On the other hand the lack of a clear neutral pronoun can lead to awkward sentence construction.

PRACTICE 18: *Choosing Transition Signals*

A. STEP 1 Choose the transition signal that best shows the relationship between the sentences in each group from the choices given in parentheses. Write the signal in the space.

STEP 2 Add punctuation and change capital letters to small letters if necessary.

Note: All of the transition signals in this practice are sentence connectors. This is to give you more practice in using and punctuating this type of transition signal correctly.

Example:

A recent article in *Era* magazine suggested ways to reduce inflation. The article suggested that the president reduce the federal budget; furthermore, it suggested that the government reduce federal, state, and local taxes. (however, in contrast, furthermore)

1. The same article said that the causes of inflation were easy to find ________ the cure for inflation was not so easy to prescribe. (however, for example, therefore)
2. *Era* also suggested that rising wages were one of the primary causes of inflation ________ the government should take action to control wages. (however, therefore, for example)
3. In physics, the weight of an object is the gravitational force* with which the Earth attracts it ________ if a man weighs 150 pounds, this means that the Earth pulls him down with a force of 150 pounds. (moreover, therefore, for example)

---

epidemic: rapidly spreading disease
controversy: disagreement
women's lib: abbreviation for women's liberation movement
gravitional force: the force that pulls things toward the earth

4. The farther away from the Earth a person is, the less the gravitational force of the Earth ________________ a man weighs less when he is 50,000 miles from Earth than when he is only 5,000 miles away. (in conclusion, therefore, however)
5. A *tsunami* is a tidal wave produced by an earthquake on the ocean floor. The waves are very long and low in open water, but when they get close to land, they encounter friction* because of the shallow water ________________ the waves increase in height and can cause considerable damage when they finally reach land. (on the other hand, as a result, for example)

B. STEP 1 Fill in each blank with an appropriate transition signal from the following list. Use each only once.

for instance, however, moreover, but, furthermore, for example, in conclusion, such as

STEP 2 Use correct punctuation.

Internationalization of Japan

For many years, Japanese consumers have been very slow in accepting foreign goods, mainly because they are very selective and will only purchase high-quality products. Lately ________________ the consumer market has been changing. According to a recent article in **The Wall Street Journal**, **kokusaika**, which is defined as "internationalization," is influencing young Japanese consumers, who are very eager to purchase and enjoy products from countries around the world. The greatest access* into the Japanese market has been by the food industry. Traditionally, the protein staple* in Japan has been fish products, ________________ in the last decade or so, the Japanese have been consuming more beef. In fact, annual per capita* consumption is expected to be about 7 kilos by the mid-1990s. ________________ they have acquired a taste for imported beverages, both of the nonalcohol or low alcohol varieties, like beer drinks and "light" wines imported from England, Germany, Switzerland, the United States, and Australia. ________________ young people, especially women who are aware of the importance of health and fitness, are eating Western-style breakfasts. ________________ they enjoy fruit, milk, and bran-type cereals imported from the United States.

Not only Western countries but also Asian nations ________________ South Korea, Taiwan, Hong Kong, Singapore, and Thailand have been benefitting from the changing diet of the Japanese consumer. ________________ Japan is importing eels (fish) from Taiwan, asparagus (vegetable) from Thailand, and mangoes (fruit) from the Philippines. ________________ the Japanese trend toward internationalization should become even greater as we approach the twenty-first century. It will certainly increase international trade, which will definitely be advantageous to many countries of the world.

---

friction: resistance
access: increase or growth
staple: main food source
per capita: per person

PRACTICE 19: *Using Transition Signals*

Choose one of the topic sentences below and write a paragraph that develops it. Use transition signals to connect the supporting sentences smoothly. You may use the transition signals suggested for each topic, or you may use others not listed. Add other sentences without transitions if you need to in order to explain the topic completely.

1. The rowdiness* of soccer fans at international games is getting out of control.
   Two years ago
   Last year
   More recently
   As a result
2. There are two noticeable differences between British and American English.
   The first difference
   For example
   The second difference
   For example
   In conclusion, although
3. Some people enjoy solitude.*
   For instance
   Moreover
   On the other hand
   Therefore

Logical Order

In addition to using transition signals and repeating key nouns and pronouns, a third way to achieve coherence is to arrange your sentences in some kind of logical order. Since there are different kinds of logical relationships, there are different ways to organize the ideas and sentences in a paragraph. Your choice of one kind of logical order over another will, of course, depend on your topic and on your purpose. You may even combine two or more different logical orders in the same paragraph. The important point to remember is to arrange your ideas in some kind of order that is logical to a reader accustomed to the English way of writing.

Some common kinds of logical order in English are *chronological order, logical division of ideas, comparision and contrast,* and *cause and effect.* In this chapter, you will learn to recognize some of the logical orders; in later chapters, you will learn to write them.

Each kind of order has its own special words and phrases to show the relationships among the ideas. For example, in a piece of writing using chronological order, you would expect to find a lot of time expressions:

- first, next, after that, finally, before the last war, after 1950, since then, in 1990, while working on the project, etc.

In a paragraph describing differences (contrast), you would find these expressions:

- the most noticeable difference, larger than, unlike, on the other hand, in contrast, differ from

rowdiness: rough, disorderly behavior **solitude:** being alone

In a paragraph showing similarities (comparison), you would find these expressions:

- similarity, similarly, as expensive as, just as, just like, compare with, in comparison

Logical division of ideas is another common method of organizing ideas to give a paragraph coherence. Ideas are put into groups, and each group is discussed one after the other. Transition words such as *first, second, third* introduce each group.

PRACTICE 20: *Recognizing Kinds of Logical Orders*

Read the following paragraphs and decide which kind of logical order is used in each: comparison/contrast, chronological order, or logical division of ideas. Be able to discuss the reasons for your choice.

Paragraph 1: Translation by Computer

Powerful computers capable of translating documents from one language into another have recently been developed in Japan. The process of machine translation is complex. To translate a document from English into Japanese, for example, the computer first analyzes an English sentence, determining its grammatical structure and identifying the subject, verb, objects, and modifiers. Next, the words are translated by an English-Japanese dictionary. After that, another part of the computer program analyzes the resulting awkward jumble* of words and meanings and produces an intelligible sentence based on the rules of Japanese syntax* and the machine's understanding of what the original English sentence meant. Finally, the computer-produced translation is polished by a human bilingual editor.

Kind of logical order: ______________________________

Reasons for your choice: ______________________________

____

Paragraph 2: The Cost of Business Letters

The cost of dictating and transcribing the average business letter is $8.46 when the letter is dictated to a live secretary. By comparison, when the same letter is dictated into a machine, the cost of the letter drops to $6.08, according to the Dartnell Institute of Business Research. The fixed costs of a business letter, including typing supplies, mailing costs, and maintenance are the same for both machine-dictated and secretary-dictated letters. In both cases, they total $2.38. The difference in costs occurs in labor costs. For a machine-dictated letter, the dictator's time, based on 7.2 minutes and a salary of $644 per week costs $1.93. When the same dictator dictates the same letter to a live secretary, in contrast, the cost of the dictator's time increases to $2.71. Similarly, the cost of the secretary's time rises from $1.29 for a machine-dictated letter to $1.68 for a letter dictated in person, and nonproductive labor costs increase from 48¢ to 65¢. These figures make it clear that dictating to a machine is far less costly than dictating to a person.

Kind of logical order: ______________________________

Reasons for your choice: ______________________________

____

jumble: confused mixture **syntax:** sentence structure

Paragraph 3: The Expanding Deserts

Three factors have combined to cause deserts to expand in size in many areas of the world. The first factor is overpopulation. Overpopulation puts too much demand on the amount of land available for growing food. The second factor is unwise use of the land. The cutting down of trees for firewood, overgrazing (too many animals eating grass on too little land), and insufficient crop rotation* are examples of unwise land use practices. The third factor that has led to an increase in the size of many deserts around the world is continued drought.*

Kind of logical order: ______________________________

Reasons for your choice: ______________________________

Paragraph 4: Types of Business Organizations

A sole proprietorship and a general partnership are two forms of business ownership. A sole proprietorship is a business owned by a single person. In contrast, a general partnership is an association of two or more persons who own a business jointly. Both sole proprietorships and general partnerships are common in retailing and personal service businesses such as law, accounting, and medicine. Also, of course, the principals* in both types of businesses work equally hard to make their companies successful. There are, however, major differences in the organizational structure and daily operation of sole proprietorships and general partnerships. For example, a sole proprietor has the absolute freedom to make decisions. On the other hand, a majority of the partners must agree on any business decision before action can be taken. Furthermore, a sole proprietor is responsible for all of the managerial duties necessary to run the business, whereas the managerial functions in a partnership are divided among all the partners. Both types of businesses are terminated* in the same way, however. A sole proprietorship is legally terminated by the death or declaration of bankruptcy* of the owner. Similarly, the death or withdrawal* of any one of the partners in a general partnership usually terminates it. In conclusion, the choice depends on the business skills of the individual and the capital needed to start the business.

Kind of logical order: ______________________________

Reasons for your choice: ______________________________

Review

These are the important points you should have learned from this chapter:

1. Every good paragraph has coherence. Coherence is achieved by:
   - repeating key nouns frequently.
   - using pronouns consistently.
   - using transition signals to show the relationship of one idea to the next.
   - stating your ideas in some kind of logical order.
2. Transition signals can be transition phrases, conjunctive adverbs, coordinating conjunctions, subordinating conjunctions, prepositions, adjectives, or nouns. Each type of transition signal is punctuated differently.
3. Some common kinds of logical order in English are chronological order, logical division of ideas, and comparison/contrast.

---

crop rotation: changing the crops planted in the same place each year
drought: lack of rainfall
principal: owner
terminated: ended
bankruptcy: financial ruin
withdrawal: departure

WRITING PRACTICE

Choose one of the topics below and write one paragraph about it. Focus on making your paragraph coherent. The ideas should flow smoothly from beginning to end.

STEP 1: Narrow the topic and brainstorm to develop ideas by listing, freewriting, or clustering.

STEP 2: Develop an outline, including a topic sentence and a concluding sentence (if necessary). Underline them.

STEP 3: Decide where transition signals would be appropriate and write them in the margin of your outline.

STEP 4: Write a rough draft, and check it against the Paragraph Checklist below for organization. Circle your transition signals.

STEP 5: Write a second draft and check it for grammar and mechanics.

STEP 6: Write your final copy and hand it in.

Topic Suggestions

Cheating
Drinking laws
Drugs
Marriage
A current fad or fashion

Paragraph Checklist

Form:	______ Does your paragraph have a title?
	______ Did you write on the correct side of the paper?
	______ Did you indent?
	______ Did you write on every other line?
	(Refer to the Assignment Format on page 18 for complete instructions.)
Topic Sentence:	______ Does your topic sentence contain a controlling idea?
Supporting Sentences:	
Unity:	______ Do all of your sentences support your topic sentence?
Coherence:	______ Do you repeat key nouns frequently and use pronouns appropriately?
	______ Do you use transition signals at appropriate points to make your sentences flow smoothly?
	______ Are your ideas arranged in some kind of logical order?
Concluding Sentence:	______ Does your paragraph have a concluding sentence?

WRITING UNDER PRESSURE

Choose one of the following topics and write a paragraph about it. Your instructor will give you a time limit.

Suggested time limits

1.	Brainstorm for ideas.	5 minutes
2.	Develop a rough outline.	3 minutes
3.	Write your paragraph.	10 minutes
4.	Check your paragraph.	2 minutes
		20 minutes

Topic Suggestions

An unusual pet
Your favorite leisure-time activity
Your favorite kind of food
Your best friend
A bad habit

CHAPTER 5

Kinds of Logical Order

In Chapter 4, you learned that writing your ideas in some kind of **logical order** is necessary to achieve coherence. You also learned to recognize three of the common "logical orders" in English—chronological order, comparison/contrast, and logical division of ideas. In this chapter, you will practice writing paragraphs using chronological order, logical division, and order of importance.

Chronological Order

Chronological order is one of the easiest methods of organization to master. *Chronos* is a Greek word meaning time. Chronological order, therefore, is a way of organizing the ideas in a paragraph in the order of their occurrence in time.

Chronological order is used for something as simple as a recipe and for something as complex as a history book. In academic writing, chronological order has many uses. One of the primary ways you might use it is to write a historical review of the subject of a term paper. For example, you might review the history of labor unions before you discuss the current situation.

However, chronological order is not just used for historical events; it is also used in business, science and engineering to explain processes and procedures. For example, chronological order would be used to explain how to solve a math problem, how to perform a chemistry experiment, or how to set up an accounting system. Such paragraphs are called "how to" or "process" paragraphs.

Here are some typical test questions and/or term paper topics for which you could use chronological order as a method of organization:

Economics: Trace the growth of labor unions in the United States since 1900.
Business: Describe the procedure for taking a year-end inventory in a small retail business.

Chemical Engineering: Describe the process of desalinization.*
Biochemistry: Discuss the function of the enzyme* pepsin in the digestion of food.

There are two keys to writing a good chronological paragraph:

1. Discuss the events (in a history) or the steps (in a process) in the order in which they occur.
2. Use chronological transition signals to indicate the sequence of events or steps.

Analyze the following model paragraphs for their organization by time. Circle any words or expressions that indicate time order (*first, next, after that, in 1971,* etc.). The first paragraph reviews very briefly the history of computers. The second paragraph is an example of a process paragraph. It tells how to perform part of a simple chemistry experiment.

MODEL: *Chronological Order*

The Evolution of Computers*

In the relatively short span of forty-five years, there has been an incredible evolution in the size and capabilities of computers. Today, computers smaller than the tip of your fingernail have the same capabilities as the room-sized machines of forty-five years ago. The first computers were developed around 1945. They were so large that they required special air-conditioned rooms. About twenty years later, in the 1960s, desk-sized computers were developed. This represented a gigantic advance. Before the end of that same decade, however, a third generation of computers, which used simple integrated circuits and which were even smaller and faster, had appeared. In 1971, the first microprocessor, less than one square centimeter in size, was developed. Today, electronic engineers predict that even smaller and more sophisticated computers will be on the market before the twenty-first century.

A Neutralization Experiment

To perform a neutralization experiment, proceed in the following manner. First, measure out about 2 cc. of laboratory NaOH solution. Second, pour the solution into a small casserole.* Next, add portions of HCl solution, stirring after each addition until the solution is acid when tested with litmus paper.* Then, place the casserole containing the solution on a wire gauze over a Bunsen burner and heat it until the solution begins to boil. When it does, reduce the size of the flame immediately and allow the solution to boil gently. As it approaches dryness, sputtering* may occur. At this point, cover the casserole loosely with a watch-glass. Then, hold the casserole above the flame and move it back and forth until no further water vapor* is expelled.* Finally, allow the dish and residue* to cool.

---

desalinization: removal of salt from sea water
enzyme: protein substance vital to cell metabolism
evolution: development
casserole: baking dish
litmus paper: a treated paper used to test acidity and alkalinity
sputtering: spitting out of small particles
water vapor: steam
expelled: given off
residue: remaining solid matter

Writing Technique Questions

1. What are the two uses of chronological order that the two model paragraphs exemplify?
2. What are the main time divisions in the paragraph about computers? How would you outline it?
3. What transition signals and time expressions are used in the first paragraph to show chronological order? Circle them.
4. What transition signals and time expressions are used in the second paragraph to show the steps in the process? Circle them.
5. What verb forms are used in the second paragraph? Why?

Topic Sentences

Notice that the topic sentence of a chronological paragraph in some way indicates the time order. In paragraphs such as the one on computers, phrases such as *the development of, the growth of,* or *the evolution of* give the reader a hint that this is a chronological paragraph.

In a "how to" or process paragraph such as the one on page 54 about the chemistry experiment, the process to be described is named in the topic sentence. Again, this is a hint to the reader to expect a chronological paragraph.

PRACTICE 21: *Chronological Topic Sentences*

STEP 1 Put a check in the space to the left of every topic sentence suggesting that a chronological paragraph will follow.

STEP 2 In the sentences you have checked, circle the word or words that indicate chronological order.

Example:

__✓__ (In the past forty-five years) (developments) in the field of electronics have revolutionized the computer industry.

_____ **1.** A person's intelligence is the product of both heredity* and environment.

_____ **2.** The tensions* that led to last year's student riots had been building for several years.

_____ **3.** The life cycle of the Pacific salmon is a fascinating phenomenon.*

_____ **4.** There are two main reasons I believe women should be drafted* into the army along with men.

_____ **5.** Surviving a major earthquake is possible if you follow certain procedures.

_____ **6.** The worst day in my life was the day I left my family and my friends to come to the United States.

_____ **7.** American directness often conflicts with Asian modesty.

_____ **8.** The two most important holidays in the United States are, first, Christmas and, second, Thanksgiving.

---

heredity: characteristics received from one's parents (hair color, eye color, height, etc.)
tensions: stresses
drafted: called into military service
phenomenon: an unusual or scientific fact or event

_____ **9.** The traditions of Christmas originated in several different countries.

_____ **10.** Every year, our family celebrates Christmas Day in the same way.

_____ **11.** The preparation of the poisonous puffer fish for eating is not for amateur chefs.

_____ **12.** To make a perfect cup of coffee, follow these easy directions.

Transition Signals

Transition signals are especially important in a chronological paragraph. You have to be very clear about the sequence of events: did one event happen before, at the same time as, or after another event?

Some of the most common chronological transition signals are given in the chart below.

Transition Signals for Chronological Order

Transition Words/Phrases	Subordinators	Others
first (second, third, fourth, etc.)	before	the first (+ noun)
next, last, finally	after	the second (+ noun)
first of all	while	before the (+ noun)
after that	until	in the year _____
since then	as soon as	since the (+ noun)

Keep in mind, however, that *any* time expression can serve as a chronological transition signal, such as these:

Later,
In 1989,
Twenty-five years earlier,
Before the telephone was invented,
In the next ten years,
Yesterday,
From 1950 to 1975,

PRACTICE 22: *Chronological Transition Signals*

Add appropriate chronological transition signals to the following essay and punctuate them. Consult the list in the preceding table or use others with which you are familiar.

How to Reduce the Danger of Smoking

The Department of Health, Education and Welfare (HEW) has outlined some steps to take some of the danger out of smoking for those people who are unable to quit smoking outright.* __________ choose a cigarette with less tar and nicotine to reduce your intake of these pollutants. __________ don't smoke your cigarette all the way down. Smoke halfway, and you will inhale only about 40 percent of the total tar and nicotine. Remember, 60 percent of these substances* is contained in the last half of the cigarette. __________ take fewer draws on each cigarette; that is, reduce the number of puffs on each cigarette. This will cut down on your smoking. __________ reduce your inhaling. Don't open your lungs by inhaling deeply. Take

outright: all at once **substances:** materials

short, shallow puffs. ____________ smoke fewer cigarettes each day. This may be the most difficult step of all. However, just follow these directions:

1. Pick a time of day to start, and don't smoke before that time.
2. Don't think of it as cutting down; think of it as postponing.*
3. Carry your cigarettes in a different pocket, or put them in a different place so that you can't reach for them automatically.

____________ think about the terrible diseases you are opening yourself up to each time you smoke a cigarette. ____________ if you follow each of these steps without cheating, you should be able to at least control the number of cigarettes you smoke daily. Who knows, this might be the beginning of the end—of your smoking, that is.[1]

Writing a Chronological Paragraph

To write a chronological paragraph, whether it is a history or a process:

1. Make a simple outline that lists the events (in a history) or the steps (in a process) in the order of their occurrence.
2. Add transition signals at appropriate points in the left margin of your outline.
3. Write a topic sentence that names the event or the process.
4. Write the paragraph, following your outline. Add enough details to make the chain of events or steps in the process very clear.

WRITING PRACTICE

STEP 1 Choose a topic from the suggestions listed below.

STEP 2 Write an outline, listing the main steps or main events that you will explain in your paragraph.

STEP 3 Add chronological transition signals at appropriate points in the left margin of your outline.

STEP 4 Write your paragraph from your outline.

Topic Suggestions

A. Process Topics
How to study for a test, take a test, or find a book in the library
How to cure the hiccoughs, a hangover, "the blues," "the blahs"*
How to jump-start a car, wash and wax a car, change a tire
How to make a perfect cup of coffee, cup of tea, dry martini

B. Historical Topics
Use some or all of the following data to write a brief history of manned space flights.

---

postponing: delaying
"the blahs": don't care attitude

[1]DHEW Publication No. (CDC) 78-8705, U.S. Government Printing Office, 1978, 0-252-573.

Manned Space Flights

Crew/Date of Mission	Mission Name	Comments
Yuri Gagarin April 12, 1961	Vostok 1	First manned orbital* flight.
John Glenn, Jr. February 20, 1962	Mercury-Atlas 6	First American in orbit.
Valentina Tereshkova June 16–19, 1963	Vostok 6	First woman in space.
Aleksei Leonov March 18, 1965	Voskhod 2	First "space walk" (10 minutes).
3 U.S. astronauts July 20, 1969	Apollo-Saturn 11	First landing on the moon.
2 Russian cosmonauts and 3 U.S. astronauts July, 1975	Soyuz 19 and Apollo 18	U.S.–U.S.S.R. joint flight. Crews linked up in space.
Sally Ride June 18, 1983	Space Shuttle Challenger	First American woman in space.
7 American astronauts January 28, 1986	Space Shuttle Challenger	Exploded after liftoff. All aboard killed.

Logical Division of Ideas

Logical division is one of the most common ways to organize ideas in English. When you use logical division, you group related ideas together and discuss each group, one after the other. You already learned something about logical division when you divided the brainstorming list on the problems of Metropolitan City into groups A, B, and C in Chapter 3. In everyday life, things are divided into groups. Grocery stores separate items into groups: produce (fresh fruits and vegetables) are in one section, milk products (milk, butter, cheese) are in another section, meats in another, and so on. Corporations divide themselves into departments: marketing, research, accounting, etc. Authors divide books into chapters.

There is usually more than one way to divide things. Suppose, for example, you are asked to divide the members of your class into groups. How many different ways could you divide them? Make a list:

By gender (male, females)
By age
By ______________
By ______________
By ______________

The order of your group makes no difference. In the model about "Problems of Metropolitan City" in Chapter 1, traffic, public transportation, and the cost of housing are all more or less equally important in the mind of the writer. Therefore, they could be discussed in any order. The important point to know about logical division as a method of organization is that each group should be unified within itself. In other words, you shouldn't put meat in the produce section.

orbital: in a circle around the Earth

MODEL: *Logical Division of Ideas*

Life in Space

Living aboard a space station in orbit around the Earth for months at a time poses problems for astronauts' bodies as well as for their minds. One major problem is maintaining astronauts' physical health. Medical treatment may be days or even weeks away as there may not be a doctor on board. Illnesses such as appendicitis or ulcers, routinely treated on Earth, could be fatal in space because of the delay in getting to a doctor. Furthermore, surgery may be impossible because blood would float around inside the operating room. Another health problem is the potential for bone deterioration.* In a weightless environment, the body produces less calcium. Astronauts would have to exercise at least three hours a day to prevent bone loss. A second major problem is maintaining astronauts' mental health. Being confined for long periods of time in dark and hostile* space will undoubtedly produce anxiety.* Loneliness and boredom are other psychological concerns. Finally, how will astronauts "let off steam"* when interpersonal* conflicts develop? It is clear that space-station duty will require astronauts who are not only physically but also mentally strong.

Writing Technique Questions

1. How many main groups is the topic of this paragraph divided into? What are they?
2. Does the topic sentence tell you the topics of the divisions? Does the concluding sentence?
3. How many points are discussed in the first group?
   How many points are mentioned in the second group?
4. What transition signals indicate the divisions? Where else are transition signals used? What is their purpose?
5. In your opinion, would it make any difference if mental health were discussed before physical health? Do you think that one is more important than the other, or are they approximately equal in importance?
6. In your opinion, could this paragraph be split into two paragraphs? Where?

Transition Signals for Logical Division

Transition signals used in logical division include many that you already know.

Sentence Connectors	Others
first, second, third, etc.	the first (+ noun)
next, last, finally	the/a second (+ noun)
in addition, moreover	one (+ noun)
furthermore	another (+ noun)
also	an additional (+ noun)

deterioration: reduction in amount
hostile: unfriendly
anxiety: fear, worry
"let off steam": get rid of anger, frustration (idiom)
interpersonal: between or among people

- *First,* maintaining astronauts' physical health is a concern.
- *In addition,* sanitation* is a problem in weightless space.
- *A second* concern is maintaining astronauts' mental health.
- *An additional* problem caused by weightlessness is the potential for bone loss.

Order of Importance

Another very common way to organize ideas in a paragraph is to discuss them in the order of their importance. This method is very similar to logical order; the only difference is that you discuss each item in order of its importance (in your mind). You can discuss the most important item first and work down to the least important, or you can begin with the least important and end with the most important. Both ways can be effective.

MODEL: *Order of Importance*

The Challenges of Overpopulation

World population is increasing at an alarming rate. In fact, according to the United Nations, by the year 2060, the Earth will have 10 billion people. Governments, particularly governments of developing countries, will face four major challenges to provide for their expanding populations. The first challenge will be to provide an adequate food supply. Hungry, undernourished* people lack the energy, the time and the will* to improve their lives. A second challenge is to build adequate housing. The population needs access to affordable housing to keep people off the streets. Another challenge is to provide jobs. Since rural* areas provide only limited job opportunities, many people migrate to the cities in hopes of finding employment. If employment is not available, these people quickly become burdens on the urban* society. The final and most important challenge is to provide education for all the people. As the population increases, more schools will have to be built, and good teachers and administrators will have to be trained to operate these schools. Not only do young children need an education, but adults also need training in various skills and trades* that will translate into jobs to benefit themselves and their countries. In conclusion, the challenges of rapid population growth must be met by all countries, especially developing ones. In my opinion, the most important one is education, for without education, there can be no progress.

Writing Technique Questions

1. How do you know that this is "order of importance" rather than "logical division"?
2. What transition signals are used for order of importance? Which ones are the same as those used for logical division? Which ones are different?
3. How many challenges does this writer discuss? Does this paragraph begin or end with the most important challenge? Do you agree with this order?

Transition Signals for Order of Importance

Transition signals used for order of importance include all of those used for logical division, and a few new ones.

---

sanitation: cleanliness
undernourished: lacking enough healthful food
will: determination, resolve
rural: in the country (not city)
urban: in the city
trades: occupations requiring skill such as carpentry

Sentence Connectors	Others
first, second, third, etc.	the first (+ noun)
next, last, finally	the/a second (+ noun)
in addition, moreover	one (+ noun)
furthermore	another (+ noun)
also	an additional (+ noun)
more importantly	the most important (+ noun)
most importantly	the second most important (+ noun)
more significantly	the most significant (+ noun)
above all	the third most significant (+ noun)
primarily	the primary (+ noun)

PRACTICE 23: ***Transition Signals for Logical Division and Order of Importance***

Reread the model paragraphs "Life in Space," page 59 and "The Challenges of Overpopulation," page 60. Circle all of the transition signals you can find.

Topic Sentences for Logical Division and Order of Importance

The topic sentence of logical division and order of importance paragraphs often indicates the number of groups the topic is divided into.

- Gold, a precious metal, is prized for two important characteristics.
- Inflation has three causes.

The topic sentence may even tell what the groups are.

- Gold, a precious metal, is prized not only for its beauty but also for its utility.
- Inflation has three causes: an increase in the supply of paper money, excessive government spending, and unrestrained consumer borrowing.

The topic sentence for order of importance differs only in that it may contain an order-of-importance transition signal:

- Gold, a precious metal, is prized not only for its beauty but, *more importantly,* for its utility.

PRACTICE 24: ***Logical Division and Order of Importance Topic Sentences***

A. Put a check (✓) in the space to the left of every topic sentence that suggests logical division as a method of organization. Put a double check (✓✓) if the sentence suggests order of importance organization. Some are neither, so leave these unchecked.

_____ **1.** My eighteenth birthday was a day I will never forget.

_____ **2.** On his eighteenth birthday, an American male receives two important rights/responsibilities: he can vote and he can be drafted into the army.

_____ **3.** In most occupations, women lag behind men in three areas: salary, power, and status.

_____ **4.** Living in a dormitory offers three advantages to a newly arrived foreign student.

_____ **5.** Photosynthesis is the process by which plants manufacture their own food.

_____ **6.** Television game shows are insulting to the educated viewer because they are poorly disguised commercials but more importantly, because they require such a minimal level of knowledge.

_____ **7.** Some meteorologists* believe that another ice age* is approaching.

_____ **8.** Earthquake prediction is still an inexact science although seismologists* learn more each time they monitor* a quake.

_____ **9.** A college degree in international business today requires, first, a knowledge of business procedures and, second, a knowledge of cultural differences in business methods.

_____ **10.** A computer is both faster and more accurate than a human.

_____ **11.** Teenagers demonstrate their rebellious attitude in several ways.

_____ **12.** Small cars have three advantages over large ones.

B. Suggest changes to the topic sentence of the model paragraph "Life in Space" on page 59 to make it an order-of-importance paragraph. Also suggest changes to the transition signals.

*Two Topic Sentence Tips**

Here are two tips to help you write topic sentences for logical division and order of importance paragraphs:

1. Use a colon [:] in front of the names of the groups. (For more information about the use of colons, see Appendix A.)

Inflation has three causes: an increase in the supply of paper money, excessive government spending, and unrestrained consumer borrowing.

2. Use paired (correlative) conjunctions when there are only two groups.

Paired conjunctions are *both . . . and . . . , not only . . . but also . . . , either . . . or . . . , neither . . . nor . . . .*

Remember that paired (correlative) conjunctions follow the rule of parallelism. If you put a noun after the word *both,* you **must** put a noun after the word *and.* If you use a prepositional phrase after *not only,* you **must** use one after *but also.* (See pages 168–171 for further information and practice.)

Here are some examples of logical division topic sentences with these special conjunctions.

- Gold, a precious metal, is prized not only *for its beauty* but also *for its utility.* (prepositional phrases)
- To stay healthy, you should both *eat nutritious food* and *exercise daily.* (verbs)
- In my opinion, drivers arrested for speeding should have the choice of either *spending* time in jail or *working* in a hospital emergency room. (*-ing* verb forms)
- In my opinion, neither *wealth* nor *beauty* guarantees happiness. (nouns)
- *I want to be a flight attendant* because the work is challenging *and* because I can travel around the world. (dependent clauses)

---

meteorologist: person who studies the weather
ice age: time period millions of years ago, when ice covered large areas of the Earth
seismologist: person who studies earthquakes
monitor: observe, check with instruments
tip: helpful advice

Review

These are the important points you should have learned from this chapter:

1. You can achieve coherence in writing by stating your ideas in logical order. There are several kinds of logical orders. Chronological order, logical division of ideas, and order of importance are three common ones in English.
2. Each kind of logical order has special words and expressions.

WRITING PRACTICE

Choose one of the topics below and write a paragraph about it. Use either logical division or order of importance to organize your ideas.

STEP 1 Brainstorm your topic for ideas.

STEP 2 Develop an outline.

STEP 3 Write a rough draft.

STEP 4 Revise your rough draft, using the Paragraph Checklist below as a guide. Be sure to use transition signals.

STEP 5 Revise your second draft, proofreading it for grammar, sentence structure, and mechanics.

STEP 6 Write or type the final copy to hand in.

Topic Suggestions

Ways to improve your English speaking skills
The most important freedoms in your country
Qualities of a marriage partner

Paragraph Checklist

Form:	_______	Does your paragraph have a title?
	_______	Did you write on the correct side of the paper?
	_______	Did you indent the first line?
	_______	Did you write on every other line?
		(Refer to the Assignment Format on page 18 for complete instructions.)
Topic Sentence:	_______	Does your topic sentence contain a controlling idea?
Supporting Sentences:		
Unity:	_______	Do all of your sentences support your topic sentence?
Coherence:	_______	Do you repeat key nouns frequently and use pronouns appropriately?
	_______	Do you use transition signals at appropriate points to make your sentences flow smoothly?
	_______	Are your ideas arranged in logical order?
Concluding Sentence:	_______	Does your paragraph have a concluding sentence?

WRITING UNDER PRESSURE

Choose one of the topics below and write a paragraph about it using chronological order, logical order, or order of importance. Your instructor will give you a time limit.

Suggested Time Limits

1. Brainstorm for ideas	5 minutes
2. Develop a rough outline	3 minutes
3. Write your paragraph	10 minutes
4. Check your paragraph	2 minutes
	20 minutes

Topic Suggestions

The most exciting day in my life
The worst day in my life
Important people in my life
Important events in my life

CHAPTER 6

Concrete Support

One of the biggest problems in student writing is that student writers often fail to prove their points. They fail because they do not support their points with concrete details. Their papers are too often full of opinions and generalizations without the factual details needed to support them.

A paragraph contains **concrete support** for the topic sentence. Support your topic sentence by using specific and factual details.

Facts Versus Opinions

Facts are objective statements of truths.

- At sea level, water boils at 100 degrees Celsius.
- Women live longer than men.
- Lung cancer among women is increasing.

Opinions are subjective statements based on a person's beliefs or attitudes.

- Men are better drivers than women.
- Engineering students do not need to take a lot of English courses.
- Americans are only superficially* friendly.

It is certainly acceptable to express opinions in academic writing. In fact, most professors want you to express your own ideas. However, you must support your opinions with factual details. Moreover, the more specific you are, the better.

In very formal academic writing, even some statements that are considered facts need further support. In other words, they need specific supporting details in order to be completely convincing.

superficially: on the surface

Here are some examples of statements that need further support to be acceptable in formal academic writing, and of the additional necessary supporting detail.

Unsupported "Fact":	On the average, heavy smokers die earlier than nonsmokers.
Concrete Supporting Detail:	The life expectancy of a two-pack-a-day smoker at age 25 is 8.3 years less than that of a nonsmoker.
Unsupported "Fact":	Smoking causes lung cancer.
Concrete Supporting Detail:	The U.S. Surgeon General's 1964 report on smoking and lung cancer states: "Cigarette smoking is causally related to lung cancer in men.... The risk of developing lung cancer increases with duration of smoking and the number of cigarettes smoked per day and is diminished by discontinuing."

PRACTICE 25: *Facts Versus Opinions*

A. Decide whether each of the following statements is a fact or an opinion. Write F for fact, O for opinion. Next, decide if the facts need additional supporting details. Write NFS for "needs further support" next to those that do.

_____ **1.** Smoking is relaxing.
_____ **2.** Smoking is unhealthy.
_____ **3.** Some people enjoy smoking because it relaxes them.
_____ **4.** Dr. Kathleen Parker, a well-known cancer specialist, recently admitted in an interview, "Although I see the harmful effects of smoking nearly every day in my work, I still enjoy relaxing with a cigarette after dinner."
_____ **5.** Cigarette smoke causes chemical changes in your lung cells which can lead to emphysema* and cancer.
_____ **6.** Young men between the ages of 16 and 30 are reckless drivers.
_____ **7.** Young men between the ages of 16 and 30 have 2.7 times as many accidents as young women in the same age group do and receive 5 times as many tickets for speeding.
_____ **8.** Young men between the ages of 16 and 30 should be required to take a drivers' training class, which emphasizes safety and responsibility.
_____ **9.** Young men who take such a class will become safer drivers.

B. Discuss with your classmates what specific supporting details you might use to support the sentences you marked O (opinion) or F-NFS (fact—needs further support).

---

emphysema: a lung disease

Concrete Supporting Details

There are several kinds of concrete supporting details that you can use to support or prove your topic sentence. Among the most common are examples and illustrative incidents, statistics, and quotations. In academic writing, quotations are perhaps the kind of support most often used, but many academic disciplines* require the occasional use of statistics as well. The other two—examples and illustrative incidents—are also useful for explaining or proving your point.

Read the following article about the growing refugee problem in the world. Notice how the four different types of concrete supporting details support the author's main points.

MODEL: *Concrete Supporting Details*

World Refugees

Illustrative Incident

Duc Trong knew that the voyage would be risky, but he also knew that he had no choice. If he and his family stayed in their country, there was little hope for their future. So one night, he, his wife, and ten other members of his family boarded a small, rickety* boat, taking with them only what they could carry, and set sail along with thirty-six other Vietnamese. Their voyage was a nightmare. Before they reached safety, they were attacked by two different groups of pirates, and during a terrible storm, their supplies were washed overboard. Eleven of the older people died, and the survivors were delirious* from lack of food and water.

Statistics

The rising tide of refugees around the world is rapidly becoming a flood. According to figures published by the United Nations, there are more than 6.2 million refugees and an additional 2.6 million people who are classified as "displaced persons." That makes a total of nearly 9 million.

Examples and Statistics

No corner of the Earth is without a refugee problem although the African continent has so far produced the greatest number. Ethiopia, with its 1.6 million refugees, has produced three times as many refugees as Vietnam and Cambodia combined. The Middle East has its Palestinian and, more recently, Afghan refugees. In the Western Hemisphere, Haiti, Cuba, and the Central American countries of El Salvador and Guatemala are producing refugees by the thousands.

Quotation

The refugees present problems not only for themselves but also for the countries that take them in. As Victor Palmieri, the U.S. coordinator for refugee affairs, has put it, "The worldwide refugee explosion is a massive tragedy in human terms and a growing crisis in financial terms for the countries bearing the burden."

Writing Technique Questions

1. What does the incident about Duc Trong in the first paragraph illustrate? What, then, is the author's main point in this paragraph? Notice that, even though it isn't stated directly in a topic sentence, the main idea is clear from the incident. What topic sentence could you write for this paragraph?
2. What is the main idea in the second paragraph? What statistics are given?
3. What is the main idea in the third paragraph? How is this supported?
4. What is the main idea in the last paragraph? What kind of specific supporting detail is given to support it? What is the source of the quotation?

---

academic discipline: major field of study **delirious:** temporarily crazy
rickety: in poor condition

In the following sections, you will practice using each kind of concrete supporting detail.

Examples and Illustrative Incidents

Examples and illustrative incidents are perhaps the easiest kind of supporting details to use. You don't have to search in the library for information; you can often take examples from your own knowledge and personal experiences. Furthermore, examples and illustrative incidents are usually interesting and make your writing enjoyable to read. Finally, since it is easy to remember a striking example or a good story, your reader is more likely to remember your point.

However, there are two cautions you should keep in mind if you use examples and illustrative incidents for support. First, remember that in formal academic writing—research papers, theses, and the like—examples and illustrative incidents are considered the weakest kind of support, so use them sparingly.* Second, be sure that your examples really prove your point. For instance, if you are trying to prove that, on the average, men are better drivers than women, don't use famous racing car drivers as examples of superior drivers because they aren't average.

Study the two models to see how examples and illustrative incidents can be used to support a topic sentence.

MODEL: *Examples*

*Language and Perception**

Although we all possess the same physical organs for perceiving the world—eyes for seeing, ears for hearing, noses for smelling, skins for feeling, and mouths for tasting—our perception of the world depends to a great extent on the language we speak. In other words, we cannot perceive things that we have not named. Each language is like a pair of sunglasses through which we "see" the world. A classic example of the relationship between language and perception is the word **snow.** In the English language, there is only that one word to describe all of the possible kinds of snow. In Eskimo languages, however, there are as many as thirty-two different words for snow. For instance, the Eskimos have different words for falling snow, snow on the ground, snow packed as hard as ice, slushy snow, wind-driven snow, and what we might call "cornmeal" snow. In contrast, cultures that rarely experience cold weather and snow may have only one word to express several concepts that are differentiated in English. For example, the ancient Aztec languages of Mexico used only one word to mean snow, cold, and ice.

Writing Technique Questions

1. What is the main idea of this paragraph? Where is it stated?
2. How many supporting examples are given?
3. What transition signals introduce the examples?

---

sparingly: infrequently **perception:** knowledge derived from the five senses

MODEL: *Illustrative Incidents*

*Nonverbal Communication**

Nonverbal communication, or "body language," is communication by facial expressions, head or eye movements, hand signals, and body postures. It can be just as important to understanding as words are. Misunderstandings—often amusing but sometimes serious—can arise between people from different cultures if they misinterpret nonverbal signals. Take, for example, the differences in meaning of a gesture* very common in the United States: a circle made with the thumb and index* finger. To an American, it means that everything is OK. To a Japanese, it means that you are talking about money. In France, it means that something is worthless, and in Greece, it is an obscene* gesture. Therefore, an American could unknowingly offend a Greek by using that particular hand signal.

The following incident illustrates how conflicting nonverbal signals can cause serious misunderstandings. While lecturing to his poetry class at Ain Shams University in Cairo, a British professor became so relaxed that he leaned back in his chair and revealed the bottom of his foot to the astonished class. Making such a gesture in Moslem society is the worst kind of insult. The next day the Cairo newspapers carried headlines about the student demonstration that resulted, and they denounced British arrogance* and demanded that the professor be sent home.

Writing Technique Questions

1. What is the main point of these two paragraphs? In which two places is it stated directly?
2. What examples are given to support the main point?
3. What story is told to support the main point?
4. What words and phrases are used to introduce the examples and the illustrative incident?
5. Why do you think this article was divided into two paragraphs?

Tips for Using Examples and Illustrative Incidents

When you use examples and illustrative incidents to support a point:

1. Make sure that your example or illustration really supports your point.
2. Introduce them with appropriate transition signals. Three common ones are *for example, for instance,* and *e.g.* (from Latin *exempli gratia,* for example).

---

nonverbal communication: communication without words
gesture: hand signal
index finger: the finger next to the thumb
obscene: indecent, disgusting
arrogance: too much pride

WRITING PRACTICE

Choose either A or B below and write a paragraph using examples and/or illustrative incidents to explain your topic sentence.

STEP 1 Choose your topic and write a topic sentence.

STEP 2 Freewrite to generate supporting sentences. Your supporting sentences should include at least two specific examples or illustrative incidents. This is a rough draft.

STEP 3 Circle the transition signals that introduce your examples and illustrations.

STEP 4 Rewrite your rough draft if necessary after checking it against the Paragraph Checklist on page 73 for organization.

STEP 5 Check your paragraph for grammar and mechanics.

STEP 6 Write a final copy to hand in.

A. Describe a body-language signal from your own culture that is different from English body language. Explain the confusion that can be caused when other people misunderstand it.

B. Explain a proverb* from your language by using examples. Some proverbs in English are

A stitch in time saves nine.
Early to bed, early to rise, makes a man healthy, wealthy, and wise.
People who live in glass houses shouldn't throw stones.
An apple a day keeps the doctor away.
A rolling stone gathers no moss.

Figures and Statistics

In business, engineering, and the sciences, figures and statistics are often used for support. This section will give you practice in using figures and statistics from charts and graphs to support your ideas.

Study the chart on World Population Growth, and then read the paragraph which explains its significance. Notice that the source of the information is given in the sentence which begins, "According to . . .".

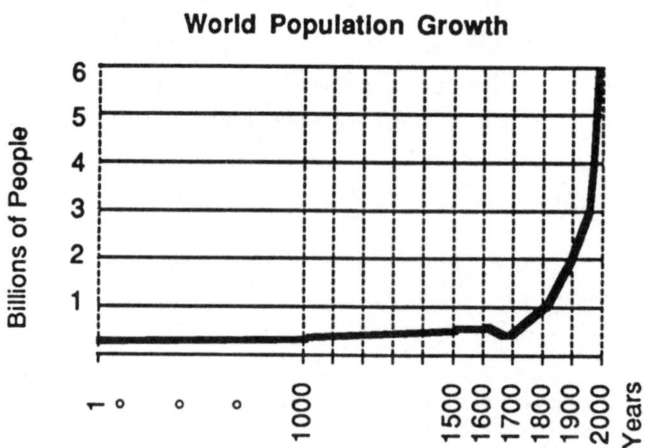

proverb: wise saying that gives a practical rule for living

MODEL: *Figures and Statistics*

World Population Growth

The world's population is growing at an ever-increasing rate. According to estimates and statistics compiled* by the World Health Organization, it took 1,600 years for the Earth to acquire its first one-half billion people. It took only 200 years, or until 1800, for its population to double to one billion. It gained another billion people by 1930, a time span of only 130 years. The third billion was gained by 1964 after only 34 years, and the fourth billion after only ten years, in 1974. Population growth has slowed somewhat, so it took 13 years for the Earth to acquire its five billionth citizen. WHO estimates that the world's population will reach the six billion mark before the end of the century.

PRACTICE 26: *Using Figures and Statistics*

Study the graph below, which shows the amount of carbon emissions* measured in millions of metric tons for different groups of nations around the world. Then, use the information in the graph to complete the paragraph.

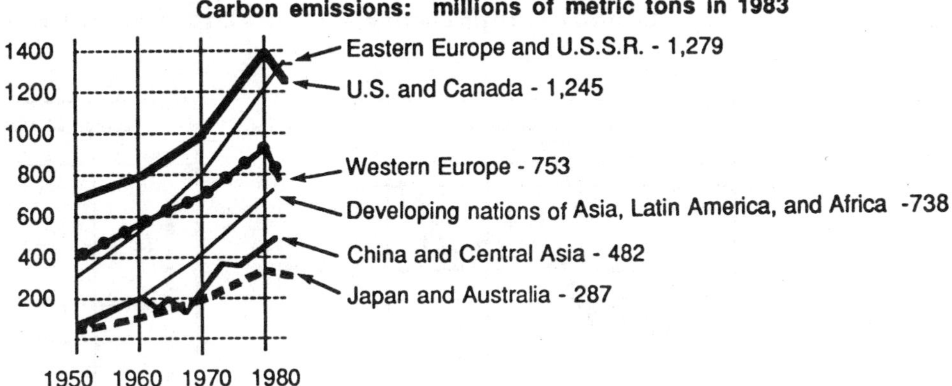

Global Distribution of CO2 Emissions

During the past two centuries, carbon dioxide (CO2) in the atmosphere has increased dramatically. One of the causes appears to be the burning of fossil fuels (oil, coal, and gas). Nations of North America and Western and Eastern Europe, including the Soviet Union, ______________

____

Eastern Europe and the U.S.S.R. produced the most, emitting ______________

____ in 1983.

Of the industrialized nations, Japan and Australia emitted ______________

____

---

compiled: collect facts, information **emission:** something released, sent out

Since 1980, however, the U.S., Canada, Japan, Australia, and the countries of Western Europe ____

____

By contrast, rapidly developing nations of Asia, Latin America, and Africa continue ______

____

____

WRITING PRACTICE

Choose either pair of graphs and write a paragraph explaining the significance of the pair.

STEP 1 Decide what main idea the graphs illustrate and write this idea as a topic sentence.

STEP 2 Write five to eight supporting statements, using the statistical information shown in the graphs.

STEP 3 Check your paragraph against the Paragraph Checklist on page 73 before handing it in.

A. Global Temperature/Carbon Dioxide in the Atmosphere

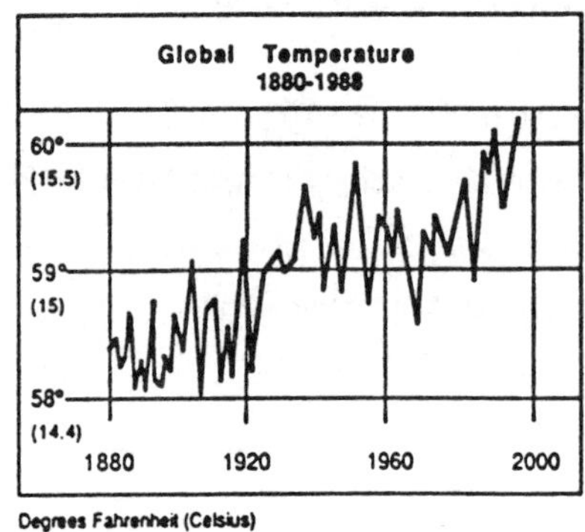

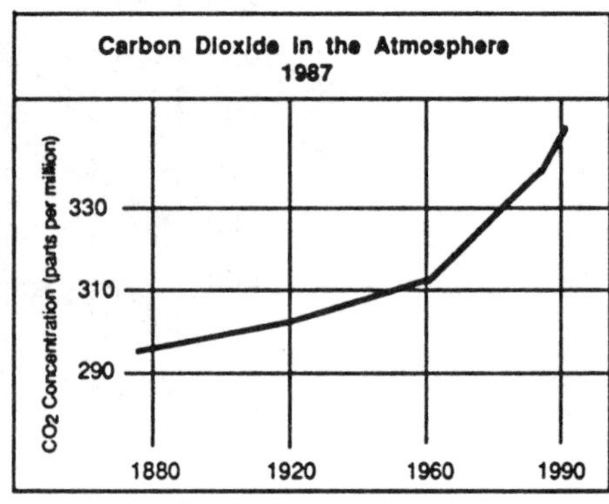

B. Pay Gap Narrows Slowly

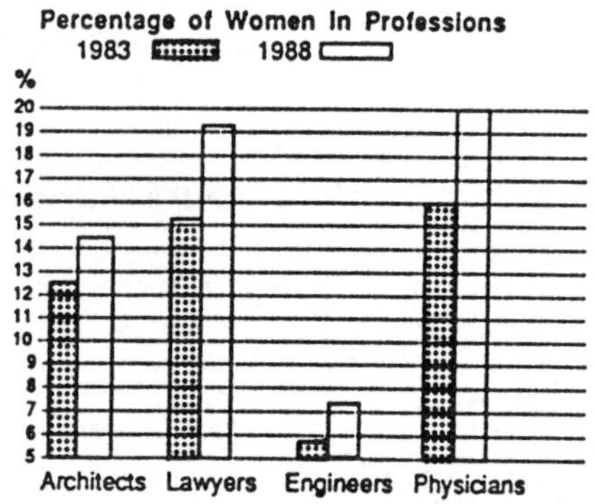

Review

These are the important points you should have learned from this chapter:

1. Use concrete supporting details to prove your points.
2. Do not use opinions for support.
3. Use examples, illustrative incidents, or figures and statistics to support your points.

Paragraph Checklist

Form:	_______	Does your paragraph have a title?
	_______	Did you write on the correct side of the paper?
	_______	Did you indent the first line?
	_______	Did you write on every other line?
Topic Sentence:	_______	Does your topic sentence contain a controlling idea?
Supporting Sentences:		
Unity:	_______	Do all of your sentences support your topic sentence?
Coherence:	_______	Do you repeat key nouns frequently and use pronouns appropriately?
	_______	Do you use transition signals at appropriate places to make your sentences flow smoothly?
	_______	Are your ideas arranged in logical order?
Concrete Support:	_______	Does your paragraph contain enough specific supporting details to prove your main points?
Concluding Sentence:	_______	Does your paragraph have a concluding sentence?

WRITING UNDER PRESSURE

Make a general opinion statement about one of the groups of people listed below under Topic Suggestions and support your opinion with specific supporting details. Your goal is to convince your reader that your opinion is correct, so you must present very strong arguments.

Your instructor will give you a time limit.

Suggested Time Limits:

1. Brainstorm for ideas	5 minutes
2. Develop a rough outline	3 minutes
3. Write your paragraph	10 minutes
4. Check your paragraph	2 minutes
	20 minutes

Topic Suggestions

Americans
English teachers
Politicians
In-laws
Businesspeople
Rock musicians
Engineers
Professional athletes
Astronauts

PART

Writing an Essay

CHAPTER 7

The Essay

Writing an Essay

An **essay** is a piece of writing several paragraphs long instead of just one or two paragraphs. It is written about one topic, just as a paragraph is. However, the topic of an essay is too long and too complex to discuss in one paragraph. Therefore, you must divide the topic into several paragraphs, one for each major point. Then you must tie all of the separate paragraphs together by adding an introduction and a conclusion.

Writing an essay is no more difficult than writing a paragraph except that an essay is longer. The principles of organization are the same for both, so if you can write a good paragraph, you can write a good essay.

An essay has three main parts:

1. An *introductory paragraph*
2. A *body* (at least one, but usually two or more paragraphs)
3. A *concluding paragraph*

The **introductory paragraph** consists of two parts: a few *general statements* about your subject to attract your reader's attention and a *thesis statement* to state the specific subdivisions of your topic and/or the "plan" of your paper. A thesis statement for an essay is just like a topic sentence for a paragraph: it names the specific topic and the controlling ideas or major subdivisions of the topic.

The **body** consists of one or more paragraphs. Each paragraph develops a subdivision of your topic, so the number of paragraphs in the body will vary with the number of subdivisions. The paragraphs of the body are like the main supporting points of a paragraph. Furthermore, just as you can organize the ideas in a paragraph by chronological order or by order of importance, you can organize the paragraphs in an essay in the same ways.

The **conclusion** in an essay, like the concluding sentence in a paragraph, is a summary or review of the main points discussed in the body.

The only additional element in an essay is the linking expressions between the paragraphs of the body. These are just like transitions within a paragraph. You use transitions *within* a paragraph to connect the ideas between two sentences. Similarly, you use transitions *between* paragraphs to connect the ideas between them.

You can see that writing an essay is essentially the same as writing a paragraph; an essay is just longer. The chart below shows you how the parts of a paragraph correspond to the parts of an essay.

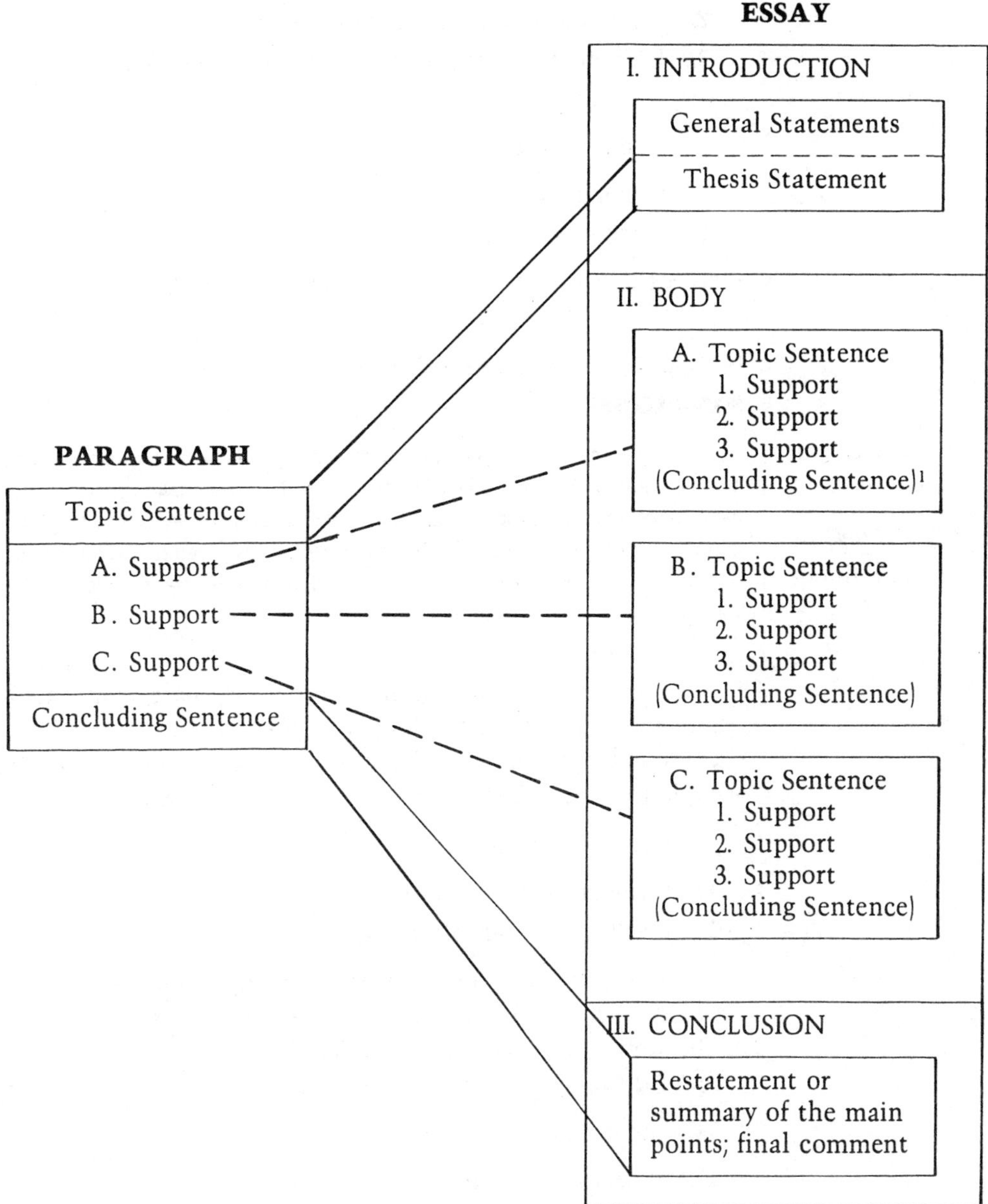

Note: The body is the longest part of the essay and can contain as many paragraphs as necessary to support the controlling ideas of your thesis statement.

[1]A concluding sentence is not always necessary.

The Introductory Paragraph

All writers (even professionals) complain that the most difficult part of writing is getting started. How many times have you wasted valuable minutes during an essay examination trying to think of your first sentence? Getting started, or writing an introduction,[1] can be easy if you remember that an introduction has four purposes:

1. It introduces the topic of the essay.
2. It gives a general background of the topic.
3. It often indicates the overall "plan" of the essay.
4. It should arouse the reader's interest in the topic.

The introduction has two parts:

1. General statements
2. A thesis statement

Notice the two parts of the introductory paragraph in the following model.

MODEL: *The Introductory Paragraph*

General Statement

Thesis Statement

A person born in the twentieth century has seen a lot of changes take place in almost all areas of human life. Some people are excited by the challenges that these changes offer; others want to return to the simpler, less automated life style of the past. Living in the twentieth century has certain advantages such as a higher standard of living, but it also has some disadvantages such as a polluted environment, the depersonalization of human relationships, and the weakening of spiritual values.

The first sentence in an introductory paragraph should be a very general comment about the subject. Its purpose is to attract the reader's attention and to give background information on the topic. Each subsequent sentence should become more specific than the previous one and finally lead into the thesis statement.

General statements:

1. introduce the topic of the essay.
2. give background information on the topic.

The thesis statement is the most important sentence in the introduction. It states the specific topic and lists the major subtopics that will be discussed in the body of the essay. Furthermore, it often indicates the method of organization such as chronological order or order of importance.

The thesis statement:

1. states the main topic.
2. lists the subdivisions of the topic.
3. may indicate the method of organization of the entire paper.
4. is usually the last sentence in the introductory paragraph.

[1]*Note:* A writer doesn't always have to write the introduction first; it can be written even after the other paragraphs have been completed.

To sum up, an introductory paragraph is like a funnel: very wide at the top, increasingly narrow in the middle, and very small at the neck or bottom.

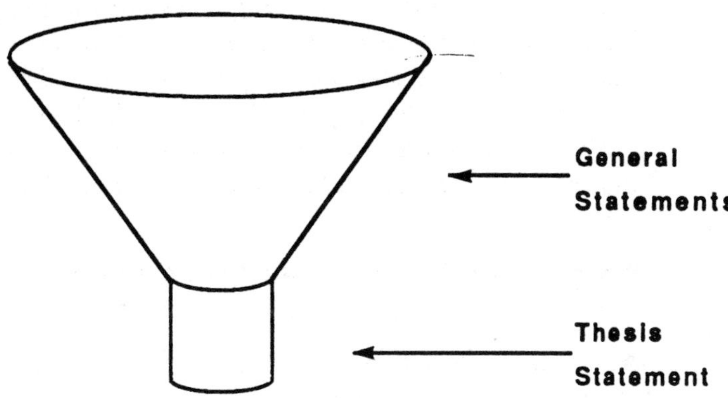

PRACTICE 1: ***Recognizing the Parts of an Introduction***

STEP 1 Read the following introductory paragraphs, each of which is in scrambled order.

STEP 2 Rewrite each paragraph, beginning with the most general statement first. Then add each sentence in the correct order until the introduction becomes more specific. Write the thesis statement last.

Paragraph 1

(1) The heavy traffic problem can be solved by building rapid transit systems from the suburbs to the cities, by improving public transportation systems within the cities, and by forming car pools. (2) Traffic congestion is caused by the thousands of cars that come into the cities from the suburban areas as well as from the thousands of cars within the city limits. (3) One of the most serious problems facing most big cities is traffic congestion. (4) This mammoth problem must be resolved* before it gets worse.

Paragraph 2

(1) However, in others, the nuclear family is the norm, with only the parents and young children sharing the same house. (2) People in different cultures all over the world have different systems for family life. (3) In most cultures, people live in extended families, in which several generations share the same house. (4) If this new system becomes widespread, it could have enormous effects on American society. (5) On the positive side, living together might reduce the divorce rate in the United States; on the negative side, it might lead to the eventual disintegration* of the family altogether. (6) In the United States, some people are experimenting with still another system of family life: living together without marriage.

resolved: solved **disintegration:** falling apart

Paragraph 3

(1) Although scientists have experimented with different methods of prediction, from observing animal behavior to measuring radio signals from quasars,* they have not proven successful. (2) Earthquakes are the most destructive natural disasters known to man, in terms of the millions of deaths and billions of dollars in property loss that they cause. (3) Despite these heavy losses, scientists are still unable to predict earthquakes. (4) This paper will review the history of the science of earthquake prediction, then discuss each of the methods in more detail, and finally present data indicating the success–failure ratios of each method.

PRACTICE 2: *Thesis Statements I*

A. Study these thesis statements from two different essays on the topic of the status of women in Xanadu, an imaginary country. Which method of organization (chronological order or comparison and contrast) does each one indicate?

1. Beginning in World War II and continuing through the period of economic boom,* the status of women in Xanadu has changed remarkably.

   Method of organization: ______________________________

2. Although the status of women in Xanadu has improved remarkably in recent years, it is still very low when compared to the status of women in the countries of the Western world.

   Method of organization: ______________________________

B. In the following two thesis statements, both the method of organization and the major subdivisions of the topic are indicated. Each subdivision will be the topic of a paragraph in the body. How many paragraphs will the body of each essay probably contain? Underline the topics of each paragraph.

1. The status of women in Xanadu has changed remarkably in recent years due to increased educational opportunities and changes in the country's laws.

   Probable number of paragraphs: ____

2. The status of women in Xanadu has improved remarkably in recent years in the areas of economic independence, political rights, educational opportunities, and social status.

   Probable number of paragraphs: ____

C. Analyze the following thesis statements.

STEP 1 Locate the main topic and the subtopics in each of the following thesis statements.

STEP 2 Underline the subtopics.

STEP 3 Draw a circle around the words or punctuation marks that are used to introduce the subtopics.

Example:

Capital punishment should be abolished (not only) because it deprives another person of life (but also) because it does not stop crime.

---

quasars: star-like objects in space **boom:** rapid development

1. Women generally live longer than men for two main reasons: they tend to take better care of their health, and they lead less stressful lives.
2. Drug and alcohol abuse among teenagers can be traced to the following causes: lack of parental supervision, lax* enforcement of drug laws, and the social and psychological problems of teenagers themselves.
3. In choosing a major, a student has to consider various factors, such as personal interest, job opportunities, and the availability of training institutions.
4. An architect should be both an artist and an engineer.
5. The purpose of this report is to analyze the influence of Chinese culture on Japanese language and literature.

PRACTICE 3: *Thesis Statements II*

STEP 1 Complete the following thesis statements by adding topics to them.

STEP 2 Circle your topics. If you use correlative conjunctions (both . . . and, not only . . . but also, etc.), be sure your structures are parallel. (See "Parallelism," pages 168-171.)

1. The life expectancy of the average person is increasing because of ________

   ____

2. Technology is changing our lives in three important areas: ________

   ____

3. Foreign students have a difficult time taking notes in class due to ________

   ____

4. A teacher must have the following qualities: ________

   ____

5. The purpose of this paper is to ________

   ____

6. Television commercials are insulting to the average viewer because ________

   ____

7. Owning an automobile is a necessity both ________

   ____

8. The basic causes of inflation are ________

   ____

9. Poverty creates negative consequences for society, such as ________

   ____

---

lax: not strict

10. Living together before marriage is becoming increasingly popular for three reasons: ____

____

WRITING PRACTICE

Write a clear thesis statement for essays on each of the following topics:

Leaving home	Choosing a career
Foreign travel	Your own choice of a topic
Space exploration	

The Concluding Paragraph

The final paragraph is the conclusion, a very important part of the essay. In this paragraph you tell the reader that you have completed the essay. This is achieved by either writing a summary of the main points discussed in the body of the essay or by rewriting the thesis statement in different words. Then you add your final comments on the subject—food for thought.* Since this is your last opportunity to make your point, you should write a strong, effective message that the reader will remember.

The concluding paragraph consists of:

1. a summary of the main points, or
   a restatement of your thesis in different words, and
2. your final comment on the subject, based on the information you have provided.

Be sure to introduce the concluding paragraph with a transition signal.

Study the introduction and conclusion for the following model essay on the advantages and disadvantages of living in the twentieth century. Is the concluding paragraph a summary of the main points of the essay, or is it a paraphrase* of the thesis statement? Is there a final message for the reader?

MODEL: *The Concluding Paragraph*

Introduction

A person born in the twentieth century has seen many changes take place in almost all areas of human life. Some people are excited by the challenges that these changes offer; others long to return to the simpler, less automated life style of the past. Living in the twentieth century has certain advantages, such as a higher standard of living, but it also has some disadvantages, such as a polluted environment, the depersonalization of human relationships, and the weakening of spiritual values.

---

food for thought: something to think about
paraphrase: restatement using different words

Conclusion

In conclusion, although the twentieth century has indeed given us a lot of advantages by making us richer, healthier, and freer to enjoy our lives, it has, in my opinion, not made us wiser. The twentieth century has also made our Earth dirtier, our people less humane, and our spiritual lives poorer. We should continue to enjoy the benefits of technological advancements because they free us to pursue our interests and goals. However, we must make a concerted* effort to preserve our natural environment for future generations. Moreover, we should take the time now to make our lives more meaningful in an increasingly impersonal, mechanized world.

PRACTICE 4: *Concluding Paragraphs*

A. Write concluding paragraphs for the following introductions.

STEP 1 Summarize the main points or paraphrase the thesis statement. Be sure to begin with a conclusion signal.

STEP 2 Add your own comments as a final message to the reader.

Paragraph 1

The busy schedules that most adults face from day to day have created a rising health problem in the modern world. Stress affects almost everyone, from the highly pressured executive to the busy homemaker or student. It can cause a variety of physical disorders, ranging from headaches to stomach ulcers and even alcoholism. Stress, like a common cold, is a problem that can't be cured; however, it can be controlled. A person can learn to control stress by setting realistic goals, enjoying a hobby and/or physical exercise, and by maintaining a good, warm relationship with family and friends.

Paragraph 2

Television is the most popular form of entertainment in many households. People of all ages use this medium to entertain themselves for an average of four hours a day. Thus, television has had a tremendous influence on its viewers, especially children. Scientists now say that children can be adversely* affected by constantly watching television. This is due to the fact that they participate less in physical activities, spend less time reading and studying, and see a world of violence that can affect their own feelings of security.

B. Write concluding paragraphs for introductory paragraphs 1, 2, and 3 that you reorganized in Practice 1, pages 79-80.

Essay Outlining

Because an essay is longer and more complex than a paragraph, it is even more important to organize your thoughts and to plan your essay before you begin to write. The best way to do this is to make an outline.

The principles and techniques that you have already learned for paragraph outlining can be applied to essays. You may be required during the course of your academic writing career to produce a formal outline. The number/letter system for a formal outline is illustrated in the model outline below.

Notice that subgroups are indented to the right. As you move to the right, the ideas become more and more specific.

---

concerted: joint, united
adversely: unfavorably

MODEL: *Essay Outline*

I. The Americas
  A. North America
    1. Canada
      a. Alberta
        (1) Edmonton
        (2) Calgary
        (3) Medicine Hat
          Etc.
      b. British Columbia
        (1) Vancouver
        (2) Victoria
          Etc.
      c. Quebec
        (1) Quebec City
        (2) Montreal
        (3) Sherbrooke
          Etc.
    2. United States
      a. California
        (1) Sacramento
        (2) Los Angeles
        (3) San Francisco
          Etc.
      b. New York
        (1) New York City
        (2) Buffalo
          Etc.
    3. Mexico
      a. Sonora
        (1) Hermosillo
        (2) Guaymas
          Etc.
      b. Jalisco
          Guadalajara[1]
  B. Central America
    1. Guatemala
    2. Nicaragua
      Etc.
  C. South America
    1. Argentina
      a. Buenos Aires
        (1) Buenos Aires
        (2) La Plata
        (3) Bahia Blanca
          Etc.
    2. Brazil
      a. Sao Paulo
        (1) Sao Paulo
        (2) Santos
      b. Rio Grande do Sul
        (1) Santa Maria
        (2) Porto Alegre
          Etc.
      c. Rio de Janeiro
        Etc.
    3. Chile
      Etc.

II. Africa
  A. Egypt
  B. Ethiopia
  C. Liberia
  Etc.

III. Asia

PRACTICE 5: *Essay Outlining*

Make an outline using a different area of the world (Africa, Europe, Asia, the Middle East, etc.). Follow the model above.

[1]If there is no 2, you do not use the numeral *1*. Also, if there is no *b*, there is no *a*.

Study the following model outline for an essay on the advantages and disadvantages of living in the twentieth century. Only the thesis statement in the introductory paragraph has been given; only the paragraphs of the body of the essay have been outlined.

MODEL: ***Essay Outline***

The Advantages and Disadvantages of Living in the Twentieth Century

I. Living in the twentieth century offers certain advantages, such as a higher standard of living, but it also has some disadvantages, such as a polluted environment, the depersonalization of human relationships, and the weakening of spiritual values.

II. The biggest advantage of living in the twentieth century is the high standard of living we enjoy.
   - A. More money for less hard work.
      1. More office workers than manual laborers
      2. Higher salaries
      3. Increased government services
         - a. Social security
         - b. Unemployment benefits
         - c. Disability insurance
   - B. Longer life expectancy
      1. Better medical care
         - a. More hospitals, doctors, nurses
         - b. Advances in medical technology
      2. Improved nutrition
      3. More leisure time
   - C. Modern conveniences
      1. Communication
         - a. Telephones
         - b. Radio and television
      2. Labor-saving machines in the home
         - a. Dishwashers
         - b. Washing machines/dryers
         - c. Vacuum cleaners
      3. Faster transportation

III. One of the main disadvantages of living in the twentieth century is that we are living in an increasingly polluted environment.
   - A. Air pollution
      1. Smog
      2. Nuclear fallout
   - B. Water pollution
      1. Chemical wastes from factories
         - a. Dead fish
         - b. Contaminated drinking water supplies
      2. Raw sewage from cities
      3. Oil spills from ships

IV. A second disadvantage of living in the twentieth century is the depersonalization of human relationships.
   - A. People and machines
      1. Automated vending machines, banks, etc.
      2. Tape recorded telephone answering
      3. Computerized dating services

B. People and numbers
1. Social security numbers
2. Credit card numbers

V. The final disadvantage of living in the twentieth century is the weakening of spiritual values.
A. Materialistic culture
B. Faith in science instead of in religion

VI. In conclusion, although the twentieth century has indeed given us a lot of advantages by making us richer, healthier, and freer to enjoy our lives, it has, in my opinion, not made us wiser. The twentieth century has also made our earth dirtier, our people less humane, and our spiritual lives poorer. We should continue to enjoy the benefits of technological advancements because they free us to pursue our interests and goals. However, we must make a concerted effort to preserve our natural environment for future generations. Moreover, we should take the time now to make our lives more meaningful in an increasingly impersonal, computerized world.

Writing Technique Questions

1. How many paragraphs will this essay contain?
2. How many paragraphs are in the *body* of the essay?
3. Look at the contents of paragraph II. How many main points are given? Do you think there are too many ideas for one paragraph? Would you recommend dividing it into several paragraphs? How many? What would your new topic sentences be?

Transition Signals Between Paragraphs

Transition signals are important not only *within* paragraphs but also *between* paragraphs. If you write two or more paragraphs, you need to show the relationship between your first and second paragraph, between your second and third paragraph, and so on.

Think of transitions between paragraphs as the links of a chain. The links of a chain connect the chain; they hold it together. Similarly, a transition signal between two paragraphs links your ideas together.

Two paragraphs are linked by adding a transition signal to the topic sentence of the second paragraph. This transition signal may be a single word, a phrase, or a dependent clause that repeats or summarizes the main idea in the first paragraph.

Study the following model, and notice how the paragraphs are linked by a single word, a phrase, or a clause.

MODEL: *Paragraph Transitions*

Flextime

Introduction

One of the most important changes that management has made in industry in recent years is the scheduling of flexible work hours for their employees. Workers are given the option* of choosing when they will work. This allows them more leisure time for family and fun. Flextime has obvious advantages for both workers and management although it may not be practical in all types of businesses.

---

option: choice

Transition Word The <u>first</u> advantage is increased production per work hour.

(+ supporting sentences)

Transition Word A <u>second</u> advantage is that factory workers are happier.

(+ supporting sentences)

Transition Phrase <u>In addition to increased output and worker satisfaction</u>, factory managers report that absenteeism has declined.

(+ supporting sentences)

Transition Clause <u>Although flextime has produced these three positive results in some industries</u>, it is not as advantageous in all types of businesses.

(+ supporting sentences)

Conclusion To summarize, flextime has resulted in increased production and happier workers who are less likely to miss work, and it works well in manufacturing and retail industries. It works less well in service industries such as the restaurant and health care industries.

PRACTICE 6: *Transitions Between Paragraphs*

A. Connect the ideas in the following paragraphs by adding a transition word, phrase, or clause to the topic sentences of the second, third, fourth, and fifth paragraphs. Try to vary the linking expressions that you use. You may rewrite the topic sentences if necessary.

Icebergs—A Potential Source of Water

The supply of fresh water has not been a major problem for most countries in the world because a rainy season is part of their yearly climatic conditions. However, in countries where the rainfall is very sparse,* scientists must constantly seek ways to increase fresh supplies of this precious element. Government planners in South America and the Middle East have been trying to devise new ways of increasing their nations' supplies of fresh water. The first method being considered is the use of desalinization plants, which would remove salt from sea water. Another method being considered is towing icebergs. According to this method, large icebergs from Antarctica would be wrapped in cloth or plastic, tied to powerful tugboats by strong ropes, and towed to the dry country. While this plan may have some potential, there are certain practical problems that must be solved.

The first problem (handwritten) ______________________ is the expense. According to estimates, it would cost between $50 and $100 million to tow a single 100-million-ton iceberg from Antarctica to, for example, the coast of Saudi Arabia.

______________________ is the possibility that the iceberg would melt en route.* No one knows if an iceberg could be effectively insulated during such a long journey. At the very least, there is the possibility that it would break up into smaller pieces, which would create still other problems.

______________________ there is the danger that a huge block of ice off an arid* coast could have unexpected environmental effects. The ice could drastically* change the weather along the coast, and it would almost certainly affect the fish population.

---

sparse: small in amount
en route: during the journey
arid: dry
drastically: extremely

____

____________ the cost of providing fresh water from icebergs would be less than the cost of providing water by desalinzation, according to most estimates. It would cost between 50¢ and 60¢ per cubic meter to get water from an iceberg, as opposed to the 80¢ per cubic meter it costs to get the same amount by desalinization.

In conclusion, before icebergs can become a source of fresh water in the future, problems involving cost, overall practicality, and, most importantly, environmental impact* must be solved.

B. Add transition words, phrases, or clauses to the topic sentences of the paragraphs in this essay. Rewrite the topic sentences if necessary.

*Technology and Ethics**

Recent advances in the fields of medicine and biotechnology have brought about situations that could scarcely be imagined only a generation ago. Battery-operated plastic hearts can be implanted* into people. People can be kept alive indefinitely by machines. Exact duplicates of animals can be made. While such scientific achievements may ultimately benefit mankind, they have also created complex legal and ethical issues.

____ involves doctors' ability to intervene in human reproduction. A well-known example is the case of Baby M. A man paid another woman to bear a child for him and his wife, who could not have children. They signed a contract, but after the baby was born, the woman wanted to keep the baby. The father said the baby was his, but the woman said it was hers. It took the courts many months to decide who was right.

____

____________________, another ethical dilemma* has arisen because doctors are now able to keep people who are in comas* alive for years by attaching their bodies to machines. This gives great power and great responsibility to the people who control the machines. How does a person decide whether another person whose heart cannot beat on its own and whose lungs are pumped by a machine is still alive or not? As a result of this power, society has had to develop a new definition of death.

____ is the ability to transplant* organs from one person into another. Doctors are now able to transplant hearts, lungs, livers, and kidneys from one human to another. Should doctors also be allowed to transplant organs from animals to humans? Such an operation was actually performed in 1987, when doctors transplanted a baboon's heart into a dying human baby. The ethics of this experiment is still being debated.

____, the ability of biotechnologists to produce new forms of life in their laboratories is another area with profound* ethical consequences. Isn't a scientist who creates, for example, a new bacterium "playing God"? Furthermore, is it even safe to introduce new life forms into the Earth's atmosphere? Is there a risk that such life forms could get out of control? Some people fear so.

____, scientists are now able to duplicate living organisms, cell by cell, through a process called cloning. Recently, twin horses that were clones were born in Colorado; that is, they were exact duplicates of each other. How long will it be before biotechnologists can clone people? Should they be allowed to? Who should control this?

---

impact: effect
ethics: the study of right and wrong
implanted: put in
dilemma: difficult problem
comas: states of unconsciousness (can't see, hear, move)
transplant: take out of one person and put into another
profound: important, serious

____________________ revolutions—political or technological—cause upheaval* and force change. Our new ability to create and prolong life is raising questions and forcing changes in our very concept of life, an issue involving not only legal but also profound moral considerations.

The Writing Process (Continued): Writing and Revising the Essay

In Chapter 1, you were introduced to writing and revising drafts of a single paragraph, important steps in the writing process. You learned that writing a good paragraph takes time and effort. You were also taken through the steps of the revision process by studying the drafts of the model paragraph on pages 12-15.

In this section, you will write multiparagraph essays. Just as you wrote several drafts of your paragraphs before your final copy, you will also continue to write and revise several drafts of your essays until you have produced a final copy that you can be proud of.

The following model shows you how one student worked through the process of writing and revising drafts of a multiparagraph essay before arriving at the final copy.

MODEL: *Essay Outline*

Metropolitan City

I. Introduction
Although Metropolitan City is a culturally rich city and an important center of national and international business, it still has several serious problems.

II. Body
- A. The first problem is the city's unreliable public transportation system.
  - 1. Schedules are unreliable
    - a. Late bus arrivals
    - b. Arrival in bunches
  - 2. Passengers are victims
    - a. Late to work, appointments, classes
    - b. Extra waiting time
- B. The second problem is the shortage of affordable housing for young people and immigrants.
  - 1. Shortage of rentals
  - 2. High rents
- C. The final problem is the extremely congested condition of the city's streets.
  - 1. Heavy downtown traffic
    - a. Cars and trucks within city
    - b. Commuter traffic from suburbs
    - c. Accidents
  - 2. Traffic jams
  - 3. City officials' pleas
    - a. Use of public transportation
    - b. Use of transit system

III. Conclusion
In conclusion, Metropolitan City's public transit system is in bad shape. Furthermore, the high cost of housing and massive traffic jams are all negative aspects of this beautiful city.

---

upheaval: social disturbance

From this outline, the student wrote a first rough draft of the body paragraphs.

MODEL: *The First Rough Draft*

AUDIENCE: English Instructor, classmates
PURPOSE: To describe the most serious problems of Metropolitan City

Problems of Metropolitan City

The first ^and most important^ problem is Metropolitan's inadequate public transportation system. Thousands of residents rely on the city's buses and streetcars to travel throughout this large city. ~~Some people must transfer to other lines more than once before they finally arrive at their destinations.~~ *take out* Metro Transportation System's daily schedules are totally unreliable. A bus or streetcar that is supposed to arrive at 7:45 A.M. It may not arrive eight o'clock or even later. Unfortunately passengers become unhappy victims of the waiting game. *add details* This causes them to be late for work or to miss important appointments; For instance, once I waited so long in incredibly cold weather, ^that^ I caught a bad cold and ended up in bed for a week. Then, on the day of my psychology exam, the streetcar was thirty minutes late. In order to get to their destinations on time, people must leave home earlier to allow for waiting time at the bus and streetcar stops.

Rewrite more clearly The second problem is the lack of reasonable housing in Metro City. In the first place, there is a big shortage of rental units, so naturally rents skyrocket.* This is a fasinating city, and it offers an exciting lifestyle for the young and ambitious business people. Moreover, immigrants are attracted to this city because it offers unskilled job opportunities. All of these would-be residents need affordable rentals apartments, flats, and single family houses. However, rents are very high. Therefore, people leave the city. ← *Add example*

Move to second body paragraph The final problem is the extremely congested condition of the city streets. There is simply too many cars everywhere. Today most families own at least one car or even more. Beside the heavy traffic caused by city residents, many comuters drive on the freeways and bridges leading into the city from the suburbs. This added traffic cause even greater traffic jams. To clear up the congested streets, city officials want city residents to leave their cars at home. They want them to use public transportation. They have pleaded with out-of-towners to use the transit systems coming into this huge metropolis. However, their please have fallen on deaf ears because residents know that public transportation is bad, and people from the suburbs like the convenience of driving which gives them the freedom to come and go as they please.

Comments on the First Draft

The writer has decided to classify the three problems in order of importance and has designated the first one as "The first and most important problem." Furthermore, several unwanted sentences have been crossed out. Then, in the middle of the first paragraph, the writer wants to add more information to develop the main idea of the city's poor public transportation. In addition, the sequence of ideas in the second paragraph is unclear; therefore, the writer has made a note to rewrite this part. He/she has also decided to add an example to prove that rents are high.

MODEL: *The Second Draft: Proofreading*

The first and most important problem is Metropolitan's inadequate public transportation system. Thousands of residents rely on the city's buses and streetcars to travel throughout this large city, but Metro Transportation System's daily schedules are totally unreliable. A bus or streetcar that

---

skyrocket: rise rapidly

is supposed to arrive at 7:45 A.M. It may not arrive untill eight o'clock or even later. Sometimes three buses or streetcars will arrive in bunches, one after another. Moreover, it is not unusual for a bus driver or a streetcar conductor to pass up groups of people anxiously waiting in the snow in freezing weather because he is behind schedule and wants to make up for lost time. Unfortunately passengers become unhappy victims of the waiting game. ~~This causes~~ them to be late for work or to miss important appointments; ~~for~~ instance, once I waited so long in incredibly cold weather I caught a bad cold and ended up in bed for a week. Then, on the day of my psychology exam, the streetcar was thirty minutes late. In order to get to their destinations on time, people must allow for waiting time at the bus and streetcar stops.

The second serious problem is the extremely congested condition of the city streets. There is simply too many cars everywhere. Besides the heavy traffic caused by city residents, many ~~comuters~~ drive on the freeways and bridges leading into the city from the suburbs. This added traffic causes even greater traffic jams. To clear up the congested streets, city officials want city residents to leave their cars at home and ~~using~~ public transportation. They have pleaded with out-of-towners to use the transit systems coming into this huge metropolis. However, their pleass have fallen on deaf ears because residents know that city's public transportation is poor ~~and people from the suburbs~~ like the convenience of driving which gives them the freedom to come and go as they please.

The final problem is the lack of reasonable housing in Metro City. ~~In the first place,~~ this is a fasinating city that offers an exciting lifestyle for young and ambitious business and professional people. ~~Moreover~~, immigrants are attracted to this city because it offers many unskilled job opportunities. All of these would-be residents need affordable rentals like apartments, flats, and single-family houses. But, unfortunately, because there ~~are~~ a tremendous shortage of rental units, rents skyrocket, and so people leave the city. For example, Kathleen and Suzy's rent for a two-bedroom flat was recently raised from $750.00 to $1,000.00 per month, so Suzy moved to Vallejo where she teaches. Kathleen has been looking for a studio apartment, and, so far, she has found that the rents range from $550.00 to $750.00 per month depending on the location.

Comments on the Second Draft

In the second draft, the writer has corrected punctuation, spelling, and other errors in mechanics, and has changed some vocabulary words. He/she has also corrected the grammar and improved the sentence structure. Notice that housing is now the final problem, and traffic is now the second problem. Now the final copy can be written.

The Final Copy

This is the final copy of the model essay on "The Problems of Metropolitan City." The five-step writing process is complete. The writer brainstormed the topic to get ideas (Stage I), then developed an outline (Stage II). Next, a rough draft was written (Stage III) and revised twice, once for content and organization and once for grammar and mechanics (Stage IV). At last, the writer wrote the final copy to hand in (Stage V). Although this final copy is based on the outline on page 89, it no longer follows it exactly because it has gone through several drafts and revisions.

MODEL: *The Final Copy*

The Problems of Metropolitan City

Metropolitan City is full of charm and scenic beauty, so visitors from around the world come to enjoy its famous theaters, museums, countless ethnic restaurants, and scenic wonders. Although Metropolitan City seems like a paradise, it isn't, for the city has several serious problems: poor public transportation, congested streets, and expensive housing.

The first and most important problem is Metropolitan's inadequate public transportation system. Thousands of residents rely on the city's buses and streetcars to travel throughout this large city, but Metro Transportation System's daily schedules are totally unreliable. A bus or streetcar that should arrive at 7:45 A.M. may not arrive until eight o'clock or even later. Sometimes three buses or streetcars will arrive in bunches, one after another. Moreover, it is not unusual for a bus driver or a streetcar conductor to pass up groups of people anxiously waiting in the snow in freezing weather because he is behind schedule and wants to make up for lost time. Unfortunately, passengers become unhappy victims of the waiting game, causing them to be late for work or to miss important appointments. For instance, once I waited so long in below zero weather that I caught a bad cold and ended up in bed for a week. Then, on the day of my psychology final, the streetcar was thirty minutes late. In order to get to their destinations on time, people must allow for waiting time at the bus and streetcar stops.

The second serious problem is the extremely congested condition of the city streets. There are simply too many cars everywhere. Besides the heavy traffic caused by city residents, many commuters drive on the freeways and bridges leading into the city from the suburbs. This added traffic causes even greater traffic jams. To clear up the congested streets, city officials want city residents to leave their cars at home and use public transportation. They have pleaded with out-of-towners to use the transit systems coming into this huge metropolis. However, their pleas have fallen on deaf ears because residents know that the city's public transportation is poor; moreover, suburbanites like the convenience of driving, which gives them the freedom to come and go as they please.

The final problem is the lack of reasonable housing in Metro City. This is a fascinating city that offers an exciting lifestyle for young, ambitious business and professional people. Also, immigrants are attracted to this city because it offers many unskilled job opportunities. All of these would-be residents need affordable rentals like apartments, flats, and single-family houses. But, unfortunately, because there is a tremendous shortage of rental units, rents skyrocket, and so people leave the city. For example, Kathleen and Suzy's rent for a two-bedroom flat was recently raised from $750.00 to $1,000.00 per month, so Suzy moved to Vallejo, where she teaches. Kathleen has been looking for a studio apartment, and, so far, she has found that the rents range from $550.00 to $750.00 per month, depending on the location.

In conclusion, Metropolitan City must improve its public transit system, clear up the massive traffic jams caused by slow-moving traffic in the downtown areas, and keep rentals down to affordable levels. In other words, Metropolitan City must improve its image, or it will soon become just another mediocre* city due to the lack of administrative responsibility to solve these unfortunate problems.

---

mediocre: average

Final Comments

As you can see, you must go through several stages of writing and rewriting if you want to produce a good piece of writing. The major part of the revision process includes not only checking the content and focus of the entire essay but also adding or deleting whole paragraphs, checking the development and ordering of ideas within each paragraph, adding examples, more specific information, and so on. Then, only after all of the major changes have been made should you check the more specific problems like sentence structure (correct compound and complex sentences), correct use of transitions, and mechanics such as grammar, punctuation, spelling, and capitalization. Just remember that each time you write, revise, and rewrite again, you have improved your paper.

Review

These are the important points you should have learned from this chapter.

Main Parts of an Essay

An essay has three main parts: an introduction, a body, and a conclusion.

1. The introductory paragraph attracts the reader's attention and informs the reader what your main topic of discussion will be. An introductory paragraph has two parts:
   a. Several general sentences that give background information on your subject and gradually lead your reader into your specific topic.
   b. A thesis statement that states the subdivisions (topics of each paragraph). It may also indicate your method of development.
2. The body of an essay discusses your subdivided topics, one by one. It contains as many paragraphs as necessary to explain the controlling ideas in the thesis statement.
3. The concluding paragraph reminds your reader of what you have said. Remember to use a "conclusion" transition signal. Your concluding paragraph has a summary of the main ideas or a restatement of the thesis in different words and your final comment on the topic.

Transitions Between Paragraphs

Remember to show the relationship *between* paragraphs by using appropriate linking words, phrases, or clauses.

Outlining an Essay

Always make an outline of an essay before you begin to write. Follow the model in this chapter, page 89.

Writing and Revising the Essay

1. Write the first rough draft of your essay from the outline. Skip lines in order to have enough space to make changes.

2. Check the second draft for grammar, sentence structure, etc. Write as many drafts as necessary before the final copy.

Essay Checklist

This checklist details the major points you have learned about writing paragraphs and essays. It is a good idea to keep this checklist in front of you when you are writing. It will remind you of all the essential elements of a good essay. After you have finished your first draft, check your essay for *every* item on the list. If anything is missing, add it before you write your final draft.

Essay Organization

Introduction:	______	General statements
	______	Thesis statement
Body:	______	Logical and appropriate pattern of organization for the topic (chronological order, logical division, comparison-contrast, etc.)
	______	Between-paragraph transitions
Conclusion:	______	Summary of the main points or paraphrase of the thesis and your final comments on the topic

Paragraph Organization

Topic Sentences:	______	Topic sentence for each paragraph; each topic sentence has a controlling idea. (Chapter 2)
Supporting Sentences:	______	Concrete Support: Specific factual details (Chapter 6)
	______	Unity: Only one main idea in each paragraph (Chapter 3)
	______	Coherence: Repeating key nouns, using pronouns, transition signals, and logical order (Chapters 4 and 5)
Concluding Sentences:	______	Concluding Sentence (if necessary)

CHAPTER 8

Patterns of Essay Organization

Organizing an **essay** is essentially the same as organizing a paragraph; the only difference is that instead of working with single sentences, you are working with paragraphs. You can use the same patterns (or combination of patterns) for essays as you use for paragraphs. You simply decide what information belongs in each paragraph, and then in what order you should arrange the paragraphs.

You already know something about the different patterns of organization in English. You are familiar with chronological order, logical division, and order of importance as ways of sequencing ideas. So far, however, you have practiced these different orders only within a paragraph.

In this chapter, we will analyze in some detail four of the most useful patterns of essay organization: chronological order, logical division, cause and effect, and comparison and contrast.

Chronological Order

As you know, chronological order is order by time. It is used in almost all academic fields to describe historical events as well as to write biographies and autobiographies. In addition, chronological order has an important use in scientific and technical writing. It is used in these fields to explain physical, chemical, biological, and mechanical processes, such as how a machine works, how a chemical reaction takes place, how a certain biological process occurs, and so on. It is also used to give directions or instructions—how to perform a chemistry experiment, how to operate a piece of equipment, etc.

In a chronological process essay, the main steps in the process are the topics of the paragraphs.

In this section, you will practice using chronological order to explain the steps in a technical process. The following practice essay explains the process of how a hot water system works. In the writing practice for this section, you will be asked to explain a similar process.

How Solar Collectors Use the Sun's Energy to Heat Water

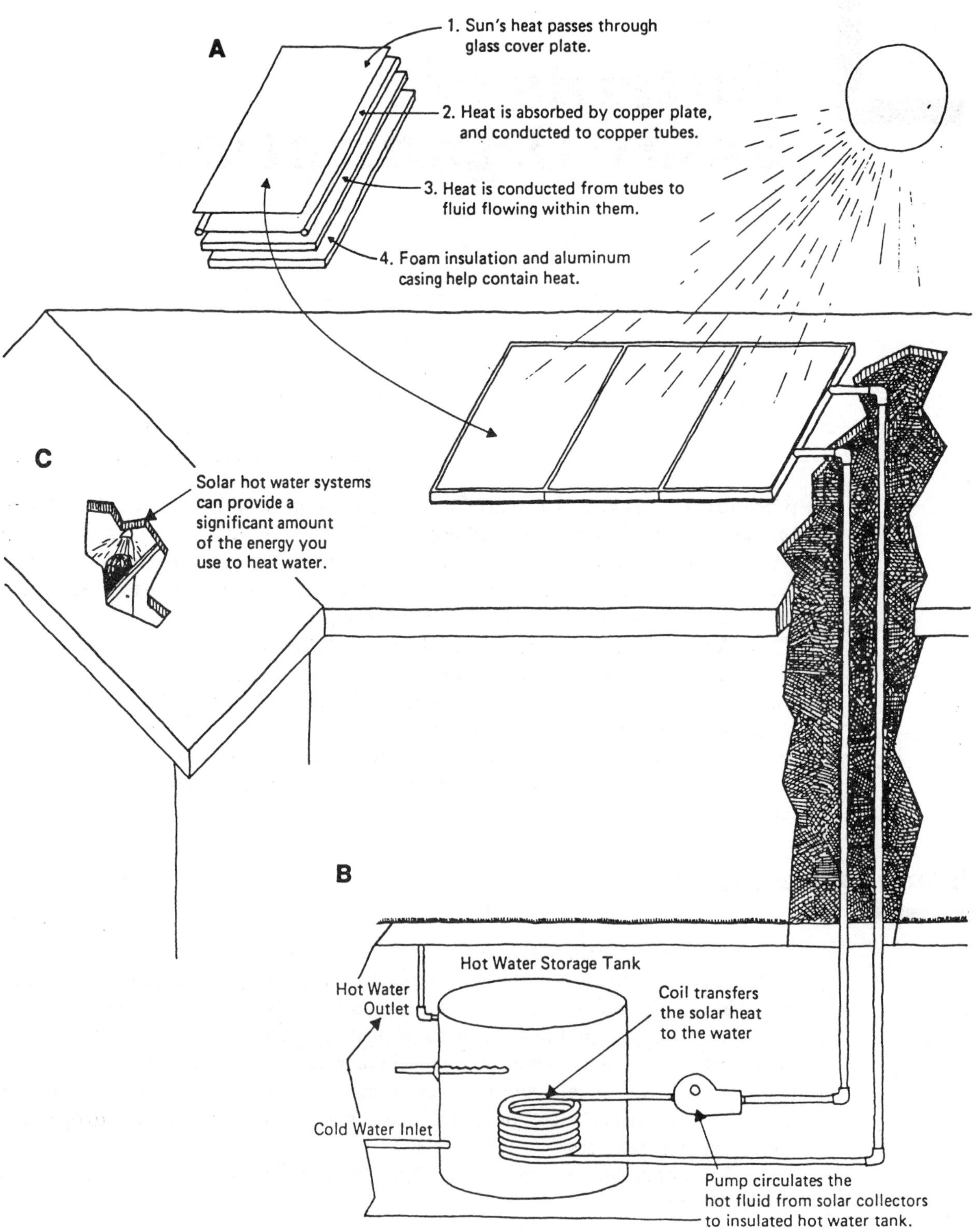

The following model essay is based on the diagram on the preceding page. Before you read the essay, study the diagram. Then, refer to it as you read the essay and follow the chronological process. Notice that this essay contains many passive verb forms.

Analyze the organization by following these steps:

STEP 1 Underline the thesis statement twice.

STEP 2 Underline the topic sentence of each paragraph.

STEP 3 Underline the passive verb forms.

STEP 4 Circle the transition signals.

MODEL: *Chronological Process*

How a Solar Hot Water System Works

A solar hot water system collects and converts* solar radiation into usable energy for the purpose of heating water. The use of solar radiation for heating water is an inexpensive and environmentally responsible substitute for heating by gas or electricity. The main parts of a solar hot water system are a collector, a hot water storage tank, and a distribution system. The main steps in the process of heating water by using the sun's rays are (1) trapping the sun's energy, (2) heating and storing the hot water, and (3) dispensing* the water at points of use.

The first step is to capture solar radiation (A). That is, the sun's energy must be absorbed* by a solar heat collector, which is usually built on a south-facing roof. The collector has several layers of material. It has a glass plate and a metal absorber plate, which is painted black to increase its ability to absorb heat. Next to the absorber plate are copper tubes, which are filled with transfer fluid. The tubes are surrounded by foam insulation and aluminum casing to help hold the heat in them. The process of trapping the sun's radiation is as follows. As the sun shines through the glass plate, its thermal* energy is absorbed by the copper absorber plate. This heat is conducted* from the plate to the tubes. The heat from the tubes is then conducted to the fluid flowing through them.

After trapping heat from the sun, the second step is to transfer this heat to water which is stored in an insulated tank (B). The hot fluid from the collector is circulated by a pump through copper coils inside the tank. The heat is conducted by the coils to the water. When the supply of solar radiation is reduced on cloudy days, an auxiliary* system can take over.

Dispensing the hot water is the final step in the process. The water flows from the outlet valve through pipes to faucets throughout the house (C).

In summary, the process of collecting and converting solar energy for use in a solar hot water system involves three steps. First, collectors absorb the sun's energy, which is then transferred to fluid in copper tubes. These tubes run from the collector to a tank, where the water is heated and stored. Finally, the hot water is distributed through pipes to wherever it is needed. Although initially expensive to install, solar heating systems are economical in the long run*—at least until utility companies figure out how to charge us for sunshine!

Writing Technique Questions

1. What are the steps in the process of heating water by solar energy? Are the steps listed both in the introduction and in the conclusion?
2. Which step has several substeps?
3. Which topic sentence begins with a between-paragraph transition?
4. Why do you think there are a lot of passive verb forms in this essay?

converts: changes to or into another form
dispensing: distributing, giving out
absorbed: taken in
thermal: related to heat
conducted: (here) transferred
auxiliary: additional, secondary
in the long run: in the end, after everything is considered

Organization

In order to write a process essay, you must have a clear understanding of the operations involved in each step and be able to explain them in logical order, using the proper terminology.* The following is a general outline which you can follow to write a well-organized process essay:

I. Introduction
   A. Give a definition of the process.
      Explain why the process is performed, by whom it is performed, and in what way it is performed. (This information gives the reader an overview of the whole process.)
   B. List the equipment, supplies, etc., needed in the process.
   C. List the main steps of the process in the order they are performed.

II. Body
   A. Write a topic sentence to introduce the first step.
      1. Define the step and state its purpose.
      2. Describe the apparatus or equipment used.
      3. Divide the main step into as many substeps as necessary.
      4. Explain the action in as many details as necessary.
   B. For all subsequent* steps, follow the same general procedure outlined above until you have explained all of the steps.

III. Conclusion
   Summarize the essay by restating what the steps of the process are, what the purpose of the process is, how it operates, and why it is important. In other words, the conclusion repeats the information given in the body of the essay, without going into specific details.

Chronological process essays are not limited to describing technical processes, however. You also use chronological order when you are writing instructions; that is, when you are telling someone how to do or make something. When you write this kind of chronological essay, you can follow the general procedure described above. However, there is a difference between an essay like the model, which describes a technical process, and a "how to" essay, which tells someone how to do or make something. A technical process essay contains many passive verb forms ("The hot water from the collector is circulated by a pump . . .). A "how to" essay, on the other hand, will contain imperatives ("Fold the paper in half . . .") and second-person singular active verb forms ("You should taste the mixture before you add salt . . .").

A third kind of writing that uses chronological order describes events over a period of time, such as a biography, autobiography, or history. Instead of explaining steps in a process, you will write about events in the order that they happen. Your paragraphs will be blocks of time: morning, afternoon, and night; or childhood, school years, and adulthood; or before the revolution, during the revolution, and after the revolution.

In *all* types of chronological order essays, you should use chronological transition signals and time expressions to make the time sequences clear to your reader.

---

terminology: technical terms **subsequent:** succeeding

Thesis Statements for Chronological Order

The thesis statement for an essay which describes a technical process names the process and indicates that it involves a series of steps:

- The desalinization of water is a complex process.

It may even name the main steps in the process:

- The main steps in the process of heating water by using the sun's rays are (1) trapping the sun's energy, (2) heating and storing the hot water, and (3) dispensing the water at points of use.

A thesis statement for a "how to" essay is similar to those above; it names the process (or product) and indicates that it involves a series of steps:

- Administering CPR (cardio-pulmonary resuscitation) is a process which requires a careful sequence of steps.
- Even a beginner can make good home videotapes if he or she follows these directions.

Although the thesis statement for a chronology does not indicate that a series of steps is involved, it should indicate chronological order. Words such as *development* and *evolution* as well as expressions of time are effective in doing this:

- The field of genetic engineering has developed rapidly in the past ten years.
- My life can be divided into three main time periods: childhood, primary school years, and high school years.

PRACTICE 7: *Chronological Order Thesis Statements*

Write a thesis statement for one of the topics in each group:

1. Scientific/technical processes:
   How the human circulatory system works
   How an automobile engine works
   How the leader of your country is chosen
   How the judicial system in your country operates
   How the educational system in your country works
   How ____________ is manufactured (any product)
   How a ____________ works (any machine or system)
2. Instructions/directions:
   How to register for classes at your school
   How to get accepted by a good college in your country
   How to check out a book from the library
   How to obtain a driver's license
   How to prepare for and survive an earthquake
   How to prepare a special dish (food) from your country
   How to learn a foreign language
   How to make ____________ (batik fabric, a ceramic sculpture, or any other interesting process which involves several steps)

3. Chronologies:
    Your autobiography
    The biography of a famous person from your country
    How your country's most important holiday is celebrated
    A traumatic* event in your life
    The chronology of an important event in your country's history (the winning of independence, a revolution, etc.)
    The process of courtship* and marriage in your country

WRITING PRACTICE

Choose one of the topics from Practice 7 above and write an essay using chronological order as a method of organization. Follow these steps to success:

1. Brainstorm by freewriting, listing, or clustering all the steps in your process or events in your chronology. (Review the Prewriting Activities on pages 3–9.)
2. Draw a simple diagram or flow chart which shows the steps and substeps in the process of chronology.
3. Develop an outline from your flow chart. Use the outline on page 89 as a guide.
4. Write your first draft from your outline. Be sure to use chronological transition signals.
5. Revise your rough draft as you have learned in Chapter 7. Check your final copy against the Essay Checklist on page 94.

Logical Division

Logical division is a form of essay organization that is used to group related items according to some quality they have in common. Logical division can be useful in planning a paper because a broad subject can be subdivided into several categories or groups that will narrow the topics for discussion. Then, each subdivided topic can be discussed in order.

For instance, as an engineer, you might write a paper in which you classify the various options available to students in the field of engineering. You might divide engineering, the main class, into the following subclasses: civil engineering, electrical engineering, mechanical engineering, space engineering, and electronic engineering. By dividing the field into subclasses, you can discuss each one separately, which simplifies the task of explaining a broad subject.

Review logical division organization in Chapter 5, pages 58–60. Then, study the model essay which discusses some of the influences of native Americans* on modern American culture. Notice that the same techniques used for logical division paragraphs can also be used for whole essays.

---

traumatic: shocking **courtship:** selection of a marriage partner
native Americans: American Indians

STEP 1 Locate and underline the thesis statement twice. How many subtopics does it list?

STEP 2 Locate the main sentence in the concluding paragraph and underline it twice. Is it a paraphrase of the thesis statement or a summary of the main points?

STEP 3 Underline the topic sentence in each paragraph once, and circle all of the transition signals. (*Note:* The topic sentence is not necessarily the first sentence in every paragraph.)

STEP 4 Notice especially the transition expressions between paragraphs. Do all of the paragraphs contain one?

MODEL: *Logical Division*

Native American Influences on Modern American Culture

When the first Europeans began to settle the North American continent, they encountered* a completely new culture: the native American tribes* of North America. Native Americans, who had a highly developed culture in many respects, must have been as curious about the strange European manners and customs as were the Europeans about native Americans. As always happens when two cultures come into contact, there was a cultural exchange. Native Americans adopted* some of the Europeans' ways, and the Europeans adopted some of their ways. As a result, native Americans have made many valuable contributions to American culture, particularly in the areas of language, art, food, and government.

First of all, native Americans left a permanent imprint* on the English language. The early settlers borrowed words from several different native American languages to name the new places and new objects that they had found in their new land. All across the country, one can find cities, towns, rivers, and states with native American names. For example, the states of Delaware, Iowa, Illinois, and Alabama are named after native American tribes, as are the cities of Chicago, Miami, and Spokane. In addition to place names, English has adopted many everyday words from various native American languages. The words **chipmunk**, **moose**, **raccoon**, **skunk**, **moccasin**, and **potato** are just a few examples.

Although the vocabulary of English is the area that shows the most native American influence, it is not the only area of American culture that was changed by contact with native Americans. Art is another area showing the mark of native American contact. Wool rugs woven by women of the Navajo tribe in Arizona and New Mexico are highly valued works of art in the United States. Also, native American jewelry made from silver and turquoise is very popular and very expensive. Especially in the western and southwestern regions of the United States, native crafts such as pottery, handcrafted leather products, and beadwork can be found in many homes. Indeed, native art and handicrafts have become a treasured part of American culture.

In addition to language and art, agriculture is another area in which native Americans had a great and lasting influence. Being skilled farmers, the native Americans of North America taught the newcomers many things about farming techniques and crops. Every American schoolchild has heard the story of how native Americans taught the first settlers to place a dead fish in a planting hole to provide fertilizer for the growing plant. Furthermore, they taught the settlers irrigation methods and crop rotation. In addition, many of the foods we eat today were introduced to the Europeans by native Americans. For example, potatoes, corn, chocolate, and peanuts were unknown in Europe. Now they are staples in the American diet.

Finally, it may surprise some people to learn that Americans are also indebted* to one tribe for our form of government. The Iroquois, who were an extremely large tribe with many branches and sub-branches (called "nations"), had developed a highly sophisticated* system of govern-

---

encountered: met unexpectedly
tribes: groups of native people
adopted: took and used as their own
imprint: mark left on
indebted: owing gratitude
sophisticated: highly developed

ment to keep the various branches of the tribe from fighting one another. Five of the nations had joined together in a confederation called "The League of the Iroquois." Under the League, each nation was autonomous* in running its own internal affairs, but the nations acted as a unit when dealing with outsiders. The League kept the Iroquois from fighting among themselves and was also valuable in diplomatic relations with other tribes. When the thirteen American colonies were considering what kind of government to establish after they won their independence from Britain, someone suggested that they use a system similar to the League of the Iroquois. Under this system, each colony or future state would be autonomous in managing its own affairs but would join forces with the other states to deal with matters that concerned them all. This is exactly what happened. As a result, the present form of government of the United States can be traced directly back to a native American model.

In conclusion, we can easily see from these few examples the extent of native American influence on our language, our art forms, our eating habits, and our government. Modern Americans are truly indebted to native Americans for their contributions to their culture. Hopefully, the cultural exchange will one day prove to be equally positive for them.

PRACTICE 8: *Outlining*

Make an outline of the previous essay. Make your outline as detailed as possible. Follow the model essay outlines on pages 85, 86, and 89.

PRACTICE 9: *Transitions Between Paragraphs*

Copy the words, phrases or clauses that serve as links between the six paragraphs of the model essay.

Between 1 and 2: ______________________

Between 2 and 3: ______________________

Between 3 and 4: ______________________

Between 4 and 5: ______________________

Between 5 and 6: ______________________

Transition Signals and Thesis Statements

Review the chart of transition signals used for logical division.

Sentence Connectors	Others
first, second, third, etc.	the first (+ noun)
next, last, finally	the/a second (+ noun)
in addition, moreover	one (+ noun)
furthermore	another (+ noun)
also	an additional (+ noun)

autonomous: independent, self-governing

Also review the section on how to write topic sentences for logical order paragraphs on pages 61–62. The same principles apply for writing thesis statements except that, of course, an essay topic is larger, so the subtopics will be larger as well. If you want to name the subtopics in the thesis statement, you can use the same techniques, namely, paired (correlative) conjunctions and the colon (:).

- A college education is a necessity in today's competitive world for two main reasons. (subtopics not named)
- A college education is a necessity in today's competitive world not only because of the knowledge you gain but also because of the personal contacts you make. (subtopics named)
- To many men, an automobile symbolizes three things: money, power, and success. (subtopics named)

WRITING PRACTICE

A. Write an essay in which you explain the influence of one culture on another. Choose two cultures with which you are familiar. For example, you might write about the influence of your country's culture on another country such as the United States or the influence of U.S. culture on your country's culture. (Remember that cultural exchanges work in both directions.)

Follow these steps to success:

1. Write your thesis statement at the top of your paper.
2. Brainstorm by freewriting, listing, or clustering all the influences that come to your mind. (Review Prewriting Activities on pages 3–9.)
   language
   food
   clothing
   music
   family customs
   business methods
   etc.
3. Go through your list and choose three or four influences you wish to write about in your essay.
4. Then, brainstorm for ideas to support each of these influences.
5. Write an outline from your brainstorming activity. (See outlining model on pages 85, 86, and 89.)
6. Write your first rough draft from your outline. Be sure to use transition signals both *within* and *between* paragraphs.
7. Revise your rough draft as you have learned in Chapter 7 (pages 89–93). Check your final essay against the Essay Checklist on page 94.)

B. Write an essay in which you discuss some of the customs or traditions of your culture you wish to preserve as a part of your lifestyle, such as food, religion, holidays, etc. Follow the same steps to success as in the writing exercise above.

Cause and Effect

Another common method of organizing an essay is by cause and effect. In a cause and effect essay, you discuss the reasons for something, and then you discuss the results.

The following are examples of typical cause and effect essay examination questions.

Sociology: Discuss the causes of alienation* in modern society.
Environmental Studies: Discuss the causes of smog.
Business and Economics: Discuss the reasons for the 1987 stock market crash.
History: Discuss the reasons behind the Iranian Revolution in 1979.
Psychology: Explain the high suicide rate of Scandinavia.

Indeed, cause and effect (which can also be called reasons and results) is one of the most-used forms of organization in academic writing. In this section, you will learn about two different ways to write about causes and effects.

Organization

There are basically two main ways to organize a cause and effect essay: "block" organization and "chain" organization. In *block organization*, you first discuss all of the causes as a block (in one, two, three, or more paragraphs, depending on the number of causes). Then you discuss all of the effects together as a block. In *chain organization*, you discuss a first cause and its effect, a second cause and its effect, and a third cause and its effect, in a "chain."

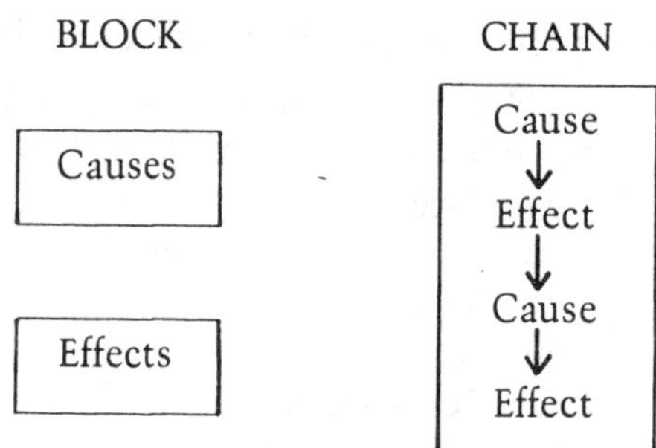

The type of cause and effect organization you choose will depend on your topic. Some topics are more easily organized one way, and some the other way. A chain pattern is usually easier if the causes and effects are very closely interrelated. The chain pattern also works better with smaller topics. With larger topics, and when there is no *direct* cause and effect relationship, the block style is usually easier. Some topics require a combination of block and chain organization as in the model essay on Women's Liberation, which follows.

Transition Paragraphs

In block organization, there is often a short paragraph that separates the "causes" part from the "effects" part. This is called a transition paragraph.

---

alienation: feeling of separation from society

The function of transition paragraphs is to conclude the first part of the essay and introduce the second part. It is not always necessary to write a transition paragraph, but it is helpful when your topic is long and complex.

If the transition paragraph is only one sentence, as in the following model, it could be placed at the beginning of the next paragraph or at the end of the previous one.

Analyze the organization of the model essay by following these steps:

STEP 1 Underline the thesis statement twice and the topic sentences once.

STEP 2 In which paragraph does the discussion change from causes to effects?

STEP 3 Circle all of the cause and effect structure words in the essay. (See page 108 for a list of them.)

MODEL: *Block Organization*

Women's Liberation

Since the middle of this century, women around the world have been seeking greater independence and recognition. No longer content with their traditional roles as housewives and mothers, women have joined together to create the so-called "women's liberation movement." While the forces behind this international movement vary from culture to culture and from individual to individual, the basic causes in the United States can be traced to three events: the development of effective birth-control methods, the invention of labor-saving devices for the home, and the advent* of World War II.

The first cause of the liberation of women was the development of effective birth-control methods, freeing women from the endless cycle of childbearing and rearing. As a result of having a choice as to **when** and **if** to bear children, women acquired the freedom and the time to pursue interests outside of the home. Because of the development of birth control, women could delay having children or avoid having them altogether; consequently, women had the opportunity to acquire an education and/or pursue a career.

Another event was the development of mechanized labor-saving devices for the home, resulting in more leisure time and freedom for women. For example, fifty years ago, a housewife spent an average of twelve to fourteen hours per day doing housework. Due to the invention of machines such as vacuum cleaners, washing machines and dishwashers, a housewife can now take care of her daily housework in about five hours.

The final event that, at least in the United States, gave impetus* to the liberation of women was World War II. During the war, most men were serving in the military. Consequently, women had to fill the vacancies in the labor force. Women by the thousands went to work in factories and then took over businesses for their absent husbands. This was a great change for the majority of American women, for they discovered that they could weld* airplanes and manage businesses as well as change diapers and bake cookies.

These three events planted the seeds of great change in society, and the effects of this change are being felt at all levels: in the family, in business, and in government.

One of the biggest effects of the greater independence of women is being felt in the home. The traditional husband-wife relationship is undergoing a radical transformation.* Because so many women are working, men are learning to share the household tasks of cooking, cleaning, and even caring for children. In some families, there has been a complete reversal of the traditional roles: the husband stays home, while the wife earns the family's income. It should be pointed out, however, that this is the exception, not the rule. In most families in the United States, the husband still earns most of the money, and the wife still does most of the housework.

The effects of women's liberation are being felt not only in the home but also on the job. More and more women are working, and they are demanding equal salaries and equally

---

advent: arrival
impetus: stimulation
weld: to join metal parts using heat
radical transformation: extreme change

responsible positions. It is not uncommon for a woman to be the president of a corporation these days. Many businesses encourage women to advance to high management positions, and every year, the nation's schools produce more women doctors, lawyers, and accountants.

Politics and government are still other areas that are feeling the effects of the women's movement. Although the United States doesn't appear ready to accept a woman president, as some countries of the world have, women are being elected to public office in increasing numbers. The United States currently has several women governors, which is the highest office in a state. A few years ago, this would have been unthinkable.

In conclusion, women in the United States are acquiring greater independence, which is causing sweeping changes in society—at home, at work, and in politics. While men may not be happy with these changes, they should always remember that it was they, the men, who created the conditions leading to the liberation of women: men made war, male scientists developed birth control, and businessmen earned a lot of money selling vacuum cleaners and dishwashers.

Writing Technique Questions

1. Which paragraphs discuss the causes of the liberation of women in the United States? Which paragraphs discuss the effects?
2. What is the function of the paragraph that begins on line 25?
3. Does the thesis statement list both causes and effects, or just causes?
4. Does the conclusion review both causes and effects, or just effects?

PRACTICE 10: *Block Organization*

Fill in the boxes for the "block" cause and effect organizational pattern of the essay on "Women's Liberation."

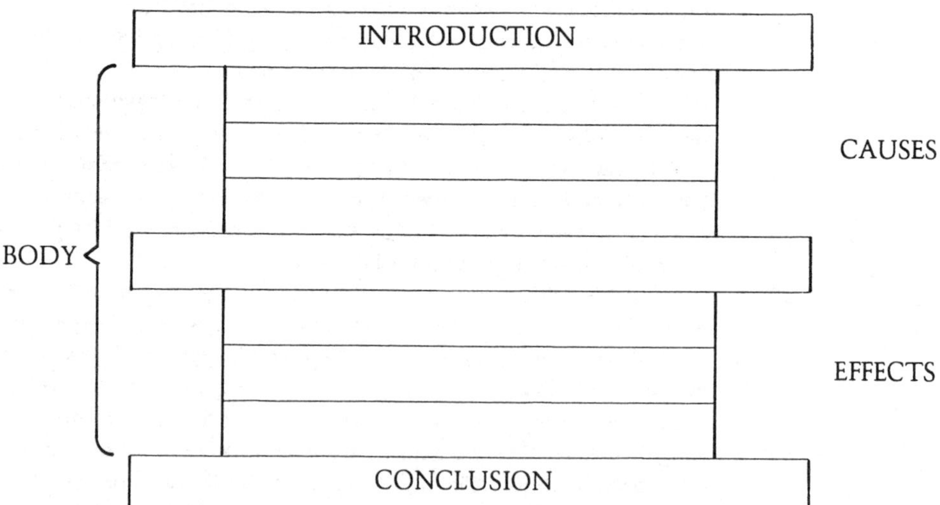

Chain Organization

The other organizational pattern that you might use to write about causes and effects is "chain" organization. One event causes a second event, which in turn causes a third event, which in turn causes a fourth event, and so on. The following short essay describes a simple chain reaction.

MODEL: *Chain Organization*

SAD

When winter arrives, some people get sad, even suicidal.

Doctors have recently started to study the causes of a medical disorder which they have appropriately named SAD, or **s**easonal **a**ffective **d**isorder. People who suffer from SAD become very depressed during the winter months. Their depression appears to be the result of a decrease in the amount of sunlight they are exposed to. Doctors theorize that decreased sunlight affects the production of melatonin, a hormone manufactured in the brain, and serotonin, a chemical that helps transmit nerve impulses. Depression may result from the ensuing* imbalance of these two substances in the body. Also, doctors believe that a decrease in the amount of sunlight the body receives may cause a disturbance in the body's natural clock, which could, in turn, result in symptoms such as listlessness, oversleeping, weight gain, anxiety, and irritability—all symptoms of depression.

Since absence of light seems to be the cause of this disorder, a daily dose of light appears to be the cure. Doctors advise patients to sit in front of a special light box which simulates* natural light for a few hours every day.

In conclusion, this revelation* may help explain the high suicide rate of the Scandinavian countries, and more importantly, it may suggest a remedy:* when the days grow short, turn on the lights.

Writing Technique Questions

1. What causes the days to grow shorter?
2. What is the effect of shorter days?
3. What does this cause?
4. What other change results from a decrease in the amount of light?
5. What is the final result?

PRACTICE 11: *Chain Organization*

Fill in the boxes to complete the flow chart, which illustrates the chain reaction described in "SAD."

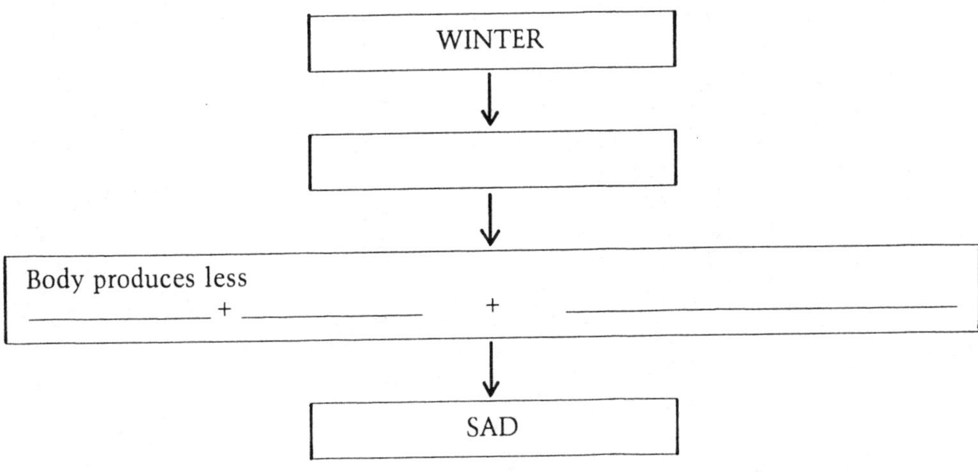

ensuing: following immediately
simulates: gives the effect of, imitates
revelation: fact that is made known
remedy: cure

Cause and Effect Structure Words

Just as there are transition signals that show time and order of importance relationships, there are words and phrases that show cause and effect relationships. They are called cause and effect structure words.

In writing a cause and effect essay, there are many possible structure words you can use. These words show whether you are discussing a reason or result.

You are probably already familiar with many.

Cause structure words	Effect structure words
The first cause ______	The first effect ______
The next reason ______	As a result ______
Because of ______	Therefore ______

To keep clear the difference between these two different groups of signals, remember that cause structure words signal a reason for something:

- In 1975, the speed limit in the U.S. was lowered from 70 to 55 miles per hour.

Conversely, effect structure words signal the result of some action:

- The number of traffic deaths in the U.S. decreased sharply in 1975.

The first sentence is the *reason* for the decrease in the number of traffic deaths. The second sentence is the *result* of the lowering of the speed limit.

Many of the most common cause and effect structure words are listed in the chart below. Learn to use different ones so that you don't always use *because* or *as a result* in your sentences.

Cause and Effect Structure Words

	Sentence Connectors	Clause Connectors		Others
		Coordinators	Subordinators	
To introduce a cause or reason		1) for	2) because since as	3) to result from (+ noun) 4) due to (+ noun) because of (+ noun) 5) the result of (+ noun) the effect of (+ noun) the consequences of (+ noun) 6) as a result of (+ noun) as a consequence of (+ noun)
To introduce an effect or result	7) as a result as a consequence therefore thus consequently hence	8) so		9) to result in (+ noun) to cause (+ noun) to have an effect on (+ noun) to affect (+ noun) 10) the cause of (+ noun) the reason for (+ noun)

Note: The numbers correspond to the numbers in the chart on the facing page.

Examples: Cause Structure Words

1. In 1986, the government raised the speed limit again on some highways, *for* most people were ignoring the 55 MPH limit.
2. In 1986, the government raised the speed limit again on some highways *because* most people were ignoring the 55 MPH limit.
   since
   as
3. The raising of the speed limit again on some highways
   resulted from the general public's disregard for the 55 MPH limit.
   was the result of
4. In 1986, the government raised the speed limit again on some highways *because of* the general public's disregard for the 55 MPH limit.
   due to
5. The *effect of* the general public's disregard for the 55 MPH limit was that the government raised it again on some highways.

   The *consequence of* the general public's disregard for the 55 MPH limit was that the government raised it again on some highways.
6. *As a result of* the general public's disregard for the 55 MPH speed limit, the government raised it again on some highways.

   As a consequence of the general public's disregard for the 55 MPH speed limit, the government raised it again on some highways.

Examples: Effect Structure Words

7. The government lowered the speed limit to 55 MPH;
   as a result, the number of traffic deaths decreased.
   as a consequence,
   therefore,
   thus,
   consequently,
   hence,
8. The government lowered the speed limit to 55 MPH, *so* the number of traffic deaths decreased.
9. The lowering of the speed limit to 55 MPH
   resulted in a decrease in the number of traffic deaths.
   caused

   The lowering of the speed limit to 55 MPH
   had an effect on the number of traffic deaths.
   affected
10. The lowering of the speed limit to 55 MPH was the
    cause of the decrease in the number of traffic deaths.
    reason for

PRACTICE 12: *Recognizing Cause Structure Words*

STEP 1 Underline the sentence that states a cause.

STEP 2 Circle the word or words that introduce the cause.

STEP 3 Be able to discuss the use of each structure word or phrase that you have circled. What kind of grammatical structure follows each one? Notice especially the difference between the use of *because* and *because of.*

Example:

The computer is a learning tool (since) it helps children to master math and language skills.

1. Due to the ability of computers to keep records of sales and inventory, many big department stores rely on them.
2. A medical computer system is an aid to physicians because of its ability to interpret data from a patient's history and provide a diagnosis.*
   (How would you rewrite this sentence using *because* instead of *because of*?)
3. Lowering the speed limit to 55 MPH has caused a sharp decrease in the number of traffic deaths.
4. Public transportation is becoming popular because the cost of gasoline has been rising.
   (How would you rewrite this sentence using *because of* instead of *because*?)
5. Since carpools cut expenses, many commuters are joining them.
6. Smog results from chemical air pollutants being trapped under a layer of warm air.
7. The patient's death was the result of the doctor's negligence.*
8. Little is known about life on the ocean floor, for scientists have only recently developed the technology to explore it.
9. One effect of prolonged weightlessness is the loss of muscle tone,* which can be a problem for astronauts who spend long periods of time in space.

PRACTICE 13: *Recognizing Effect Structure Words*

STEP 1 Underline the part of the sentence that states an effect.

STEP 2 Circle the word or words that introduce the effect.

STEP 3 Be able to discuss the use of each structure word or phrase. What kind of grammatical structure follows each one? How is the sentence punctuated?

1. The performance of electric cars is inferior to the performance of cars with conventional internal combustion engines; consequently, some improvements must be made in them if they are to become popular.
2. However, electric cars are reliable, economical, and nonpolluting; therefore, the government is spending millions of dollars to improve their technology.

---

diagnosis: identification of a disease **muscle tone:** healthy elastic quality
negligence: carelessness

3. Electric cars use relatively inexpensive electricity for power; thus, they cost less to operate than cars that use gasoline.
4. His refusal to attend classes resulted in his dismissal from the school.
5. The cost of gasoline is rising; as a result, many people are using their cars less often.
6. The cause of the patient's death was the doctor's negligence.
7. When he finally arrived, he gave no reason for his tardiness.*
8. It has been documented that heavy cigarette smoking affects the heart as well as the lungs.
9. Cold water is denser than warm water and will therefore sink.
10. Fresh water is less dense than salt water, so it tends to float on the surface of a body of salt water.

PRACTICE 14: *Cause and Effect Structure Words*

Using various cause and effect structure words from the chart on page 108, combine these sentences to emphasize a cause or an effect relationship as indicated. Use different structure words in each sentence, and circle the words you use. Change nouns to pronouns (and pronouns to nouns) when necessary.

Example:

The death rate among women from lung cancer is increasing. Women are smoking more.

Emphasize the cause: *Because women are smoking more, the death rate of women from lung cancer is increasing.*

Emphasize the effect: *The increase in the death rate of women from lung cancer is the result of their smoking more.*

1. Cancer is increasing in industrialized nations. Air pollution and the use of chemicals in food are increasing in these countries.

   Emphasize the cause: ____________________

   Emphasize the effect: ____________________

tardiness: lateness

2. Mr. Williams received a promotion last week. Mr. Williams is a clever administrator, a capable personnel manager, and a financial wizard.*

   Emphasize the cause: ______

   Emphasize the effect: ______

3. The saltiest water is found at the bottom of the ocean. Salt water, being denser than fresh water, sinks.

   Emphasize the cause: ______

   Emphasize the effect: ______

4. Heat energy is carried by electrons. Metals have many free-moving electrons. Metals are good conductors of heat.

   Emphasize the cause: ______

   Emphasize the effect: ______

5. Some businesses now have flexible working hours. Productivity has increased. Absenteeism has decreased.

   Emphasize the cause: ______

   Emphasize the effect: ______

---

wizard: a gifted or clever person

WRITING PRACTICE

Choose one of the suggested topics that follow and write an essay that discusses it in terms of cause and effect. Use either block or chain organization or a combination of both. If you use block organization, be sure to insert a transition paragraph between the two parts of the body of the essay.

Follow these steps to success:

1. Write your thesis statement at the top of your paper.
2. Brainstorm by using one of the prewriting techniques that you prefer. (See Prewriting Activities on pages 3–9.)
   Hint: Divide your paper into two columns. List the causes in the first column and the effects in the second column.
3. Then, brainstorm for ideas to support each cause and effect.
4. Write an outline from your brainstorming activity. (See outlining models on pages 85, 86, and 89.)
5. Write your first rough draft from your outline. Be sure to use a variety of cause and effect structure words, and begin each paragraph with a transition expression.
6. Revise your rough draft as you have learned in Chapter 7. Check your final essay against the Essay Checklist on page 94.)

Topic Suggestions

Culture shock	Rising divorce rate
Pollution	Sex discrimination/racial discrimination
Inflation	Increasing life expectancy in a country
Stress	The refugee problem
Why women outlive men	Student cheating

Any social, economic or political problem in your country or in the United States that interests you.

Comparison and Contrast

A very common and useful method of essay organization is comparison and contrast. It is a form of writing that is used frequently in college work, and in business and the professions as well. Anything can be compared or contrasted such as periods in history, characters in stories, kinds of equipment, or the qualifications of two job applicants. The only important rule to observe is to compare or contrast things of like nature, or else the comparison or contrast will not be valid. In other words, you can compare and contrast apples and bananas, but you can't compare apples and typewriters.

When you make a comparison, you show how certain aspects of one item are similar to the same aspects of another item in the same general class. A comparison answers the question, "What features do X and Y have in common?" or "How are X and Y similar?"

When you contrast two things, you point out the differences between them; i.e., you point out how they are *not* alike. A contrast answers the question, "What are the differences between X and Y?" or "How are X and Y different?"

As with every other kind of writing, there are specific techniques you need to learn in order to write good comparison and contrast essays. The two major techniques are

1. Appropriate use of comparison and contrast structure words.
2. Logical organization of the points of comparison and contrast.

Analyze the following comparison/contrast model essay about the cultures of Japan and the United States.

STEP 1 Locate and underline the thesis sentence twice and the topic sentences once. Does the thesis statement indicate comparison/contrast?

STEP 2 Circle all of the structure words for comparison/contrast. (Refer to the charts on pages 116 and 119.)

STEP 3 Analyze the organization: Which paragaraph discusses similarities? Which paragraphs discuss the differences? Is there a transition between the two parts? What is the purpose of the conclusion?

MODEL: *Comparison and Contrast*

Japan and the United States

The culture of a country is an integral* part of its society whether it is a remote Indian village in Brazil or a highly industrialized city in Western Europe. Basically, culture is reflected in a country's language, literature, art, music, and dance. However, culture also includes the patterned ways in which people conduct themselves in their relationships with others. Japan and the United States are two highly industrialized nations in the world. Although their cultures have a few similarities, there are greater differences between these nations of the East and West.

First of all, Japan and the United States have several similarities. The United States is a democracy and Japan is, too. The United States' Constitution is the supreme law of the land, just as the Japanese Constitution is in Japan. Also, Japan's Diet is similar to the U.S. Congress. In addition, both Japan and the United States have made a mutually enriching exchange of cuisine.* There are Japanese restaurants in America, where diners can enjoy food like sashimi (raw fish), tempura (fried vegetables and prawns), and noodles. Similarly, Japanese enjoy American fast foods like McDonald's hamburgers and French fries, Kentucky fried chicken, and Mrs. Fields' cookies. Finally, the Western sport of baseball is popular not only in the United States but also in Japan. The Japanese have their major leagues as the Americans do, and they have their version of the World Series games. Baseball heroes are important to Japanese spectators, just as they are to American fans.

Despite these similarities, the United States and Japan have some very significant cultural differences.

One important difference is the people. Japan is a homogeneous* society of one nationality and a few underrepresented* minority groups like Chinese and Koreans. As a result, all areas of government and society are controlled by the Japanese majority. In contrast, although the United States is a country with European roots originally, its liberal immigration policy has resulted in its becoming a heterogeneous* society of many nationalities—Europeans, Africans, Asians, and Hispanics.* They are represented in all facets* of American society, including business, education, and politics.

---

integral: necessary for completeness
cuisine: food
homogeneous: alike
underrepresented: not well represented in government
heterogeneous: mixed
Hispanics: Spanish-speaking people
facets: areas

Another difference is in the two countries' use of transportation. Japan and the United States have modern transportation systems which use the latest technology. However, the means of transportation used by the masses* in Japan is different from that used by the masses in the United States. The majority of Japanese use an efficient network of public transportation for pleasure and for commuting from the outlying areas to the cities or from city to city. Thus, the train and subway systems are extremely overcrowded during peak* hours. By comparison, Americans rely less on public transportation and prefer instead to drive their own cars or to ride in carpools.* Although the average Japanese family owns one car, the typical American family owns at least two cars or more, depending on the number of children of legal driving age. Finally, a common sight in Japanese cities is neatly dressed women on motorized scooters riding on busy streets to do their shopping. Bicycles are also a very popular form of daily transportation. In contrast, Americans usually do their errands* by car and ride their bikes mostly for exercise or pleasure.

The final and most important difference is that in modern Japan, traditional customs are still largely observed. In fact, surprisingly, many young people still prefer an arranged marriage, in which a couple meet through the combined efforts of parents and friends of relatives. By comparison, young American people seek their own marriage partners. In addition, married Japanese couples have more clearly defined roles than their American counterparts.* A Japanese wife has greater control over the household and family decisions than an American wife. For example, a Japanese wife decides on the family's residence, major expenditures, and the children's schools. The strong role of a Japanese wife is understandable since the husband, as primary breadwinner,* is a very busy man. His loyalty is first to his workplace, and he must expend all of his energy and waking time to his career or job. Thus, he may not arrive home until late at night, so his wife must discipline the children and make important decisions to keep the household running smoothly. On the other hand, an American couple, who more or less maintain a 50/50 relationship, generally have a more democratic approach and make decisions together.

It is clear that although there are some important similarities between Japan and the United States, there are significant differences as well. The extent to which Japan has accepted some aspects of Western culture reveals the country's desire to absorb new customs. Indeed, the cultural exchanges of Japan and the United States have benefited both nations dramatically and will continue to do so in the future.

Writing Technique Questions

1. On how many points are the two cultures compared and contrasted? What are they? Where are they named?
2. In which paragraph(s) are the similarities discussed? In which paragraph(s) are the differences discussed?
3. What is the function of the third paragraph? Could it be attached to the second or fourth paragraphs?
4. Is the organization of this essay similar to cause and effect block style organization, discussed in the last section?

Comparison Structure Vocabulary

The first key to writing successful comparison and contrast essays is the appropriate use of comparison and contrast structure words. These are words that introduce points of comparison and points of contrast.

The table on the following page lists some of the words and phrases used to write about similarities.

---

the masses: the ordinary people
peak: most traffic
carpools: several riders in one car
do errands: make short trips to the store, the bank, the post office, etc.
counterpart: person in the same role in the other country
breadwinner: money earner

Comparison Structure Words

Sentence Connectors	Clause Connectors		Others
	Subordinators	Coordinators	
1) similarly likewise also too	2) as just as	3) and	4) like (+ noun) just like (+ noun) similar to (+ noun) 5) (be) similar to (be) the same as (be) alike 6) not only . . . but also both . . . and 7) to compare to[1] to compare with

Examples:

likewise,

1. Human workers can detect malfunctions in machinery; *similarly,* a robot can be programmed to detect equipment malfunctions.

   Human workers can detect malfunctions in machinery; a robot can *also.*

   Human workers can detect malfunctions in machinery; a robot can, *too.*

2. Robots can detect malfunctions in machinery *just as* human workers can.

   as

3. Robots *and* human workers can detect malfunctions in machinery.

4. Robots, *like* human workers, can detect malfunctions in machinery.

   just like
   similar to

5. Robots are *similar to* human workers because they can both detect malfunctions in machinery.

   Robots and humans are *similar* because they can both detect malfunctions in machinery.

   Robots are *the same as* human workers in that they can both detect malfunctions in machinery.

   Robots and human workers are *alike* in that they can both detect malfunctions in machinery.

   Robots and humans are *alike* in their ability to detect malfunctions in machinery.

   Both *and*

6. *Not only* human workers *but also* robots can detect malfunctions in machinery.

   be compared with

7. Robots can *be compared to* robots in their ability to detect malfunctions in machinery.

[1]In strict usage, there is a difference between *compare to* and *compare with*. *Compare to* is used to express similarities only:

In this poem, the poet compares love to a rose.

Compare with is used to express both similarities and differences:

Compared with some languages, English has a simple grammar.

PRACTICE 15: *Recognizing Comparison Structure Words*

The following sentences discuss the similarities between the British and the American systems of government.

STEP 1 Underline the items being compared in each sentence.

STEP 2 Circle the comparison signal.

STEP 3 Identify the kind of grammatical structure that follows the comparison signal: noun phrase, clause, etc.

Example:

The United States has a democratic form of government, just as Great Britain does. (clause)

1. The United States operates under a two-party system; Great Britain does also.
2. Similar to the British Parliament, the United States Congress has two separate houses, the Senate and the House of Representatives.
3. The U.S. House of Representatives is like the British House of Commons, and the U.S. Senate is similar to the British House of Lords.
4. The members of the U.S. House of Representatives are elected by district, just as the members of the British House of Commons are.
5. The method of selecting cabinet members is the same in both countries.
6. In Great Britain, there is a cabinet appointed by the prime minister; similarly, the U.S. president also appoints a cabinet.
7. Both the British monarch and the U.S. president have the right to veto* any law.
8. The U.S. Congress can override* a veto by the president. In theory, the British Parliament could also override a veto by the monarch, but this has never happened because the British monarch has never vetoed a law.
9. The method of getting a law passed in Great Britain is almost the same as the method of getting a law passed in the United States.

PRACTICE 16: *Using Comparison Structure Words*

Add comparison structure words to the following sentences and connect them. Rewrite each sentence, and use a variety of comparison words. Circle the words you use.

1. A bicycle is an excellent form of transportation. A moped* is an excellent form of transportation.

    ____

    ____

---

veto: not approve　**moped:** motorized bicycle
override: overrule

2. A bicycle is constructed of a metal frame with two wheels, a handlebar for steering, a saddle seat, and two pedals. A moped has the same basic construction.

3. A bicycle is propelled by pedalling. A moped can be pedalled.

4. A bicycle requires almost no maintenance. A moped needs little upkeep.*

5. New York City has a nickname; it is called "The Big Apple." San Francisco is called "The City by the Golden Gate."

6. New York has several famous bridges that connect Manhattan to the other boroughs.* San Francisco has two bridges that connect it to neighboring counties.*

7. New York is well known for its Chinatown, Harlem, and Little Italy. San Francisco has many ethnic districts, such as North Beach (Italian), Chinatown, Japantown, and the Mission District (Hispanic).

8. New York has a financial district called Wall Street. San Francisco's financial district is called Montgomery Street.

---

upkeep: maintenance
boroughs: civic divisions of New York City
counties: civic divisions of a state

Contrast Structure Vocabulary

Contrast structure words fall into two main groups according to their meaning. The first group shows concession and/or an unexpected result:

Contrast (Concessive) Structure Words

Sentence Connectors	Subordinators	Coordinators	Others
however	although	but	despite (+ noun)
nevertheless	even though	yet	in spite of (+ noun)
nonetheless	though		
still			

Examples:

1. A robot has a memory; *however,* it has to be programmed by a human.
   nevertheless
   nonetheless
   still
2. *Though* a robot has a memory, it has to be programmed by a human.
   Even though
   Although
3. A robot has a memory, *but* it has to be programmed by a human.
   yet
4. *Despite* having a memory, a robot has to be programmed by a human.
   In spite of

The other group of contrast structure words shows strong contrast, even direct opposition. As you can see, *however* and *but* belong to both groups.

Contrast (Strong Opposition) Structure Words

Sentence Connectors	Subordinators	Coordinators	Others
however	while	but	to be different from
in contrast	whereas		to differ from
in (by) comparison			
on the other hand			to compare with
			to be dissimilar
on the contrary			to be unlike

Examples:

1. A human worker has to take breaks to eat and sleep; *however,* a robot can work around the clock.
   in comparison,
   on the other hand[1]

   A human worker cannot work around the clock; *on the contrary,* he/she has to take breaks to eat and sleep.
2. A human worker has to take breaks to eat and sleep, *while* a robot can work around the clock.
   whereas
3. A human worker has to take breaks to eat and sleep, *but* a robot can work around the clock.

[1]*on the contrary*: relates direct opposites; *on the other hand*: relates points not necessarily opposite

is different from

4. A robot *differs from* a human worker because it can work around the clock. *Compared with* a human worker, a robot is less expensive.

dissimilar

A robot and a human worker are *unlike* (each other) because a robot doesn't need breaks to eat and sleep.

PRACTICE 17: *Recognizing Contrast Structure Words*

STEP 1 Underline the items being contrasted in each sentence.

STEP 2 Circle the contrast structure words.

STEP 3 Identify the kind of grammatical structure that follows each signal: noun phrase, clause, etc.

Example:

The governments of Great Britain and the United States are quite (dissimilar) in several aspects. (Prepositional phrase)

1. Whereas the chief executive in Great Britain is called the prime minister, the chief executive in the United States is called the president.
2. In the United States, the president fulfills the functions of both political leader and head of state, while these two functions are separate in Great Britain.
3. In other words, Great Britain has both a monarch and a prime minister, but the United States has only a president.
4. The president of the United States may be of a different political party than the majority of Congress; in contrast, the British prime minister is the head of the political party that has the most seats in Parliament.
5. Unlike the United States, which has a written constitution, Great Britain has no written constitution.
6. The scheduling of elections in the two countries is quite different.
7. In the United States, elections are held on a regular schedule, no matter how popular or unpopular the government is. In Great Britain, on the other hand, elections are held whenever the prime minister loses a vote of confidence.*
8. The members of the U.S. Senate are elected; however, the members of the British House of Lords are appointed or inherit their positions.
9. As you can see, the two systems of government, although they are both democracies, differ in several major aspects.

---

vote of confidence: vote indicating approval

PRACTICE 18: *Using Contrast Structure Words*

Add contrast structure words to each of the following pairs of sentences.

STEP 1 Choose a signal of the type suggested for each group.

STEP 2 Write it in the blank space and add any necessary punctuation marks. Also, change the capitalization, if necessary.

A. Use a sentence connector.

1. Junior colleges offer programs that can be completed in two years ____________________ colleges and universities offer programs that take four years to complete.
2. Junior colleges award associate of arts degrees to their graduates ____________________ colleges and universities award baccalaureate degrees, master's degrees, and Ph.D.'s.
3. Many junior colleges are free ____________________ almost all colleges and universities charge tuition.

B. Use a subordinator.

4. Active solar heating systems require mechanical means to harness* the sun's energy ____________________ passive systems rely on natural forces to collect solar radiation.
5. Passive systems work well only in hot, dry climates ____________________ active systems can work efficiently in any area.
6. ____________________ passive systems are limited by seasonal conditions, active systems work throughout the year.

C. Use a coordinator.

7. An electric car is designed to carry a maximum of four people ____________________ a medium-sized gasoline-powered car can carry up to six passengers comfortably.
8. It takes six hours to recharge the batteries of an electric car ____________________ it takes less than five minutes to fill up the gas tank of a conventional car.

D. Use any type of contrast signal, and rewrite the sentences.

9. The analog computer is used mainly for scientific work. The digital computer is useful in business.

____

____

____

10. The analog computer is used to measure temperatures, flows, and voltages. The digital computer can count, print, reproduce facts, sort data into numerical order, and so on.

____

____

____

harness: control

11. The output from the analog computer is represented as a continuous, unbroken flow. The output from the digital computer is in the form of discrete* letters and numbers.

____

____

____

____

E. Write four sentences of your own, using contrast structure words from the groups labeled "Others" in the tables on page 119. Write sentences contrasting the subjects given.

12. computers/humans

____

____

13. English/your language

____

____

____

14. taking public transportation/driving a car

____

____

____

15. city life/country life

____

____

____

Organization

Just as there are two ways to organize a cause and effect essay, there are at least two ways to organize a comparison and contrast essay. You may use block organization or point-by-point organization. Each type of organization is illustrated in the following models. Study each model very carefully. Notice how the thesis statement tells the reader what type of organization will be used.

In block organization, you discuss all of the similarities in one block (which can be one or more paragraphs), and all of the differences in another block (which can be one or more paragraphs). The essay on Japan and the United States on pages 114–115 is an example of block organization.

Suppose you needed to compare two jobs. You might compare them on these points: salary, fringe benefits,* opportunities for advancement, and workplace atmosphere. If you use block organization, your outline might look like this:

---

discrete: individual
fringe benefits: employment benefits other than salary (vacation time, health insurance, etc.)

MODEL: *Block Organization*

Thesis Statement One way to decide between two job offers is to evaluate what the similarities and differences are before making a decision.

I. The salary and fringe benefits of Job X and Job Y are almost the same.
   A. Salary (Job X and Job Y)
   B. Fringe benefits (Job X and Job Y)
II. Although the salary and fringe benefits are equal, there are big differences in the areas of workplace atmosphere and opportunity for advancement.
   A. Workplace atmosphere
      1. Job X
      2. Job Y
   B. Opportunity for advancement
      1. Job X
      2. Job Y

Conclusion

Of course, you could discuss the differences first and the similarities last. It is more usual, however, to discuss similarities first.

In point-by-point organization, you make a sentence-by-sentence comparison of the features in any order that seems appropriate for the topic. You might even use order of importance (most important feature first or last.)

MODEL: *Point-by-Point Organization*

Thesis Statement One way to decide between two job offers is to make a point-by-point comparison of their features.

I. The salaries of Job X and Job Y are approximately equal.
   A. Job X's salary
   B. Job Y's salary
II. Job X offers the same fringe benefits as Job Y.
   A. Job X's fringe benefits
   B. Job Y's fringe benefits
III. In contrast to Job Y, Job X offers good opportunities for advancement.
   A. Job X's opportunities for advancement
   B. Job Y's opportunities for advancement
IV. Unlike the high-pressure and competitive atmosphere at Company X, the atmosphere at Company Y seems congenial* and supportive.
   A. Atmosphere at Company X
   B. Atmosphere at Company Y

Conclusion

With both types of block organization, as you discuss each feature of Job Y, refer back to the same feature of Job X and use comparison and contrast structure vocabulary to show whether they are the same or different. In other words, it is not

congenial: friendly

sufficient simply to describe each job or each feature; you must constantly refer back and forth to make the similarities and differences clear.

Like Job X, Job Y . . .
In contrast to Job X, Job Y . . .
Job X and Job Y both have . . .

When you write about similarities and differences:

1. Arrange your points of comparison and contrast in logical order. Use either point-by-point or block organization.
2. Use enough comparison and contrast structure vocabulary to make the points of comparison and contrast very clear.

WRITING PRACTICE

Choose one of the suggested topics that follow and write an essay that discusses it in terms of comparison and contrast. Use either point-by-point or block organization. If you use block organization, be sure to insert a transition paragraph between the two parts of the body of the essay.

Follow these steps:

1. Write your thesis statement at the top of your paper.
2. Brainstorm by using one of the prewriting techniques that you prefer. (See Prewriting Activities on pages 3–9.)
   Hint: Divide your paper into two columns. List the comparisons in the first column and the contrasts in the second column.
3. Then, brainstorm for ideas to support each comparison and contrast.
4. Write an outline from your brainstorming activity. (See outlining models on pages 85, 86, and 89.)
5. Write your first rough draft from your outline. Be sure to use a variety of comparison and contrast structure words, and begin each paragraph with a transition expression.
6. Revise your rough draft as you have learned in Chapter 7. Check your final essay against the Essay Checklist on page 125.)

Topic Suggestions

Two cultures, or one aspect of two cultures:
- Schools in your country and another country
- Child-raising practices in your country
- Dating, courtship, and wedding customs

Two languages/two cities
Living at home/living away from home
Two jobs you have had
High school/college
Public/private schools

Two classes, teachers, friends
You and a brother or sister
Computers/humans
Robots/human workers
Your choice of any two people, places, or things

Essay Checklist

This checklist details all the things you have learned about writing paragraphs and essays. It is a good idea to keep this checklist in front of you when you are writing. It will remind you of all the essential elements of a good essay. After you have finished your first draft, check your essay for *every* item on the list. If anything is missing, add it before you write your final draft.

Essay Organization

Introduction:	_______	General statements
	_______	Thesis statement
Body:	_______	Logical and appropriate pattern of organization for the topic (chronological order, logical division, comparison-contrast, etc.)
	_______	Between-paragraph transitions
Conclusion:	_______	Summary of the main points or paraphrase of the thesis and your final comments on the topic

Paragraph Organization

Topic Sentences:	_______	Topic sentence for each paragraph: Each topic sentence has a controlling idea. (Chapter 2)
Supporting Sentences:	_______	Concrete Support: Specific factual details (Chapter 6)
	_______	Unity: Only one main idea in each paragraph (Chapter 3)
	_______	Coherence: Repeating key nouns, using pronouns, transition signals, and logical order (Chapters 4 and 5)
Concluding Sentences:	_______	Concluding Sentence (if necessary)

Review

The four common patterns of essay organization in English you should have learned in this chapter are

Chronological order
Logical division of ideas
Cause and effect
Comparison and contrast

With each pattern, you use special transition signals and structure words to help your reader understand your ideas and follow your discussion. It should be noted that there are other patterns of organization in academic writing such as definition and argumentation. It should also be noted that you may need to use a combination of patterns at times, especially for long essays or term papers.

PRACTICE 19: *Answering Essay Examination Questions*

A. Following is a list of essay questions from English placement tests and from college courses. Read each one, and decide what pattern of organization you might use to answer it.

1. Briefly discuss the events leading up to the dismantling* of the Berlin Wall. (history, political science)
2. What can be done to improve international understanding, in your opinion? (general)
3. Discuss the advantages and disadvantages of government-owned utilities. (government, economics)
4. Outline the procedure for taking a year-end inventory in a small retail business. (business)
5. Compare the straight-line with the declining-balance method of depreciation. (accounting)
6. Discuss the function of the enzyme pepsin in the digestion of food. (biochemistry)
7. Explain the "greenhouse effect." (environmental science)
8. Discuss the ways in which the advent of computers affects the life of the average person today. (general)
9. Discuss the effects of deregulation of the airline industry. (government, economics)
10. Compare the health-care systems in Great Britain and the United States. (government, economics)

B. As a class, compile a list of essay examination questions which you and your classmates have encountered in your other classes. Bring them to class and discuss methods of organizing written answers to them.

---

dismantling: taking down

PART 

Using Outside References

CHAPTER 9

Quotations, Paraphrases, and Summaries

When you write papers from your own personal experiences, you enjoy freedom of expression and the use of informal language. However, as college students, you must learn to use expository forms of writing that are required for your academic courses. For example, you may decide to write a paper about the unhealthy effects of dirty air because you remember reading an article about it. If you decide to write that paper based on your recollection of that article, you may run out of information because you can't remember all the facts that you read. Because academic writing requires that you write about a subject knowledgeably and accurately, you cannot rely totally on your memory about a past course, a newspaper or magazine article, or a television documentary. Besides the possibility of reporting information inaccurately, your knowledge may also be out of date. So, what should you do? Dr. Samuel Johnson, an eighteenth-century writer and critic, said, "Knowledge is of two kinds. We know a subject ourselves or we know where we can find information on it." A library is a good place to get more information on any topic.

While reading articles in magazines, newspapers, and books you will find important information that you may wish to include in your paper. You must know how to borrow that author's words without plagiarizing* the information, so using quotations and writing paraphrases and summaries are important tools in academic writing, which you will learn in this chapter. In addition, Part III also explains how to use the library.

Quotations

Quotations are essential in academic writing. In all kinds of academic writing, from term papers to doctoral dissertations, you are expected to use quotations to support

plagiarizing: using someone else's ideas as your own

your ideas. The reason for this is that although your own ideas and opinions are valid, quoting an authority who agrees with you makes your arguments more convincing.

Your goals in studying this section are to learn how to insert quotations smoothly into a paragraph by using various "reporting" verbs and phrases and to punctuate them correctly.

Read the following models and study how quotations are used to support the topic sentences.

MODEL: *Quotations*

The Population Time Bomb[1]

The dangers of overpopulation cannot be underestimated. As Dr. David Doom, Director of the United Nations Task Force on Population and Food Supply, believes, "The world will be uninhabitable* by the year 2100 unless the rate of growth is reduced." According to Dr. Doom, the world's food production cannot meet the needs of 8 billion people, so famine* is an inevitable* consequence of uncontrolled population growth. (Doom, p. 45) The World Health Organization agrees with Dr. Doom. In a recently published report, it noted, "Famine already exists in many parts of Africa and Asia." (**World Population,** p. 12)

The Crime of the Future

The increased use of computers in business has been accompanied by a corresponding increase in computer crime. The costs to the victims of computer crime are very high. In his book, **Crime by Computer,** computer expert Donn B. Parker stated, "The financial losses to business from computer thefts will exceed $10 billion in 1988." Although Parker's estimate is based on documented cases, no one really knows the extent of computer crime because thefts using computers are almost impossible to discover. "There is just no reliable way to detect computer thefts," Parker said. "It is not just the money they control; they control data, and data is power." (Smith and Gomer)

Writing Technique Questions

1. How many quotations does the first paragraph contain? What reporting verbs and phrases are used?
2. How many quotations are used in the paragraph on computer crime? What main idea do they support?

There are two kinds of quotations: direct and indirect. In this chapter, you will only use direct quotations. In a direct quotation, another person's words are quoted exactly and are enclosed in quotation marks.

The rules for punctuating quotations can become very complex. For general purposes, the rules are as follows:

> Place a comma after the reporting phrase, and put quotation marks before and after the actual words quoted. Capitalize the first word of the quotation as well as the first word of the sentence.

- He said, "Since 1980, famine has killed 3 million people around the world."

---

uninhabitable: unable to support life
famine: widespread lack of food
inevitable: certain, sure

[1]The information in this paragraph is fictional.

If you break a quotation into two parts, enclose both parts in quotation marks and separate the parts with commas. Capitalize only the first word of the sentence.

- "Since 1980," he said, "famine has killed 3 million people around the world."

(For further information on how to punctuate quotations, see Punctuation, pages 260–261.)

Reporting Verbs and Phrases

Reporting verbs and phrases are used to introduce a quotation or any other information that has been borrowed. Some of the more common ones and their usage are shown below:

These expressions are followed by a direct quotation.

As the prime minister said, "______________________."
As . . . reported, "______________________."
As . . . stated, "______________________."
As . . . mentioned, "______________________."
As . . . maintained, "______________________."
As . . . insisted, "______________________."
As . . . declared, "______________________."
As . . . wrote, "______________________."

It is a good idea to include *where* the person said it:

- As Dr. Douglas Woodbury declared in a speech before the World Health Organization last November, "The AIDS epidemic is an international problem."
- As Dr. Michael Jackson wrote in an article in the June, 1985 issue of *Issues for the 90's*, "Refugees are overwhelming* the resources of many already-struggling nations."

You may also use these and other reporting verbs without *as*, in either present or past tense. Follow them with a direct quotation.

The prime minister said, "______________________."
. . . further stated, "______________________."
. . . later insisted, "______________________."
. . . continued, "______________________."
. . . firmly believes, "______________________."

- Dr. Jackson further stated, "It is the responsibility of all developed nations to ease their burden."
- "The refugee problem can only escalate,"* he continued, "as war, famine, and political persecution persist."

The phrase "according to . . ." is followed or preceded by a complete sentence. Do not use quotation marks.

- According to the United Nations, the number of world refugees now exceeds 11 million.
- The number of world refugees now exceeds 11 million, according to the United Nations.

---

overwhelming: overpowering **escalate:** increase

Important!

When you use other people's ideas:

1. *Be accurate.* Do not change the original. If you have a good reason to omit part of a quotation, use an ellipsis (. . .) in place of the missing words.
   - "The first reason . . . is the inability of underdeveloped nations to produce enough food," Dr. Doom stated.

   If you have a good reason to add words to the original, put brackets ([ ]) around the added words.
   - "The second reason [for the inevitability of famine] is that developed nations, which have only thirty percent of the population, consume seventy percent of the food," he said.
2. *Document the source of your quotation.* In academic writing, it is *always* necessary to state the exact source of your information even when you do not use a direct quotation.

PRACTICE 1: *Punctuating Direct Quotations*

Add punctuation to the following direct quotations. Change the capitalization if necessary.

(The sentences in this practice are all about black holes, which are invisible masses in space larger than giant stars. The discovery of black holes is causing enormous excitement in the fields of astronomy and physics.)

1. Dr. John Miller, a well-known astrophysicist who has been studying black holes, said it is the greatest challenge we astrophysicists have ever faced.
2. He further explained in black holes the long-held laws of nature simply do not apply.
3. A black hole is a huge, great, enormous, big nothing explained Miller's associate, Kathleen Parker. It is an invisible vacuum cleaner in space she added.
4. Black holes are created by the death of a very large star she stated.
5. Since they cannot be seen, even with the most powerful telescopes she continued their existence can only be proven mathematically. ("Black Holes," p. 78)

WRITING PRACTICE

Write a short paragraph that explains the idea stated in each topic sentence. Use the quotation for support somewhere in the paragraph. Write a total of three paragraphs.

STEP 1 Copy the topic sentence exactly as it is given.

STEP 2 Add two or three supporting sentences of your own.

STEP 3 Incorporate the quotation in your supporting sentences, and punctuate it correctly.

a. Use different reporting verbs and phrases in each paragraph.

b. Name the source of the quotation informally in your paragraph (who said it and where it was published).

STEP 4 Document the source by putting the author's last name, a comma, and the page number in parentheses after the sentence in which you use the quotation.

Example:

Topic Sentence: The Japanese, who used to think leaving their company was similar to divorce, are learning the joys of job-hopping.*

Quotation: As hundreds of companies in Japan are seeking mid-career executives and engineers to help them diversify* into new markets, job-hopping has become the rage* in Japan. This has prompted thousands of Japanese to make the decision to move to another firm.

Author: Michael Berger

Article: "Job-Hopping Suddenly Becomes Rage in Japan"

Publication: *San Francisco Chronicle*, "Business Extra" (March 19, 1990), page C1.

The Japanese, who used to think leaving their company was similar to divorce, are learning the joys of job-hopping. Before World War II and in the post-war era, Japanese workers and company executives alike stayed with one company because it meant job security and life-time employment, with wage increases based on seniority. Today, however, the picture has been changing. Michael Berger stated in a recent article in the San Francisco Chronicle, "As hundreds of companies in Japan are seeking mid-career executives and engineers to help them diversify into new markets, job-hopping has become the rage in Japan." He added, "This has prompted thousands of Japanese to make the decision to move to another firm." (Berger, p. C1)

The topic of this practice is the "greenhouse effect," which is a warming of the Earth due to increased burning of fossil fuels (coal, gas). Heat is trapped in the Earth's atmosphere like in a giant greenhouse. The results could be disastrous for mankind. Weather patterns would change, and our coastal regions could be flooded.

1. Topic Sentence: The increase in carbon dioxide (CO_2) in the atmosphere will change the Earth's climate.

Quotation: Like panes of glass in a greenhouse, CO_2 allows most solar radiation to enter the atmosphere but prevents part of the heat reradiated by the Earth from escaping into space.

Author: Dr. Herbert Summer

Article: A Global Greenhouse

Publication: *National Geographic*, April, 1987, page 515.

---

job-hopping: changing jobs often
diversify: expand to multiply business opportunities
rage: widespread interest, enthusiasm

2. Topic Sentence: The results could be disastrous.
Quotation: Heavy rains could fall in previously dry regions such as the Sahel, and droughts could occur in rich farming areas such as the U.S. Midwest.
Author: Dr. Herbert Summer
Article: A Global Greenhouse
Publication: *National Geographic*, April, 1987, page 515.

3. Topic Sentence: The impact could be even greater on the level of our oceans.
Quotation: If the West Antarctic ice sheet melted, as it did during a previous period 120,000 years ago, ocean levels could rise 15 to 20 feet.
Author: Dr. Herbert Summer
A Global Greenhouse
Publication: *National Geographic*, April, 1987, page 515.

Paraphrasing

In the preceding section, you learned how to use someone else's ideas for support by quoting his/her words directly. Now, you will learn two other ways to use someone else's ideas: by paraphrasing and by summarizing them.

The ability to paraphrase and summarize is useful as an alternative to using direct quotations when you want to use material from books, magazines, newspapers, or other published sources. Paraphrases and summaries are very similar except that a paraphrase repeats most of the information in the original passage, whereas a summary includes only the main points.

Paraphrasing is a writing skill in which you "rephrase" (rewrite) previously published information in different words without changing its original meaning. Normally, you paraphrase only short selections such as sentences, a series of sentences, or a short paragraph. When you write a paraphrase, you state the author's thoughts *in your own words.* A paraphrase is usually as long as the original text in order to communicate its full meaning.

Two examples of paraphrases follow:

MODEL: *Paraphrasing*

Soccer Mania

Original:

"When the Maracaña soccer stadium [in Rio de Janeiro, Brazil][1] was opened to the public in 1950, and Brazil lost the World Cup to the Uruguayan team, the Brazilians were so disheartened one had the impression that the country itself had died. And people did die of sadness. Mere threats of defeat in a championship match can cause heart attacks, and the despair* of the public is so great that many beat their heads against the cement posts. Such is the Brazilians' passion for soccer." (de Moraes and Gullar p. 13)

---

despair: loss of hope

[1]Brackets [ ] show that the words inside the brackets were not part of the original quotation. This information (the location of the Maracaña stadium) was added for clarity.

Paraphrase:

In 1950, when Brazil was defeated by Uruguay for the World Cup in Soccer in their new stadium in Rio de Janeiro, Brazilians were so dejected that it seemed the whole country had perished. In fact, some citizens actually did die of sorrow. Brazilians react very strongly even to the possibility of defeat in championship soccer games; soccer fans pound their heads against cement posts and even suffer heart attacks. Such reactions prove that Brazilians are very emotional about soccer. (de Moraes and Gullar p. 13)

Notice these substitutions for the underlined words and phrases in the original:

lost the World Cup in Soccer to the Uruguayans	was defeated by Uruguay for the World Cup in Soccer
disheartened	dejected
one had the impression	it seemed
the country itself	the whole country
had died	had perished
people	citizens
sadness	sorrow
threats	possibility
match	game
public	soccer fans
beat	pound
passion (noun)	emotional (adj.)

Some words in the original cannot be changed. In this example, there are no synonyms for *soccer, stadium, World Cup,* or *championship.* Notice that the paraphrase is approximately the same length as the original passage and that all of the information is included.

Here is another example of a paraphrase:

MODEL: *Paraphrasing*

Artificial Languages

Original:

"Since the time of Descartes, it is estimated that no fewer than five hundred attempts have been made to create artificial languages for international use. The most successful by far has been Esperanto, a language constructed around the end of the nineteenth century by Dr. Zamenhof of Poland. Esperanto is a language that is extremely easy to learn and speak, with its words drawn mainly from English, German, the Romance languages, Latin and Greek." (Pei, p. 175)

Paraphrase:

Since the early seventeenth century, approximately five hundred artificial languages have been created for international communication. Esperanto, a language invented around the end of the nineteenth century in Poland by a man named Dr. Zamenhof, has been the most successful. Esperanto is very easy to learn and speak. Its vocabulary comes mainly from English, German, the Romance languages, Latin, and Greek. (Pei, p. 175)

PRACTICE 2: ***Finding Synonymous Expressions***

Words and phrases in the original paragraph titled "Artificial Languages" that have been "rephrased" are listed on the left. Find the synonymous expression for each in the paraphrase and write it on the right. The second one has been done for you.

1. Since the time of Descartes	__________
2. it is estimated that no fewer than five hundred attempts have been made to create artificial languages	approximately five hundred artificial languages have been created
3. for international use	__________
4. The most successful by far has been Esperanto	__________
5. constructed	__________
6. by Dr. Zamenhof of Poland	__________
7. Esperanto is a language that is extremely easy to learn and speak	__________
8. with its words drawn	__________

Writing a Paraphrase

Follow these steps to write a paraphrase:

STEP 1 Read the selection several times until you understand it fully. Take notes of important words such as scientific terms, names of places, people, events, etc.

STEP 2 Look up any words you do not understand and find synonyms for them. Also find other ways to express potentially unfamiliar information such as "since the time of Descartes" in the second example. (The "biographical names" section of a good dictionary will tell you that Descartes was a French philosopher who lived between 1596 and 1650. Therefore, the phrase "since the early seventeenth century" is an appropriate substitute.)

STEP 3 Rewrite each sentence, one after the other. Simplify the sentence structure of each sentence and use synonyms.

STEP 4 Review your paraphrase. Does it sound natural? Does it flow smoothly? Does it sound like your writing? Your paraphrase should reflect your understanding of the original in your own words. Does it contain most of the information in the original? Do not omit any of the author's essential ideas, and, above all, do not change the meaning of the original.

STEP 5 At the end of the paraphrase, copy the reference information in parentheses. (See the section "Documenting Your Sources" on pages 140–143.)

PRACTICE 3: *Paraphrasing*

A. Paraphrase the following passages, following the steps above and using the two models as guides. Work with a partner, and use a dictionary or thesaurus to find synonyms for the underlined words and phrases.

1. *Our Growing Deserts*

"As a result of the unsound use of land, deserts are creeping outward in Africa, Asia, and Latin America. Worse, the productive capacity of vast dry regions in both rich and poor countries is falling." (Byrnes, p. 11)

Original	**Synonym**
as a result of	______________
unsound	______________
creeping outward	______________
productive capacity	______________
vast dry regions	______________
rich and poor countries	______________

2. *Jet Lag*

"People who travel and people whose work schedules are altered drastically often suffer from jet lag, which is a disturbance of the body's time clock. Jet lag sufferers are troubled by both night-time sleeplessness and extreme daytime sleepiness, which inhibits their ability to function normally." (Simpson)

Original	**Synonym**
People who travel	______________
people whose work schedules are altered	______________
drastically	______________
suffer from	______________
disturbance	______________
troubled	______________
night-time sleeplessness	______________
sleepiness	______________
inhibits	______________

B. Work with a partner or group on the next two paragraphs. Select and underline expressions for which you can find synonyms. Then, write your paraphrase.

1. *Vitamin C*

"Vitamin C in large doses not only protects against the common cold but also offers considerable protection against other infectious diseases, both viral and bacterial. I believe that Vitamin C in adequate amounts could considerably decrease the incidence and severity of the flu." (Pauling and Robinson, p. 9)

2. *Interlingua*

"A more recent arrival on the international scene is Interlingua, scientifically constructed by a group of language experts out of Latin, the Romance languages, and English. But whereas Esperanto has a large body of people who actually speak it scattered throughout the world, Interlingua has not yet achieved much popularity." (Pei, pp. 175-176)

C. Now do the last one on your own!

Artificial Languages—Objections

"The main objection to constructed languages, like Esperanto or Interlingua, is that they have not developed all the thought-carrying machinery and shades of meaning that natural languages have had a chance to work out for themselves over a period of many centuries; also, that the artificial languages presented so far lean too heavily in the direction of the western European and American nations, and carry too little in the way of Slavic, Asiatic and African words and habits of thought." (Pei, pp. 176-177)

Summarizing

A summary is similar to a paraphrase except that a summary is shorter. When you summarize, you compress* large amounts of information into the fewest possible sentences. In order to do this, you include only the main points and main supporting points, leaving out the details. However, just as when you paraphrase, you must not change the original meaning, and you must document the source of the original.

Notice the differences between the paraphrase and the summary of the passage about artificial languages. The summary is shorter because many of the details have been omitted. The paraphrase is closer to the original.

MODEL: *Summarizing*

Artificial Languages

Original:

"Since the time of Descartes, it is estimated that no fewer than five hundred attempts have been made to create artificial languages for international use. The most successful by far has been Esperanto, a language constructed around the end of the nineteenth century by Dr. Zamenhof of Poland. Esperanto is a language that is extremely easy to learn and speak, with its words drawn mainly from English, German, the Romance languages, Latin and Greek." (Pei, p. 175)

Paraphrase:

Since the early seventeenth century, an estimated five hundred artificial languages have been created for international communication. Esperanto, a language invented around the end of the nineteenth century in Poland by a man named Dr. Zamenhof, has been the most successful. Esperanto is very easy to learn and speak. Its vocabulary comes mainly from English, German, the Romance languages, Latin, and Greek. (Pei, p. 175)

Summary:

Of the many artificial languages that have been developed, Esperanto, invented about 1900, has been the most successful. Easy to learn and speak, its vocabulary comes mainly from Western European languages, Latin, and Greek. (Pei, p. 175)

Writing a Summary

Since you include only the important ideas in a summary, it is helpful to make a brief outline of the passage first. For example, an outline of the paragraph about Brazilian soccer enthusiasm might be as follows:

---

compress: squeeze, press together

MODEL: *Writing a Summary*

Soccer Mania

Original:

"When the Maracaña soccer stadium was opened to the public in 1950, and Brazil lost the World Cup to the Uruguayan team, the Brazilians were so disheartened one had the impression that the country itself had died. And people did die of sadness. Mere threats of defeat in a championship match can cause heart attacks, and the despair of the public is so great that many beat their heads against the cement posts. Such is the Brazilians' passion for soccer." (de Moraes and Gullar p. 13)

Outline:

A. Brazil lost the World Cup in 1950.
   1. Entire country was sad.
   2. Some people died.
B. Possible defeat causes strong reaction.
   1. Some experience heart attacks.
   2. Some beat their heads.
C. Brazilians are very emotional about soccer.

From the outline, you can see that the main idea of the passage is stated last: Brazilians are very emotional about soccer (Item C in the outline). In your summary, you will write the main idea first (the more usual order). Then add one sentence for each of the two supporting ideas (Items A and B in the outline).

Summary:

The Brazilian people are very emotional about soccer. In 1950, when their team lost the World Cup to Uruguay, the entire country was saddened, and some people even died. Even the possibility of defeat may cause people to have heart attacks or beat their heads against cement posts. (de Moraes and Gullar p. 13)

Notice that some details are left out:

- that the championship match against Uruguay was held in the Maracaña soccer stadium
- that the stadium was new

Also, in a summary, repetitions of the same idea are omitted. Notice that the idea of people dying is mentioned twice in the original, but only once in the summary. Similarly, the idea of sadness is mentioned three times in the original ("disheartened," "sadness," and "despair") but only once in the summary.

PRACTICE 4: *Summarizing*

A. Read the following passage about a new American hobby and study the outline. Then write a summary. Try to summarize the passage in two sentences.

Genealogy

Original:

"For generations, Americans have researched their pasts to discover who their ancestors* were. In recent years, many more people have developed an avid* interest in their genealogy* and

---

ancestors: forefathers
avid: eager
genealogy: study of one's ancestors

the cultural heritage* of their ancestors. This interest was sparked for two reasons. First, Americans celebrated the bicentennial* of the United States in 1976 and paid tribute to* their country's history. Second, and more recently, the book **Roots,** which traces the family history of an American black man named Alex Haley back to Africa, was serialized* on national television. As a result of these two events, a new pastime for thousands of Americans was created." (Longsworth, p. 132)

Outline:

A. American interest in genealogy
   1. Ancestors
   2. Cultural heritage
B. Reasons for recent interest
   1. Bicentennial celebration
   2. **Roots**

Summary:

____

____

____

____

____

B. On a separate sheet of paper, summarize each of the following passages in as few sentences as possible. The passages discuss the basic categories of consumer goods. Follow these steps for success:

STEP 1 Make a brief outline.

STEP 2 Identify the main idea and write it first.

STEP 3 Omit unimportant details.

STEP 4 Don't repeat ideas.

STEP 5 Copy the reference information in parentheses.

Example:

*Convenience Goods**

Convenience goods may be classified as staples, impulse goods, and emergency goods. Staples are bought and used frequently without much consideration being given to their purchase. Many food products and nonprescription drug items are staple goods. Brand identification may have some weight in the buying decision, but usually easy availability will be more important than the brand. Items such as bread, milk, and aspirin are considered staples, and easy availability to consumers is important in their distribution. (Poe, p. 35)

Outline:

A. What are convenience goods?
B. What are staples?
   1. Examples
   2. Reasons for buying

---

cultural heritage: cultural background
bicentennial: two-hundred-year anniversary
paid tribute to: officially acknowledged
serialized: shown in parts on successive days
goods: items or services for sale

Summary:

Convenience goods include staples, impulse goods, and emergency goods. Staples consist of food products such as milk and bread and nonprescription medicines like aspirin. These products may be purchased not only because of their brand names but also because of their availability. (Poe, p. 35)

1. Impulse goods are items that customers buy on sight without having gone out specifically for their purchase. Their unit price is usually low. The purchase of an impulse good satisfies a need that is strongly felt at the moment. Items that customers will buy on an impulse are frequently placed near store doors or at cash registers. Candy bars, chewing gum, cigarettes, and magazines are frequently displayed in this way. (Poe, p. 35)
2. A good may be either a staple or an impulse item, depending on the purpose of the good's use and on whether the good was purchased because of an immediately felt need. Candy bars may be considered staple goods if they are purchased for lunch boxes as part of a weekly grocery shopping trip. But a candy bar might be viewed as an impulse item if it were purchased and eaten on the spot* because a person just happened to see it. (Poe, pp. 35-36)
3. Emergency goods are bought only when an urgent need is felt. In this situation price is not too important because the customer needs the goods at once. Tire chains purchased at a turnpike* service station during a snowstorm or ambulance service for the victim of a heart attack are example of emergency goods. (Poe, p. 36)
4. (Note: This passage is two paragraphs. Your summary should be only one paragraph, however, because the topic of both paragraphs is the same.)

   Shopping goods are in a totally different category. Shopping goods are compared with competing products for price, quality, style, or service by the customer before purchase. This presents an opportunity for selling by sales personnel. Shopping goods typically have a relatively high unit price and are bought less frequently than convenience goods. Examples of shopping goods include apparel,* jewelry, furniture, and appliances.*

   Since the customer will probably want to compare shopping goods with those sold by the competition, retail stores selling such goods find it desirable to be located close together. In some cases the name of the retail store is more important to the customer than the name of the manufacturer. Therefore, the retailer has considerable opportunity to increase sales of shopping goods through promotion. (Poe, p. 36)
5. Specialty goods is yet another classification of consumer items. Specialty goods are identified by customers with strong brand preference or with features that justify a special buying effort. The customer usually has knowledge of the product before the buying trip and is willing to go out of the way to find a certain brand. Examples of specialty goods include photographic equipment, expensive clothing, and stereo sets. An automobile may be considered a specialty good by the customer who has a strong preference for a particular manufacturer's models. (Poe, p. 36)

Documenting Sources

When writing a paper in which you use the ideas of others, *you must give proper credit to the writer of those ideas even when you do not use his or her exact words.* If you take another's ideas and pretend that they are your own in academic writing, or if you neglect to mention whose ideas you are using, you are guilty of the serious offense of plagiarism. In this section, you will learn how to document your sources.

---

on the spot: right there
turnpike: major highway
apparel: clothing
appliances: machines used in the home such as dishwashers, refrigerators, etc.

Citations Within the Text[1]

The first step is to document your sources. There are several possible ways to do this. One of the more commonly used ways requires you to write a brief reference to the source in parentheses immediately following the quoted, paraphrased, or summarized material. This reference is called a citation. You should give only the minimum information necessary to help your reader find the source. At the end of your paper, you will give complete information about each work you have cited.

Usually, you will need to give the author's last name and a page number:

- (Pei, p. 15)

If there are two authors, give both names:

- (de Moraes and Gullar, p. 13)

Do not give any more information than is necessary for your reader to identify the source of the material. For example, leave out page numbers if they are not necessary. If the article from which you are borrowing information is only one page long, you do not need to give a page number in the citation because you will give it in the "Works Cited" list at the end of your paper.

- (Simpson)

If you have mentioned the author's name in your summary or paraphrase, you do not even need to give his/her name in the parenthetical reference. For example, if you began your paraphrase of the paragraph on vitamin C on page 136 as follows: "According to Pauling and Robinson, . . ." you would not have had to repeat their names in the citation. You would only have had to give the page number, as shown here:

- (9)

If you have used material from more than one work by the same author, you must indicate which book the information is from. You can give either a shortened title of the work or the publication date.

- (Pei, *Language*, p. 175) or (Pei, 1954, p. 175)

If you use material from an encyclopedia, use the author's name if it is given. You do not need a page number since encyclopedia articles are arranged alphabetically and your reader will be able to find the source easily. If the author's name is not given, use the title of the article in quotation marks to identify it.

- ("Gun Control")

Preparing a List of Works Cited

The second step in documenting your sources is to compile a list of all of your sources in alphabetical order by author's family name. Include complete publishing information about each one. This list of sources is called "Works Cited."

Study the following list of works cited for material used in this chapter. Pay special attention to the punctuation and underlining, and notice that the list is double-spaced.

[1]The method for documenting sources described here has been recommended by the Modern Language Association since 1984. It replaces footnoting. Numbered footnotes are now used primarily for supplementary or explanatory comments, as in this footnote.

MODEL: *Works Cited*

Byrnes, James. "The Earth's Expanding Deserts." Bulletin of the Atomic Scientists Jan. 1978: 101-117.

"Gun Control." Academic American Encyclopedia. 1983 ed.

de Moraes, Vinicius and Ferreira Gullar. The Joy of Rio. New York: Vendome, 1980.

Longsworth, Stephen. "In Search of Roots." American Genealogical Journal 68 (1978): 130-135.

Pauling, Linus and Arthur Robinson. "When Is It Finally Going to Dawn on Us?" Interview. The Body Forum Jan. 1977: 9-10.

Pei, Mario A. All About Language. Philadelphia: Lippincott, 1954.

Poe, Edward. Enterprise of American Business. New York: Macmillan, 1978.

Simpson, Ann H. "Jet Lag." Modern Medicine 28 June 1988: 111.

Explanatory Notes[1]

Following is an example of a reference for an article from a periodical journal. (A periodical journal is a special kind of magazine, with issues published periodically: daily, weekly, monthly, or quarterly.)

> Byrnes, James. "The Earth's Expanding Deserts." Bulletin of the Atomic Scientists Jan. 1978: 101-117.

The author's family name is first, followed by a comma, his first name, and a period. The title of the article comes next. It is followed by a period and enclosed in quotation marks. Notice that the period is *inside* the quotation marks. The title of the journal is next, and it is underlined, but it is not followed by a period. Next comes information about the volume number, issue number, or date of publication. Since this article came from a journal which doesn't have a volume number, the month (abbreviated) and year are given, followed by a colon. Finally, the page numbers are given, followed by a period.

Following is an example of a reference for an unsigned encyclopedia article. Since the author is unknown, the article is identified by its title. Since this is a commonly used encyclopedia, only the year of publication of the edition and the abbreviation "ed." (for edition) is necessary.

> "Gun Control." Academic American Encyclopedia. 1983 ed.

The following is an example of a reference for a book with two authors. Notice that the first name of the second author is given before his last name. The title of the book is underlined and followed by a period. Next comes the city (and the state, if the city is not well known) of publication followed by a colon, the name of the publishing company (abbreviated if it is well known), a comma, the year of publication, and a period.

> de Moraes, Vinicius and Ferreira Gullar. The Joy of Rio. New York: Vendome, 1980.

[1]Authors' note: An explanation of all of the possible kinds of references is beyond the scope of this book. For complete explanations and examples, see any current style manual.

The following is another example of an article from a periodical journal. It differs from the first example in that it has a volume number; the month and day are therefore unnecessary. The year is enclosed in parentheses, followed by a colon and the page numbers.

Longsworth, Stephen. "In Search of Roots." American Genealogical Journal 68 (1978): 130-135.

The following is an example of a reference which was an interview published in a periodical journal. The word *interview* followed by a period is inserted between the title of the article and the title of the journal. This form may be used for speeches, lectures, and other public addresses.

Pauling, Linus and Arthur Robinson. "When is it Finally Going to Dawn on Us?" Interview. The Body Forum Jan. 19: 9-10.

PRACTICE 5: *"Works Cited" References*

A. Tell what each part of the following references means.

1. Pei, Mario A. All About Language. Philadelphia: Lippincott, 1954.
2. Poe, Edward. Enterprise of American Business. New York: Macmillan, 1978.
3. Simpson, Ann H. "Jet Lag." Modern Medicine 28 June 1988: 111.
4. Billingsley, John D. "Small Arms." The Encyclopedia Americana: International Edition. 1984 ed.
5. "Dyslexia." Encyclopedia of Educational Psychology. 1987 ed.

B. Prepare a list of "Works Cited" for the following scrambled references. Put the list in alphabetical order, and put each entry in correct form.

Example:

Introduction to Academic Writing. 2nd ed. Alice Oshima and Ann Hogue 1991 Addison-Wesley Reading, MA

Oshima, Alice and Ann Hogue. Introduction to Academic Writing. 2nd ed. Reading, MA: Addison-Wesley, 1991.

1. pages 34–41/F. R. Vellutius/Scientific American/256/Dyslexia/1987
2. Collier's Encyclopedia/Dyslexia/1980/Archie A. Silver and Rosa A. Hagen
3. Nelson-Hall (a publishing company)/Chicago/1978/Emmett C. Velten and Carlene T. Sampson/Rx for Learning Disability
4. Mapping the Brain/Joshua Fischman/Psychology Today/Sept/1985/pages 18–19
5. Boston Little, Brown (a publishing company)/Mary MacCracken/1986/Turnabout Children

Review

These are the important points you should have learned from this chapter.

1. When you include information in your paper from a book, journal, newspaper, magazine, etc., use any of the following methods:
   - Direct quotations—Use the author's exact words, and place them within quotation marks.
   - Paraphrasing—Rephrase the author's published information into your own words without changing his/her intended meaning. It is not necessary to condense the original information.
   - Summarizing—Compress large amounts of the author's published information into your own words, using as few sentences as possible. Use only the author's main points, and leave out the unnecessary details.
2. Document your sources when you use the published words and ideas of another person in order to give credit to the author and to help your reader find the source of your borrowed information.
   - Use citations within the text.
   - Prepare an alphabetical list of words cited.

CHAPTER 10

Using the Library

Time is the biggest problem of most students when they have to do library research for a term paper or report. Finding information in the library can take so much time that many students avoid it until the last possible minute.

Library research does not have to be very time-consuming. If you learn to use a library efficiently, you can save yourself a great deal of time. The exercises in this chapter are designed to familiarize you with the library so that you can find the information you need quickly.

The first and most important thing to know about a library is that when you can't find something, ask a librarian for help. Librarians are usually very helpful people. They are paid not just to shelve books but to provide information and assistance. The most helpful librarians are usually those who work in the reference room. They will help you get started on a term paper and even help you find material.

There are two basic places to begin looking for information: the card catalog and the various periodical indexes. The card catalog is a list of all the books in the library. A periodical index is a list of all the magazine and journal articles written on any subject. If you need to find a book, look in the card catalog. If you need to find a magazine article, look in a periodical index.

In the next few pages, you will study both of these sources of information.

The Card Catalog

The card catalog is a catalog of all the books in the library. Every book has at least three cards: an *author* card, a *title* card, and one or more *subject* cards. If you need a book by a particular author, look in the author catalog. If you know the title of the book you need, look in the title catalog. If you need a book on a particular subject, look in the subject catalog.

Reading the Cards

Every card contains a lot of basic information about a book. If you learn to read the cards, you won't waste time looking for books that you can't use. Read the card carefully and completely to get all the information possible from the card *before* you start to look for the book.

The most important thing to look for on the card is the date of publication. An engineering book published in 1898 is probably not worth finding. Next, look at the bottom of the card for the subjects under which the book is catalogued. Do they seem relevant to your topic? Now look for the total number of pages in the book. The length may help you decide whether it is worth your time to find the book and read it. Finally, look for the word *Bibliography,* often abbreviated *Bibliog.,* on the card. If a book is relevant to your subject and contains a bibliography, it is worth checking. The bibliography will lead you quickly to other relevant sources of information.

If you find a book in the card catalog that you think will contain the information you need, your next step is to write down three things:

1. the call number (from the upper left-hand corner of the card)
2. the author's name
3. the title of the book

All books are shelved by their call number. Be sure you copy it down accurately and completely. The call number is the key to locating a book on the library shelves.

Some cards have the abbreviation *Ref.* typed above the call number. This means that the book is a *reference book.* A reference book may be shelved alphabetically by call number, but it may also be in a special area called the reference room. You will have to look for it in both places.

PRACTICE 6: *The Card Catalog*

Study the two library cards below, and answer the questions that follow them.

Ref. Z 4708 K6 G33	KOREANS IN HAWAII - BIBLIOGRAPHY Gardner, Arthur L. The Koreans in Hawaii: an annotated bibliography by Arthur L. Gardner. Honolulu, Social Science Research Institute, University of Hawaii, 1970. 83 p. 28 cm. (Hawaii series, no. 2) 1. Koreans in Hawaii. 2. Hawaii - population.

PJ
7695
E8
M3

Manzalaoui, Mahmoud, ed.
Arabic Writing Today; the short story. Cairo, American Research Center in Egypt, 1968
407 p. 22 cm.

Bibliog: p. 403–407.

1. Short stories, Arabic-translations into English.
2. Short stories, English-translations from Arabic.

1. Type of card (subject, author, or title)
2. Call number
3. Author's name
4. Title of book
5. Date of publication
6. Number of pages
7. Size of book
8. Name of publisher
9. What are the other subjects under which each book is listed?
10. Does each book contain a bibliography? (Is the book a bibliography itself?)
11. Where can each book be found in the library?

Periodical Indexes

Periodical indexes are books that contain lists of all articles published in magazines and academic journals on every subject. These indexes do not contain the actual articles; they simply tell you where to find the articles you need in other magazines and journals. Periodical indexes are probably more helpful than the card catalog because they tell you where to find short magazine articles on your term paper topic. Isn't it easier to read a 20-page article than a 200-page book?

Periodical indexes are organized just like the card catalog. Every article is listed in at least two places: by the *author's name* and under one or more *subjects*. However, they are not listed by title.

There are several different indexes in the library. The most general and largest is the *Reader's Guide to Periodical Literature*. In addition, many fields of study have their own special indexes, such as the *Reader's Guide to the Social Sciences*, the *Education Index*, the *Business Periodicals Index*, the *Handbook of Chemistry and Physics*, and the *Civil Engineering Handbook*. Find out what indexes the library has in your field.

Indexes use a lot of abbreviations, which you should learn to recognize. You probably already know many of these common abbreviations:

bibl.	bibliography
cond.	condensed
cont.	continued
ed.	editor, edited, edition
f.	footnote
il.	illustrated
introd.	introduction
por.	portrait
v.	volume
sup.	supplement

The names of the magazines and journals are also abbreviated:

Nat Geog	*National Geographic*
Sci Digest	*Science Digest*
NY Times Mag	*New York Times Magazine*
Bsns W	*Business Week*
Harvard Bus R	*Harvard Business Review*

PRACTICE 7: *Periodical Indexes*

Study the entries on the next page and then answer the questions below.

1. **a.** How many articles about turtles are listed?
   b. How many of the articles about turtles have pictures or drawings?
2. **a.** How many subtopics are listed for the main topic drug abuse?
   b. Under which subtopic would you look for articles on the effects on babies of drug use by pregnant women?
3. Where can you look for an article about TV dinners?
4. In which article can you find a list of other articles about the 1989 California earthquake?
5. Who is the author of an article about UFOs?
6. What is the title of an article about twins?
7. **a.** In which magazine did an article appear about drug testing and racism?
   b. What is the volume number?
   c. What is the month, day, and year?
   d. On what page does the article begin?
   e. What does the + sign indicate?
   f. Does your library have this magazine?

DRUG ABUSE
See also
Cocaine
Crack (Cocaine)
Drugs and automobile drivers
Drugs and celebrities
Drugs and employment
Drugs and infants
Drugs and musicians
Drugs and politicians
Drugs and sports
Drugs and women
Drugs and youth
Marijuana
PCP
The federal drugstore [interview with M. S. Gazzaniga; cover story] il por *National Review* 42:34+ F 5 '90
International aspects
Drugs: the world picture [cover story] M. E. Sullivan. bibl il *Current Health 2* 16:4-10 F '90
Rehabilitation
See also
Hale House (New York, N.Y.)
Phoenix House
Dr. James Halikas finds that a pill made for seizures may help cocaine addicts to just say no [carbamazepine; interview] N. Stesin. il pors *People Weekly* 33:81-2 Ja 22 '90
Testing
Here come the specimen jars. il. *Time* 135:60 Ja 29 '90
NCAA tightens drug rules for collegiate gridders. *Jet* 77:48 F 12 '90
NFL drug problem faces allegations of racism. il *Jet* 77:46+ F 12 '90
Sizing up the hazards of cocaine use [hair analysis; work of Karen Graham and Gideon Koren] *Science News* 137:13 Ja 6 '90
EARTH
See also
Creation
EARTH, EFFECT OF MAN ON *See* Man—Influence on nature
EARTH CORPS (U.S.)
Forest of dreams. L. Morrow. il *Time* 135:74 F 12 '90
EARTHQUAKE PREDICTION
California aftershock model uncertainties [discussion of March 3, 1989 article, Earthquake hazard after a mainshock in California] P. A. Reasenberg and L. M. Jones. il *Science* 247:343-6 Ja 19 '90
The Loma Prieta, California, earthquake: an anticipated event. bibl f il maps *Science* 247:286-93 Ja 19 '90
There's earthquakes in the wind [research by Jerome Namias] *Science News* 137:47 Ja 20 '90
EARTHQUAKES
Prediction
See Earthquake prediction
California
See also
San Francisco Bay Area (Calif.)—Earthquake, 1989
California aftershock model uncertainties [discussion of March 3, 1989 article, Earthquake hazard after a mainshock in California] P. A. Reasenberg and L. M. Jones. il. *Science* 247:343-6 Ja 19 '90
There's earthquakes in the wind [research by Jerome Namias] *Science News* 137:47 Ja 20 '90
EARTHQUAKES AND BUILDING
Earthquake jostles the new Stanford Linear Collider. B. M. Schwarzschild. *Physics Today* 43:21 Ja '90
TURTLES
The exclusion of sea turtles [battle between shrimpers and environmentalists over Turtle Excluder Devices required on fishing nets] T. Williams. il. *Audubon* 92:24-6+ Ja '90
Safely telling she- from he-turtles [Kemps's ridley sea turtle] *Science News* 137:30 Ja 13 '90
Small things considered [signs warning motorists about box turtle crossings] R. De Villeneuve. il. *The Conservationist* 44:53 Ja/F '90
TUTU, DESMOND
about
Tutu in Israel. *The Christian Century* 107:96-7 Ja 31 '90
TV DINNERS *See* Frozen dinners
TWENTY-FIRST CENTURY
Facing the "totally new and dynamic" [interview with P. Drucker] E. Reingold. il por *Time* 135:6-7 Ja 22 '90
Where America was a century ago: history as a guide to the future. J. Center. il por *The Futurist* 24:22-8 Ja/F '90
Anecdotes, facetiae, satire, etc.
Last word [dating] L. Sunshine. por *Omni (New York, N.Y.)* 12:104 Ja '90
TWINS
Unhappiness might be inherited [University of Southern California study] *USA Today (Periodical)* 118:8-9 Ja '90
TWO CAREER COUPLES *See* Married couples—Employment
TWO THOUSAND (YEAR)
Health facts in the year 2000. R. Rodale. il. *Prevention (Emmaus, Pa.)* 42:23-4 Ja '90
Health savers of the next century [special section] il *Prevention (Emmaus, Pa.)* 42:33-40+ Ja '90
UFOS
Reporters and reporting
UFO update [sighting in Soviet Union reported by TASS] J. E. Oberg. il. *Omni (New York, N.Y.)* 12:73 Ja '90

Other Sources of Information

Other useful sources of information in a library are reference books, microfilm, and computer data banks.

Reference Books

These are books which contain all kinds of factual information. They include dictionaries, encyclopedias, atlases, and almanacs. You would look in these books if you needed the name of the hottest spot on Earth, the birthdate of your favorite movie star, or a summary of Chinese history. Reference books may not be taken out of the library.

Microfilm

Most libraries have copies of some newspapers and magazines on microfilm. You can read old newspaper and magazine articles with the help of special machines called microfilm readers.

Computer Data Banks

Libraries are increasingly using computers to store bibliographies. Having the information in the *Reader's Guide to Periodical Literature* in a computer, for example, greatly simplifies the task of doing research for a term paper. In some instances, you can just type in your topic, and the computer will produce lists of articles on your topic for you.

PRACTICE 8: *Using the Library*

Plan to spend about one hour in the library completing this assignment. Answer all questions carefully and completely.

A. Card Catalog

1. How many books written by Joyce Carol Oates does the library have? List the call number and title of one of her books. Also give the date and place of publication, and the number of pages in the book.

CALL NUMBER	TITLE	DATE AND PLACE OF PUBLICATION	NUMBER OF PAGES

Exactly where in the library can you find this book? ____________

2. Who wrote the book entitled *The Magic Mountain*? ____________

Was it originally published in another language? ____________

How many pages are in this book? ____________

3. Find the cards for two books on nonverbal communication. List their call numbers, titles, authors, and date of publication.

CALL NUMBER	AUTHOR	TITLE	DATE OF PUBLICATION

a. ______________________________

b. ______________________________

4. Look up a book written *about* Mikhail Gorbachev.

What is the title of the book? ______________________________

Who is the author? ______________________________

5. Under what subject can you find books on the following subjects?

schizophrenia ______________________________

malaria ______________________________

flight to the moon ______________________________

Samuel Clemens ______________________________

couples, unmarried ______________________________

soil conservation ______________________________

B. Periodical Indexes

6. Locate and write the names of three periodical indexes

Name of Index *Location*

a. ______________________________

b. ______________________________

c. ______________________________

7. In the *Readers Guide to Periodical Literature,* look up an article written about the Chernobyl nuclear accident in *Time* magazine in April 1990. Copy the complete reference and explain all of the abbreviations and numbers. ______________________________

____

____

____

____

8. In one of the three indexes you listed in question 6, look up an article on a subject of your choice. Copy the complete reference, and explain all of the abbreviations and numbers. ______________________________

____

____

____

____

C. **Reference**

9. Use the *World Almanac* and look up the most recent statistics on the birth rate in your country. (Your answer should be a percent of births per thousand.)

   Country: ______________________ Year: ________ Birthrate: ____________

D. **Microfilm**

10. Look up your birthdate in the *New York Times.* Write the main headline of the newspaper on that date: ______________________________________

    ____

Review

These are the important points that you should have learned in this chapter:

1. Learn to use reference sources in the library to find information quickly and easily.
   a. card catalog
   b. periodical indexes
   c. other sources (microfilm, etc.)
2. Ask a librarian to help you use the library efficiently.

PART IV
Sentence Structure

CHAPTER 11

Types of Sentences

Clauses

Clauses are the building blocks of sentences. A **clause** is a group of words that contains (at least) a subject and a verb. These are clauses:

> ecology is a science
> because pollution causes cancer

These are not clauses:

> to protect the environment
> after working all day in the language laboratory

There are two kinds of clauses: independent and dependent.

Independent Clauses

An **independent clause** contains a subject and a verb and expresses a complete thought. It can stand alone as a sentence by itself. An independent clause is like an adult person: it is independent and can "live" by itself.

An independent clause is formed with:

> Subject + Verb (+ Complement)

The following sentences show examples of independent clauses:

> Students normally spend four years in college.
> I will declare my major now, but I may change it later.
> Foreign students suffer from culture shock when they come to the United States.
> Because the cost of education has been rising, many students are having financial problems.

Dependent Clauses

A **dependent clause** begins with a subordinator such as *when, while, if, that,* or *who,* followed by a subject, verb, and complement. It does not express a complete thought and cannot stand by itself as a sentence. A dependent clause is like a little child: it cannot "live" by itself.

A dependent clause is formed with:

Subordinator + Subject + Verb (+ Complement)

These are dependent clauses:

... when the semester was over ...
... who was accepted by the university ...
... if you leave your car unlocked ...
... because I had a job interview ...
... that the experiment was a success ...

Notice that they all begin with subordinators. You should learn to recognize subordinators. A partial list of them is given on page 156. Refer to the list when you do the following practice.

PRACTICE 1: *Independent and Dependent Clauses*

Write INDEP next to the independent clauses and put a period (.) after them. Write DEP next to the dependent clauses.

_____ **1.** Jet lag affects most long-distance travelers
_____ **2.** Which is simply the urge to sleep at inappropriate times
_____ **3.** During long journeys through several time zones, the body's inner clock is disrupted
_____ **4.** For some reason, travel from west to east causes greater jet lag than travel from east to west
_____ **5.** Also, changes in work schedules can cause jet lag
_____ **6.** When hospital nurses change from a day shift to a night shift, for example
_____ **7.** Although there is no sure way to prevent jet lag
_____ **8.** There are some ways to minimize it
_____ **9.** Because jet lag is caused at least partially by loss of sleep, not just a change in the time of sleep
_____ **10.** The traveler should plan to arrive at his destination as late as possible
_____ **11.** Upon arriving, he or she should immediately go to bed
_____ **12.** Then the traveler should start to live in the new time frame immediately

Clause Connectors

Three groups of words are used to connect clauses in order to form different kinds of sentences. They are subordinators (subordinating conjunctions), coordinators (coordinating conjunctions), and conjunctive adverbs.

You don't use "," with conjunctions

Subordinators (Subordinating Conjunctions)

after	before	that	when	which
although	even though	though	whenever	while
as	how	unless	where	who
as if	if	until	wherever	whom
as soon as	since	what	whether	
because	so that			

Coordinators (Coordinating Conjunctions)

There are only seven coordinators, which you can remember by the phrase FAN BOYS:

for, **and**, **nor**, **but**, **or**, **yet**, **so**

Conjunctive Adverbs

Following is a list of commonly used conjunctive adverbs

accordingly	hence	likewise	nonetheless	for example
besides	however	meanwhile	otherwise	in addition
consequently	indeed	moreover	therefore	in contrast
furthermore	instead	nevertheless	thus	on the other hand

Kinds of Sentences

A sentence is a group of words that you use to communicate your ideas in writing or in speaking. Every sentence is composed of one or more clauses and expresses a complete thought.

There are basically four kinds of sentences in English: simple, compound, complex, and compound-complex. The kind of sentence is determined by the kind of clauses used to form it.

Simple Sentences

A **simple sentence** is one independent clause. Like an adult person, it can "live" alone.

- I enjoy playing tennis with my friends every weekend.
- I enjoy playing tennis and look forward to it every weekend.
- My friends and I play tennis and go bowling every weekend.

Notice that the second sentence has two verbs, *enjoy* and *look forward to.* This is called a compound verb. Because there is only one clause, this is a simple sentence. The third sentence has a compound subject as well as a compound verb, but it is still a simple sentence because it has only one clause.

PRACTICE 2: ***Simple Sentences***

1. Write two simple sentences with one subject and one verb.
2. Write two simple sentences with one subject and two verbs.
3. Write two simple sentences with two subjects and two verbs.

Compound Sentences

A **compound sentence** is two or more independent clauses joined together, like two adults joined together in marriage. Each clause is of equal importance and could stand alone. There are three ways to join independent clauses to form a compound sentence.

With a coordinator:

- I enjoy playing tennis, *but* I hate playing golf.

With a conjunctive adverb:

- I enjoy playing tennis; *however*, I hate playing golf.

With a semicolon:

- I enjoy playing tennis; I hate playing golf.

You will study each of these types of compound sentences in more detail.

Compound Sentences with Coordinators

A compound sentence can be formed with:

Independent Clause , + Coordinator + Independent Clause

Notice that there is a comma after the first independent clause. Remember that there are only seven coordinators: *for, and, nor, but, or, yet,* and *so,* which you can remember by the phrase FAN BOYS. The following sentences illustrate their meanings.

1. The Japanese have the longest life expectancy of any other people, *for* their diet is extremely healthful. (The second clause gives the reason for the first clause.)
2. The Japanese consume a lot of rice, *and* they eat more fish than red meat. (Both clauses express equal related ideas.)
3. Many Americans, on the other hand, do not eat a healthy diet, *nor* do they get enough exercise. (*Nor* means "and not." It is used to join two equal negative independent clauses. Notice that the "nor" clause uses question word order.)
4. In the last twenty years, Americans have reduced their smoking, *but* Europeans seem to be smoking more than ever. (The two clauses express contrasting ideas.)
5. Europeans should change their smoking habits, *or* they will risk developing lung cancer. (The two clauses express alternatives or possibilities.)
6. Many Japanese men smoke, *yet* the Japanese have long life expectancies. (The second clause is an unexpected contrast to the information in the first clause.)
7. The Japanese diet is becoming more Westernized, *so* their life expectancy will probably decrease in the future. (The second clause is a result of the first clause.)

PRACTICE 3: *Compound Sentences with Coordinators*

A. Add another independent clause to the following independent clauses to form compound sentences. Be sure to write a complete clause containing a subject and a verb. Circle the coordinator and add punctuation.

Example:

The college campus is located in the center of the city, (so) *it is very easy to do my shopping.*

1. Students can attend day classes and ______________________________.
2. Students can live in dormitories or ______________________________.
3. I have finished my math homework but ______________________________.
4. I have studied English for six years yet ______________________________.
5. My advisor suggested a typing class for ______________________________.
6. Some students do not like to write term papers nor ______________________________.
7. The instructor gave us eight weeks to write our term papers yet ______________________________.
8. Most students had not even chosen a topic nor ______________________________.
9. The instructor was very upset for ______________________________.
10. My roommate scored very high on the English placement test so ______________________________.

B. For each pair of sentences below, choose a coordinator which best fits the meaning and join the two independent clauses to form a compound sentence. Use each FAN BOYS coordinator once. Write your new sentences on a separate sheet of paper and punctuate them correctly.

Example:

Nuclear accidents can devastate* vast areas. Nuclear power plants should have strict safety controls.

Nuclear accidents can devastate vast areas, so nuclear power plants should have strict safety controls.

devastate: damage, destroy

1. The accident at the nuclear power plant at Three Mile Island in the United States created fears about the safety of this energy source. The disaster at Chernobyl in the Soviet Union confirmed* them.
2. Solar heating systems are economical to operate. The cost of installation is very high.
3. Energy needs are not going to decrease. Energy sources are not going to increase. (Use *nor* and question word order in the second clause, deleting the word "not.")
4. Burning fossil fuels causes serious damage to our planet. We need to develop other sources of energy.
5. Ecologists know that burning fossil fuels causes holes in the ozone layer. People continue to do it.
6. Poorer nations especially will continue this harmful practice. They don't have the money to develop "clean" energy sources.
7. All nations of the world must take action. Our children and grandchildren will suffer the consequences.

C. On a separate sheet of paper, write seven compound sentences of your own, using each coordinator once. Write about your family or about your classes.

Compound Sentences with Conjunctive Adverbs

The independent clauses of a compound sentence can also be joined by a conjunctive adverb such as *furthermore, however, otherwise,* and *therefore.* The punctuation of conjunctive adverbs is special: use a semicolon after the first clause and a comma after the conjunctive adverb.

A compound sentence can be formed with:

Independent Clause ; + Conjunctive Adverb, + Independent Clause

Just like the FAN BOYS coordinators, conjunctive adverbs express the relationship of the second clause to the first clause. The chart below shows the coordinators and conjunctive adverbs which express similar relationships.

Coordinating Conjunctions	Conjunctive Adverbs	Meaning
and	furthermore, besides moreover, also	additional idea
but, yet	however, nevertheless, still nonetheless	opposite idea
or	otherwise	choice; "or else"
so	consequently, therefore, thus accordingly, hence	result

confirmed: proved that they were correct

, < ; < .

The following sentences show how these conjunctive adverbs are used.

1. Junior colleges offer preparation for the professions, business, and industry; moreover, they prepare students to transfer to a four-year college or university. (equal related ideas)
2. Many junior colleges do not provide dormitories; however, they provide housing referral services. (opposite ideas)
3. Students must take the final exam; otherwise, they will receive a grade of Incomplete. ("or else")
4. Native and non-native English speakers have different needs; therefore, most schools provide separate English classes for each group. (result)

PRACTICE 4: *Compound Sentences with Conjunctive Adverbs*

A. Add another independent clause to the following independent clauses to form compound sentences. Be sure to write a complete clause containing a subject and a verb. Circle the conjunctive adverb and add punctuation. Notice that these are sentences from Practice 3A on page 158.

Example:

The college campus is located in the center of the city; (therefore) *it is very easy to do my shopping.*

1. Students can attend day classes moreover ______________________________.
2. Students can live in dormitories otherwise ______________________________.
3. I have finished my math homework however ______________________________.
4. I have studied English for six years however ______________________________.
5. The instructor gave us eight weeks to write our term papers however ______________________________.
6. My roommate scored very high on the English placement test therefore ______________________________.

B. On a separate sheet of paper, combine the pairs of sentences in items 1, 2, 4, 5, and 7 from Practice 3B on pages 158–159, using conjunctive adverbs instead of coordinators. Punctuate them correctly.

Example:

Nuclear accidents can devastate vast areas. Nuclear power plants should have strict safety controls.

Nuclear accidents can devastate vast areas; therefore, nuclear power plants should have strict safety controls.

C. On a separate sheet of paper, write four compound sentences, using each of these conjunctive adverbs once: *furthermore, however, therefore,* and *otherwise.*

Compound Sentences with Semicolons

The independent clauses in a compound sentence may also be joined by a semicolon only. This kind of sentence occurs when the two independent clauses are closely related. If they weren't closely related, they would be written as two simple sentences, separated by a period.

My older brother studies law; my younger brother studies medicine.

The Berlin Wall's construction in 1961 surprised the world; its destruction in 1989 stunned* it.

Poland was the first Eastern block country to turn away from communism; others soon followed.

PRACTICE 5: *Compound Sentences with Semicolons*

A. Place a semicolon between the two independent clauses in the following compound sentences.

1. The American way of life apparently does not foster* marital happiness half of all American marriages end in divorce.
2. Motherhood causes some women to quit their jobs others continue working despite having young children to care for.
3. America is becoming a nation of working mothers and single-parent families these changes will undoubtedly have enormous effects on the nation's children.

B. Write three compound sentences using a semicolon to join the independent clauses.

Complex Sentences

A **complex sentence** contains one independent clause and one (or more) dependent clause. It is like a mother with one or more children depending on her. In a complex sentence, one idea is generally more important than the other one. The more important idea is placed in the independent clause, and the less important idea is placed in the dependent clause.

In the following complex sentences, the independent clause is underlined with a solid line, and the dependent clause is underlined with a broken line.

1. Although women could own property, they could not vote.
2. Women could not vote although they could own property.
3. Men who are not married are called bachelors.
4. Last summer we rented a house in Luxembourg, which is a small country in Europe.

---

stunned: deeply shocked
foster: encourage

5. That the Earth's temperature is rising concerns scientists.
6. Scientists believe that the Earth's temperature is rising.

There are three kinds of dependent clauses used in complex sentences: adverb, adjective, and noun. This chapter presents an overview only. Each kind is studied in detail in Chapters 12, 13, and 14.

A **dependent adverb clause** begins with an adverbial subordinator such as *when, while, because, even though, so that, if,* etc. There are two possible positions for a dependent adverb clause: before or after the independent clause. If it comes before the independent clause, it is followed by a comma (sentence 1 above). If the dependent adverb clause comes after the independent clause, no comma is used (sentence 2).

A **dependent adjective (relative) clause** begins with a relative pronoun such as *who, whom, which, whose,* or the relative adverbs *where, when,* and *why.* A dependent adjective clause functions as an adjective; that is, it modifies a noun (sentences 3 and 4 above).

A **dependent noun clause** begins with *that,* a wh-question word, *whether,* and sometimes *if.* A noun clause functions as a noun; that is, it can be a subject (Sentence 5) or an object (Sentence 6) of the independent clause.

PRACTICE 6: *Complex Sentences*

A. STEP 1 Underline the independent clause of each sentence with a solid line.
STEP 2 Underline the dependent clause with a broken line.
STEP 3 Write SUB above the subordinator.

Example:

Sub
Because the cost of education is rising, many students must work part-time.

1. When foreign students come to the United States, they sometimes suffer from culture shock.
2. Because the cost of education has risen, many students are having financial problems.
3. Please tell me where the student union is.
4. Engineers, who have an aptitude for drafting and mechanics, must also be artistic and imaginative.
5. While the contractor follows the blueprint, the engineer checks the construction in progress.
6. Since the blueprint presents the details of the engineer's plans, it must be interpreted accurately by the contractor.
7. Students should declare a major by their junior year unless they have not made up their minds.
8. Even though I may declare my major now, I can still change it later.
9. Last year, the government report stated that the alcoholic beverage industry spent $1,340 million to advertise its products.
10. The U.S. Surgeon General is alarmed about the impact of alcohol advertising on young people, who think that drinking is risk-free.

B. STEP 1 Add a logical independent clause to each of the following dependent clauses.

STEP 2 Punctuate the sentence correctly.

1. I cannot go to my college ______ until I pay my tuition.
2. ~~I am going~~ ______________________________ unless I take twelve units.
3. It is a fact that I am the nicest boy in this country ______________________________
4. ______________________________ who is chair of the Communications Department.
5. Because I had to look for a part-time job ______________________________
6. ______________________________ if I want to get to school on time.
7. ______________________________ ______________ whether I should take international relations.
8. ______________________________ whom I met at the social club meeting last month.
9. ______________________________ when I left my country.
10. ______________________________ that my college adviser recommends.

PRACTICE 7: *Writing Complex Sentences*

Write complex sentences about the following topics.

STEP 1 Use the given surbordinator and topic in parentheses to write each sentence twice, once with the independent clause first and once with the dependent clause first.

STEP 2 Underline the independent clause of each sentence with a solid line and the dependent clause with a broken line. Punctuate each sentence correctly.

Example:

(United States/even though) I still miss my country very much even though I am enjoying the United States.
Even though I am enjoying the United States, I still miss my country very much.

1. (Writing an essay/before) ______________________________
____
____
____

2. (My country/since) ______________________________
____
____
____

3. (Studying/until) ______________________________

____

____

____

4. (Public transportation/because) ______________________________

____

____

____

5. (Grades/even though) ______________________________

____

____

____

6. (English/unless) ______________________________

____

____

____

Compound-Complex Sentences

A **compound-complex sentence** is a combination of two or more independent clauses and one or more dependent clauses. It is like a family of two adults and one or more children.

After I graduated from high school, I wanted to travel, but I had to work in my family's business.

The word root *multi*, which means *many*, comes from Latin, and the word root *poly*, which also means *many*, comes from Greek.

Although women could own property, they could not vote, nor could they be elected to public office.

PRACTICE 8: *Compound-Complex Sentences*

Write five compound-complex sentences of your own.

PRACTICE 9: *Types of Sentences*

Choose one or two paragraphs from any source—this or any other textbook, a popular magazine, a local newspaper. Your selection should contain at least twenty-five sentences. The selection "Culture, Logic, and Rhetoric" on pages 30–31 would be a good choice for this exercise.

STEP 1 Number the sentences in your selection, and number a blank sheet of paper accordingly.

STEP 2 Analyze each sentence and write down on your numbered paper whether it is simple, compound, complex, or compound-complex.

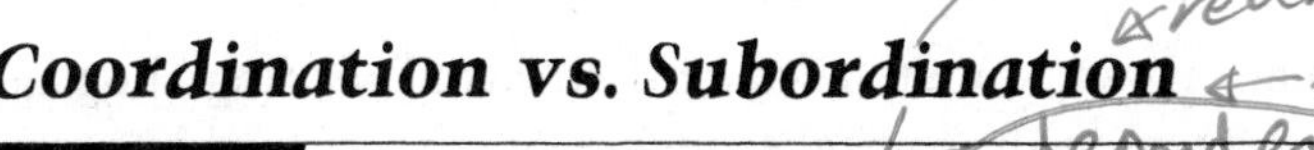

Coordination vs. Subordination

Each of the four kinds of sentences is used in academic writing, so you should develop the ability to write all of them. A composition with only one kind of sentence is boring and ineffective. Effective writing requires a mixture of sentence types.

A writer should use compound sentences (coordination) to express related thoughts which are more or less equal, and he or she should use complex sentences (subordination) to express unequal ideas. In general, however, the use of subordination is considered a more mature, interesting, and effective writing style.

The following paragraph is an example of overcoordination, or writing with too many compound sentences.

MODEL: *Overcoordination*

John F. Kennedy was the thirty-fifth President of the United States, and he was born in Brookline, Massachusetts in 1917. His father was Ambassador to England, so he was exposed to politics at an early age. Kennedy decided to enter the political arena, so he ran for Congress from Massachusetts, and he was elected to the Senate in 1953. His term ended in 1960, for he was elected President that same year at the age of 43. He was the first Roman Catholic, and he was the youngest man ever to occupy the presidency. He had planned to run again in the 1964 election year, but he was assassinated on November 22, 1963, in Dallas, Texas. Kennedy served America for such a short time, but he inspired people all over the free world because of his youth, his spirit, and his style.

The overuse of coordination in the paragraph above makes it both boring to read and difficult to focus on the ideas expressed. Note, however, that it is not necessary to completely avoid using compound sentences or even simple sentences. Compound sentences can be effective, and you should use them when you want to give equal emphasis to two ideas. Also, short sentences can add strength to your compositions. However, avoid overusing either of these kinds of sentences.

The paragraph above has been rewritten. It is now more effective because the sentences have been combined through the use of subordination as well as coordination.

MODEL: *Subordination*

John F. Kennedy, who was the thirty-fifth President of the United States, was born in Brookline, Massachusetts in 1917. Because his father was Ambassador to England, he was exposed to politics early in life. Deciding to enter the political arena, he ran for Congress from Massachusetts and was elected to the Senate in 1953. His term ended in 1960, when he was elected President that same year at the age of 43. He was not only the first Roman Catholic but also the youngest man ever to occupy the presidency. He had planned to run again in the 1964 election year, but he was assassinated on November 22, 1963, in Dallas, Texas. Although Kennedy served America such a short time, he inspired people all over the free world because of his youth, his spirit, and his style.

When using subordination, you must be careful to avoid writing illogical sentences. Sometimes, depending upon the logical sequence of events, one idea *must* be subordinated to another. Avoid illogical subordination. For example:

I was blinded by the setting sun. I drove through a boulevard* stop sign.

Incorrect: Because I drove through a boulevard stop sign, I was blinded by the sun.

Correct: I drove through a boulevard stop sign because I was blinded by the sun.

Because I was blinded by the sun, I drove through a boulevard stop sign.

PRACTICE 10: *Subordination*

Rewrite the following compound sentences into complex sentences by subordinating one of the clauses.

STEP 1 Make one clause a dependent clause introduced by the given subordinator.

STEP 2 Name the kind of relationship that exists between the dependent and independent clauses.

Example:

1. Nowadays, many American women work in full-time jobs, for they must help to support their families. (since) *Nowadays, many American women work in full-time jobs since they must help to support their families. (reason)*
2. Some women have become coal miners and construction workers, for there is less discrimination against them now. (because) ______
3. Commercials are necessary for business, but they can be a nuisance* to the public. (although) ______
4. Some people believe everything they see and hear on commercials, yet many of the advertisements give misinformation. (even though) ______
5. Many people will not buy a product, for they do not like the commercial. (if) ______
6. Camping in the mountains or on beaches is not very expensive, but you must first buy a lot of essential equipment. (although) ______

boulevard: a wide street **nuisance:** bother

7. Foreign travel is expensive, but it is worth a lot in new experiences and memories. (even though) ________________

____

____

8. Travelers must know the tipping standards of foreign countries, or they might be embarrassed. (unless) ________________

____

____

9. A three-minute phone call from San Francisco to New York City between 8 AM and 5 PM costs $1.11, but the same call between 5 PM and 8 AM costs $0.71. (whereas) ________________

____

____

Review

These are the important points in this chapter so far:

1. Clauses are the main building blocks of sentences. There are two kinds of clauses: independent and dependent.
   a. An independent clause expresses a complete thought and can stand alone as a sentence by itself.

      I hate jogging.*

   b. A dependent clause begins with a subordinator and cannot stand alone. There are three kinds of dependent clauses: adverb, adjective, and noun. Each kind is punctuated differently.

      . . . although I hate jogging . . .
      . . . which people of all ages can enjoy . . .
      . . . that people with weak bones shouldn't jog . . .

2. There are four kinds of sentences in English.
   a. A simple sentence is one independent clause.

      I hate jogging.

   b. A compound sentence is two independent clauses joined by a coordinator, a conjunctive adverb, or a semicolon alone. Punctuate compound sentences carefully.

      I hate jogging, but I love hiking.
      I hate jogging; however, I love hiking.
      I hate jogging; I love hiking.

   c. A complex sentence is one independent and one (or more) dependent clause. The punctuation of complex sentences varies according to the kind of dependent clause it contains.

      Adverb: Although I hate jogging, I love hiking.
      I love hiking although I hate jogging.
      Adjective: Hiking is a sport which people of all ages can enjoy.
      Noun: My doctor told me that people with weak bones shouldn't jog.

---

jogging: running slowly for exercise

d. A compound-complex sentence contains two independent clauses and one (or more) dependent clause.

> I hate jogging, but I love hiking because it is a sport which people of all ages can enjoy.

3. Although good writers use all four kinds of sentences, the use of subordination (complex and compound-complex sentences) is considered a more mature, interesting, and effective writing style.

Parallelism

In order to make the ideas in your sentences clear and understandable, words, phrases, and clauses should have **parallelism**—that is, the sentence structures should be grammatically balanced. Parallel construction is the repetition of grammatical patterns within a sentence or a series of sentences. By using similar grammatical forms to express equal ideas, your sentences will flow smoothly, and your writing style will improve.

Use similar grammatical structures to balance your writing. If the first structure is a noun, make all of the others nouns; if it is an infinitive verb phrase, make all of the others infinitive verb phrases; if it is a dependent clause, make all of the others dependent clauses.

Notice how the rule of parallelism is followed in the second set of sentences below. The first sentences are structurally unbalanced. The second sentences are correctly balanced: nouns with nouns, phrases with phrases, and clauses with clauses.

Incorrect:	A student needs textbooks, notebooks, and he needs pens.
Correct:	A student needs textbooks, notebooks, and pens.
Incorrect:	A student who does well in exams attends class, reads the textbook, and he reviews the notes.
Correct:	A student who does well in exams attends class, reads the textbook, and reviews the notes.
Incorrect:	The student wanted to know what the calculus problems were and the due date.
Correct:	The student wanted to know what the assigned calculus problems were and when the due date was.

All of the words in the first parallel structure do not have to be repeated in the second. You may repeat all or some of the words, depending upon what you wish to emphasize.

- Before you write a paper or (before) (you) take a test, you must organize your thoughts.

"Before" and/or "you" may be deleted from the second parallel structure.

- Before you write a paper or take a test, you must organize your thoughts.

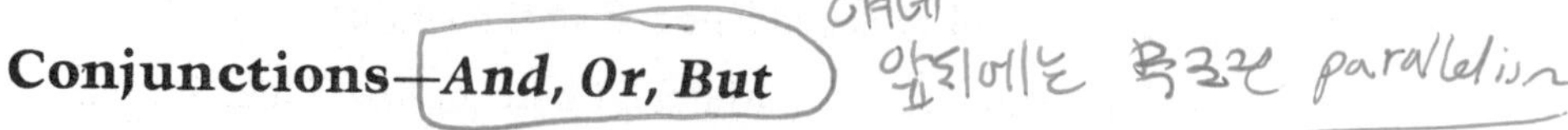

Conjunctions—*And, Or, But*

Words, phrases, and clauses that are joined by *and, or,* and *but* are written in parallel form. Notice the parallel structures joined by conjunctions in the following sentences.

- The Federal Air Pollution Control Administration regulates automobile exhausts, *and* the Federal Aviation Administration makes similar regulations for aircraft.

- The states regulate the noise created by motor vehicles *but* not by commercial aircraft.
- Pesticides must be removed from the market if they present an adverse* effect on man *or* on the environment.

Correlative Conjunctions

Use parallel forms with the correlative conjunctions *both . . . and, either . . . or, neither . . . nor,* and *not only . . . but also.*

Correlative conjunctions are placed directly *before* the elements they join in the sentence. Notice the parallel structure in these clauses joined by correlative conjunctions:

Congress has provided the means for *both* regulating pesticides *and* ordering their removal if dangerous.

Air pollutants may come *either* from the ocean as natural contaminants given off by sea life *or* from the internal combustion engines of automobiles.

If *neither* industry *nor* the public works toward reducing pollution problems, future generations will suffer.

Many people are *neither* concerned about pollutants *nor* worried about their future impact.

At the present time, air pollution is controlled through laws passed *not only* to reduce the pollutants at their sources *but also* to set up acceptable standards of air quality.

PRACTICE 11: *Parallelism I*

Grammatical elements in the following sentences are written in parallel form. Underline the words that are parallel.

Example:

The ideal conditions for skiing are <u>sunshine</u>, powdery <u>snow</u>, and uncrowded <u>slopes</u>.

A. Words

1. The XYZ Corporation manufactures copiers, duplicators, and self-correcting typewriters.
2. The corporation gathers, edits and synthesizes* information.
3. The new personal computer is the most important, useful, and exciting electronic product of today.
4. The latest self-correcting typewriter works easily, speedily, and noiselessly.
5. The company's buyers sat in the conference room with the sales representative, both listening and talking.

---

adverse: unfavorable **synthesizes:** combines parts to make something whole

B. Phrases

6. If you want to learn a foreign language well, you should try to think in the language and to speak the language as much as possible.
7. You must spend your time studying the vocabulary, listening to native speakers, and practicing new sentence structures.
8. You can learn a foreign language in the classroom, at home, or in the foreign country where the language is spoken.

C. Clauses

9. If the supply of oil drops and if the demand increases, alternative fuels will have to be found.
10. At an international seminar, participating countries discussed who the major producers of oil were and how much they would export.
11. It is a popular misconception that oil is found in vast underground pools and that it needs only to be pumped out.
12. Americans are facing a fuel crisis, but according to statistics, they are driving their cars more often.
13. Before the energy crisis began and before the government emphasized the need to save natural resources, Americans did not realize the seriousness of the situation.

PRACTICE 12: *Parallelism II*

A. Rewrite the following sentences in parallel form.

STEP 1 Underline the part of the sentence that is not parallel and correct it.

STEP 2 Circle the word or words that join the parallel structures.

Example:

Attending the symphony (or) to go to the theater is what I enjoy the most.

Attending the symphony or going to the theater is what I enjoy the most.

1. Credit cards are accepted by department stores, airlines, and they can be used in some gas stations.

2. You do not need to risk carrying cash or to risk to pass up* a sale.

3. With credit cards you can either pay your bill with one check, or you can stretch out your payments.

4. You can charge both at restaurants and when you stay at hotels.

pass up: miss an opportunity

5. Many people carry not only credit cards but also they carry cash.

6. Many people want neither to read a product's warranty nor sending it into a company.

7. Many warranties give comprehensive* coverage, but some give coverage that is limited.

8. Getting a defective* product fixed or to have it replaced is what a comprehensive warranty guarantees.

B. Write eight original sentences in parallel form, using both coordinating conjunctions (*and, or, but*) and correlative conjunctions (*both . . . and, either . . . or, neither . . . nor, not only . . . but also*).

Review

These are the main points you should have learned about parallelism:

1. Words, phrases, or clauses that are joined by coordinating conjunctions and correlative conjunctions must be written in parallel form.
2. If the first structure is a noun, make all others nouns; if it is a prepositional phrase, make all the others prepositional phrases; if it is a dependent clause, make all the others dependent clauses.
3. All of the words in the first parallel structure do not have to be repeated in the second.

Sentence Problems

In this section, you will learn to recognize some common errors in sentence structure and to correct them.

Sentence Fragments

Sentence fragments are incomplete sentences or parts of sentences. Remember that a complete sentence must contain at least one main or independent clause.

Study the following four examples of sentence fragments and the suggested methods for correcting them.

---

comprehensive: including much **defective:** not perfect

1. Because some students have part-time jobs in addition to going to school.
   Problem: This is a subordinate clause.
   To correct: Attach it to an independent clause.
   Complete Sentence: Because some students have part-time jobs in addition to full-time classwork, they have very little free time.
2. For example, the increase in the cost of renting an apartment.
   Problem: No main verb.
   To correct: Rewrite the sentence so that it has a subject and a verb.
   Complete Sentence: For example, the cost of renting an apartment has increased.
3. Having no money and being lonely in the big city.
   Problem: This is a participial phrase. It has no subject or verb.
   To correct: (a) Rewrite the phrase to include a subject and a verb.
   (b) Attach the phrase to an independent clause.
   Complete Sentences: (a) She had no money and was lonely in the big city.
   (b) Having no money and being lonely in the big city, the woman committed suicide.
4. Many people who get married before they are mature enough.
   Problem: This is a noun followed by a dependent (adjective) clause.
   Solution: Rewrite the claüse by eliminating the adjective clause aspect.
   Complete Sentence: Many people get married before they are mature enough.

Always check your own writing for sentence fragments! Pay particular attention to your sentences beginning with subordinating conjunctions (*although, since, because, if, before*, etc.). These are DANGER WORDS! Make sure that every subordinate clause beginning with these words is attached to an independent clause.

PRACTICE 13: *Rewriting Sentence Fragments*

A. Read the following sentences. Mark them FRAG if they are sentence fragments, or SENT if they are complete sentences. On a separate piece of paper, rewrite each fragment to make a complete sentence.

_____ **1.** The desire of all mankind to live in peace and freedom, for example.
_____ **2.** Second, the fact that men are physically stronger than women.
_____ **3.** The best movie that I saw last year.
_____ **4.** *Born on the Fourth of July* was the best movie that I saw last year.
_____ **5.** For example, many students have part-time jobs.
_____ **6.** Although people want to believe that all men are created equal.
_____ **7.** Finding a suitable marriage partner is a challenging task.
_____ **8.** Many of my friends who didn't have the opportunity to go to college.
_____ **9.** Working during the morning and attending classes during the afternoon.
_____ **10.** Because I don't feel that grades in college have any value.
_____ **11.** The nuclear accident that occurred in Russia in 1986, the worst nuclear accident in history.
_____ **12.** The first hint of the tragedy came two days after the accident occurred.

_____ **13.** When radiation monitors* in Sweden indicated an increase in radiation levels over Scandinavia.

_____ **14.** Radiation escaping into the atmosphere, drifting west over other countries, and causing crops and dairy products to become contaminated.*

_____ **15.** Opponents of nuclear power plants pointing to the Chernobyl disaster and the near-disaster at a U.S. plant in Pennsylvania.

B. Read the following short essay. Put brackets [ ] around any sentence fragments that you find and mark them FRAG. Then correct all fragments. Rewrite the entire essay.

Women Drivers

Male chauvinism* extends even into the area of automobile driving, it seems. Believing that they are far better drivers than women. Men consider women drivers incompetent, inattentive, and even dangerous behind the wheel.

However, statistics prove that women are, in fact, safer drivers than men. For example, insurance rates. Insurance rates for women are 20 percent lower than they are for men. Another proof is that more accidents are caused by male drivers between the ages of 18 and 25 than by any other group. Also the greater percentage of accidents involving deaths caused by men. Although women are criticized for being too cautious. They are really just being safe drivers.

The reasons for women drivers' safer driving habits can perhaps be found in the differing attitudes of the sexes toward automobiles. On the one hand, women drivers who regard the automobile as a convenience. Like a washing machine. On the other hand, men regard the automobile as an extension of their egos.* Using it as a weapon when they feel particularly aggressive. Or using it as a status symbol.

In conclusion, women are safer drivers. Because of their attitude. Men can learn to become safe drivers. If they adopt the attitude that an automobile is merely a convenience.

Choppy Sentences

Choppy sentences are sentences that are too short. They are the result of using too many simple sentences, like those that follow. Although simple sentences are quite effective sometimes, overuse of them is considered poor style in academic writing.

Choppy: We must find new sources of energy. The earth's natural sources of energy are dwindling.* Solar energy is a promising new source of energy. Solar energy is energy from the sun's radiation.

Choppy: Government and industry are spending huge sums of money to develop solar energy. Research scientists are working hard to develop economical means of converting the sun's rays into usable energy.

Choppy sentences are easy to correct. Just combine two or three simple sentences to make one compound or complex sentence. Your decision to make a compound or a complex sentence should be based on whether the ideas in the simple sentences are equal or whether one sentence is dependent on the other.

1. If the simple sentences are equal, make a compound sentence, using a coordinating conjunction (*and, or, but, so, yet, nor, for*) or a conjunctive adverb (*moreover, otherwise, however, therefore,* etc.)

---

monitors: machines to check radiation levels
contaminated: polluted
male chauvinism: belief in male superiority
egos: self-importance
dwindling: becoming smaller or less

2. If one sentence depends on the other, make a complex sentence, using a subordinating conjunction (*who, which, when, although, because, since, if,* etc.).

Compound: Government and industry are spending huge sums of money to develop solar energy, and research scientists are working hard to develop economical means of converting the sun's rays into usable energy.

Complex: We must find new sources of energy because the earth's natural energy sources are dwindling. Solar energy, which is energy from the sun's radiation, is a promising new source of energy.

Examine your own writing carefully. Do you use too many simple sentences? If you do, practice combining them.

PRACTICE 14: *Rewriting Choppy Sentences*

Improve the following choppy sentences by combining them to make either compound or complex sentences.

1. Gasoline is becoming expensive. Automobile manufacturers are producing smaller cars. Smaller cars use less gasoline.

___

___

___

2. The computer has undoubtedly benefited humanity. The computer has also created problems for humanity.

___

___

___

3. Government and private agencies have spent billions of dollars advertising the dangers of smoking. The number of smokers is still increasing.

___

___

___

4. Some students go to a vocational school to learn a trade. Some students go to college to get a degree.

___

___

___

5. The grading system at our college should be abolished.* The students don't like getting grades. The instructors don't enjoy giving grades.

___

___

___

abolished: gotten rid of, abandoned

Run-On Sentences and Comma Splices

A **run-on sentence** is a sentence in which two or more independent clauses are written one after another with no punctuation. A similar error happens when two independent clauses are incorrectly joined by a comma without a coordinating conjunction. This kind of error is also called a **comma splice.**

Run-on:	Getting married is easy staying married is a different matter.
Comma Splice:	San Francisco is a very cosmopolitan city, there are people from many cultures and ethnic groups living there.

A comma alone cannot join two independent clauses.
A run-on/comma splice sentence can be corrected by adding:

1. a period:
Getting married is easy. Staying married is a different matter.

2. a semicolon:
Getting married is easy; staying married is a different matter.

3. a coordinating conjunction:
Getting married is easy, but staying married is a different matter.

4. a subordinating conjunction:
Although getting married is easy, staying married is a different matter.

PRACTICE 15: *Run-On/Comma Splice Sentences*

Correct the following run-on/comma splice sentences using the method indicated.

1. A foreign student faces many problems, for example, he has to cope with a new culture.
a. (Add a period.) ______
b. (Add a semicolon.) ______

2. San Francisco is a very cosmopolitan city, there are people from many cultures and ethnic groups living there.
a. (Add a period.) ______
b. (Add a semicolon.) ______
c. (Add a subordinating conjunction.) ______
d. (Add a coordinating conjunction.) ______

3. Learning a new language is like learning to swim it takes a lot of practice.
(Add a coordinating conjunction.) ______

4. Ask for assistance at the reference desk in the library, there is always a librarian on duty.
(Add a semicolon.) ____

____

5. Hang-gliding is a dangerous sport you can easily break your leg.
(Add a subordinating conjunction.) ____

____

PRACTICE 16: *Recognizing Run-On/Comma Splice Sentences*

Some of the following sentences are run-ons or comma splices, and some are correct. Check each sentence. If it is incorrect, write RO or CS in the space at the left. If the sentence is correct, leave the space blank. Then, on a separate sheet of paper, rewrite the incorrect sentences correctly.

Example:

RO Two letters arrived on Monday a third one came on Wednesday.

____ 1. An encyclopedia is a valuable source of information, it contains summaries of every area of knowledge.

____ 2. Because of the rapid expansion of human knowledge, it is difficult to keep encyclopedias current.

____ 3. Almost as soon as an encyclopedia is published, it becomes obsolete.*

____ 4. Home editions of encyclopedias are shorter and more concise than library editions, they don't contain as much detailed information.

____ 5. Articles in encyclopedias are written by experts in each subject, who are often university professors.

____ 6. An editor of an encyclopedia doesn't write articles he only collects and edits* articles written by other experts.

____ 7. To find a book on a certain subject, you should look in the card catalog, but to find a magazine article on a subject, you should look in a periodical index.

____ 8. A periodical index, which is also called a periodical guide, does not contain any articles, it merely gives a list of articles and tells you where to find them.

____ 9. The reference room of the library has several periodical indexes one is the *Reader's Guide to Periodical Literature.*

____ 10. If you can't find any information on a subject, you can always ask a librarian to help you, they are paid to assist students.

PRACTICE 17: *Correcting Run-On/Comma Splice Sentences*

Locate the run-on/comma splice sentences in the following paragraphs. Mark them by writing RO or CS above them. Then, on a separate sheet of paper, rewrite both paragraphs, correcting the mistakes that you found.

---

obsolete: out of date, old **edits:** revises and makes ready for publication

Grade Inflation

Teachers at Stone Mountain State College give higher grades than teachers at twelve of the nineteen other colleges in the state college system, according to a recent report from the State Institutional Research Committee. This report showed that more than one third of the undergraduate grades awarded in the spring semester, 1987, were A's, only 1.1 percent were F's. The percentage of A's awarded to graduate students was even higher, almost two thirds were A's.

While students may be happy to receive high grades, there is evidence that this trend is having negative consequences. Investigation of the admissions criteria* of some graduate and professional schools indicates that the admissions offices of these schools are discounting high grades on the transcripts of SMSC students, this means that an A from SMSC is not equal to an A from other universities. Grade inflation may, therefore, hurt a student from Stone Mountain State College who intends to apply to a graduate or professional school, he or she may not be accepted despite a high grade point average.

Stringy Sentences

Another type of problem that students sometimes create is the **stringy sentence.** This is a sentence with too many clauses usually connected with *and, but, so,* and *because,* forming one very long sentence. The result is a sentence that seems endless.

Stringy Sentence: My roommate, Bill, goes to college and from the beginning of this semester until last week, he hadn't studied at all and the reason was because he had no exams during that period. But the day before yesterday, I was astonished* because I saw him studying and later on, he told me he had studied all day long and the reason was because he was going to have an exam the next day and he wanted to get a good grade in the exam so he decided to study.

There are several ways to correct a stringy sentence:

Stringy Sentence: Many students attend classes all morning and they work all afternoon and then they have to study at night so they are usually exhausted by the weekend.

Divide: Many students attend classes all morning and work all afternoon. Then, they have to study at night. As a result, they are usually exhausted by the weekend.

Subordinate: Many students, after they attend classes all morning, also work in the afternoon. Because they also have to study at night, they are usually exhausted by the weekend.

Subordinate and Combine: Many students, who attend classes all morning, work all afternoon, and study all night, are exhausted by the weekend.

Participial Phrases: After attending classes all morning, working all afternoon, and studying at night, many students are exhausted by the weekend.

---

criteria: standards by which a judgment is made **astonished:** surprised

PRACTICE 18: *Correcting Stringy Sentences*

Improve these stringy sentences. Use any method or combination of methods.

1. He enrolled in an advanced calculus class, but he found it too difficult, so he dropped it.

2. The tidal wave ruined the crops, and it destroyed several villages, and it caused many deaths, so it was a real disaster.

3. The analysts worked many hours on the computer program, but they couldn't find the cause of the problem, so they finally gave up, and they went home.

4. Junk food is bad for your health, and it also contains no vitamins, and it damages your stomach, so people shouldn't eat it.

5. The lack of rainfall has caused a severe water shortage, so people have to conserve water every day, and they also have to think of new ways to reuse water, but the situation is improving.

PRACTICE 19: *Sentence Problems*

The following sentences show faulty sentence structure. Identify the problem and write FRAG for fragment, RO for run-on, CS for comma splice, CHOPPY, or STRINGY in the space provided. Then correct the sentences on a separate sheet of paper.

_____ 1. The United States counts its population every ten years, and each census* reveals that the racial and ethnic mix is changing dramatically, so by the year 2050, the "average" American will not be descended from* Europeans, but the majority of U.S. residents will trace his or her ancestry* to Africa, Asia, the Hispanic world, the Pacific Islands, or the Middle East.

---

census: population count
be descended from: be the children, grandchildren, etc. of
ancestry: a person's origins (parents, country, race, culture, etc.)

_____ **2.** Once America was a microcosm* of European nationalities, today America is a microcosm of the world.

_____ **3.** The United States, no longer considered a "melting pot" society by many of its residents.

_____ **4.** Many people prefer the term "salad bowl." They use this term to describe American society. American society will soon be predominantly non-white.

_____ **5.** "Melting pot" implies that the diverse* ethnic groups blend together into one homogeneous mixture, "salad bowl" implies that nationalities, like the ingredients in a mixed green salad, retain their cultural identities.

_____ **6.** While earlier generations of immigrants believed they had to learn English quickly to survive.

_____ **7.** Many Hispanics want to retain their Spanish heritage. They want their children to learn both English and Spanish at school. They are winning the right to bilingual education in many communities. In many communities they are in the majority.

Review

Here are the important points you should have learned about sentence problems:

There are four major sentence structure problems that students often make. These are fragments, run-ons, choppy sentences, and stringy sentences.

A **fragment** is only part of a sentence. You can fix it most easily by attaching it to an independent clause.

A **run-on** or **comma splice** is two independent clauses that are not joined correctly. To fix them most easily, separate the two clauses with a period or a semicolon.

Choppy sentences result when you write a lot of simple sentences in the same paragraph. To fix this problem, join some of the sentences to make compound and complex sentences.

A **stringy sentence** results when a sentence contains too many independent clauses. Divide a stringy sentence into two or three complex or compound-complex sentences.

---

microcosm: small copy of a larger society
diverse: different, separate

CHAPTER 12

Noun Clauses

A **noun clause** is a dependent clause that functions as a noun. It can be a subject, object, or subject complement. However, you will study the noun clause only as it is used as an object.

Because a noun clause is dependent, it must be connected to an independent clause to form a complex sentence. A noun clause used as an object is preceded by an independent clause called an introductory clause. The noun clause is the object of the introductory clause verb.

INTRODUCTORY CLAUSE		DEPENDENT NOUN CLAUSE
Subject	Verb	Object
I	know	that people have different opinions about capital punishment.

Types of Noun Clauses

There are three types of dependent noun clauses:

That-clauses are made from statements.
Wh-question clauses are made from wh-questions.
Yes/no question clauses are made from yes/no questions.

The chart on the following page shows the three types of noun clauses. A noun clause is composed of:

Subordinator + Subject + Verb + Complement

The word order of most noun clauses is normal statement word order, as indicated in the following examples:

... (that) science courses require a laboratory period.
... where the student union is.
... whether our projects are due next week.
... if lunch is being served.

Note: One kind of noun clause has a slightly different pattern. In an included wh-question clause when the subordinator and the subject are the same word, the pattern is:

Subject Subordinator + Verb + Complement

... who made the error
... what happened at the U.S./U.S.S.R. summit

Noun Clauses

Introductory Clause		That-Clause
The bulletin stated	that	science courses require a laboratory period.
The credit department noted	that	Unusual Gift Shop's account was thirty days overdue.

		Wh-Question Clause
Can you remember	who	made the error?
Do you know	where	the student union is?
The professor explained	how	shock waves are formed.

		Yes/No Question Clause
I do not know	whether	our projects are due next week.
The engineer must determine	if	the given dimensions* and tolerances* are correct.

Here is a list of subordinators which introduce noun clauses.

Noun Clause Subordinators

	Subordinator	Meaning
Included Statement	that	
Included Wh-Question	who	
	whoever	whatever person
	what	
	whatever	anything or everything
	where	
	wherever	anyplace
	when	
	how much (many, often, etc.)	
Included Yes/No Question	whether (or not)	
	if	

dimensions: measurements
tolerances: difference between two limiting measurements to determine accuracy

Punctuating noun clauses is fairly simple. No comma is used to separate the introductory clause from the noun clause. The introductory clause, which may be a statement or a question, determines the end-of-sentence punctuation. If the introductory clause is a question, a question mark is used.

I don't know when he called.
Do you know when he called?

Sequence of Tenses

Before you study each of the noun clause forms, you should learn the rules governing the sequence of tenses. Sequence of tenses refers to the verb tenses in different clauses of the same sentence. The verb tense in the introductory (independent) clause determines the verb tense in the dependent noun clause.

When the verb in the introductory clause is in present tense, the verb in the dependent clause is in whatever tense expresses the intended meaning:

The president agrees that solar power is the answer to the energy crisis.
He predicts that solar power is going to be the energy source of the future.
He believes that solar energy companies have expanded operations since 1973.
A government source estimates that more than 200 solar firms began operations in the last five years.
Solar energy industries report that homeowners have to be convinced of the effectiveness of solar energy.
Homeowners think that the cost of installing this equipment may be increasing too rapidly.

When the verb in the introductory clause is in past tense, the verb in the dependent clause is usually in a past form:[1]

The president agreed that solar power was the answer to the energy crisis.
He predicted that solar energy was going to be the energy source of the future.
He believed that solar energy companies had expanded operations since 1973.
A government source estimated that more than 200 solar firms had begun operations in the last five years.
Solar energy industries reported that homeowners had to be convinced of the effectiveness of solar energy.
Homeowners thought that the cost of installing this equipment might be increasing too rapidly.

That-Clauses

That-clauses are dependent noun clauses often introduced by the subordinator *that*. Since the subordinator *that* has no grammatical function, it may be omitted.

[1]Exception: The verb in the dependent clause is in present tense when it reports a general truth.

A that-clause is composed of

(That) + Subject + Verb + Complement:

. . . (*that*) the study of the brain is fascinating.
. . . (*that*) the brain is the master control for both mind and body.
. . . (*that*) it controls sensations, moods, thoughts, and actions.

A complex sentence with an included that-clause is composed of an introductory (independent) clause and a dependent included that-clause:

I think (that) the study of the brain is fascinating.
The professor stated (that) the brain is the master control for both mind and body.[1]
He further explained (that) it controls sensations, moods, thoughts, and actions.[1]

The following is a list of some introductory clause verbs that are used to introduce that-clauses.

Introductory Clause Verbs

Group I	Group II	Group III	Group IV
agree	admit	assure	promise
answer	explain	convince	show
conclude	mention	inform	teach
notice	point out	notify	warn
realize	reply	remind	write (to)
think		tell	

The verbs in Group I do not take an indirect object.

The president concluded that he would veto* the bill.
The Senate thought that he wasn't serious.

The verbs in Group II may or may not take an indirect object. However, if an indirect object follows one of these verbs, *to* must precede it.

The president explained (to the nation) that the country faced a deficit.*
He mentioned (to the press) that he might raise taxes.

The verbs in Group III must be followed by an indirect object.

The governor told the public that the state faced a serious water shortage.
He informed the press that water rationing was necessary.

The verbs in Group IV may or may not take an indirect object.

The mayor promised (city employees) that they wouldn't lose their jobs.
He warned (them), however, that there would be no raises.

PRACTICE 20: *That-Clauses*

STEP 1 Add a verb from the table above to complete the introductory clause. Use a different verb in each sentence, and remember the sequence of tenses rule.

STEP 2 Add the subordinator *that*.

veto: prevent from becoming law by refusing to sign a bill **deficit:** not enough (money)

[1]The verb in the dependent clause is in present tense when it reports a general truth.

Example:

The president *pointed out that* coal was an increasingly important source of energy for the United States.

1. Industry ____________________ coal was regarded as energy's black gold.
2. The federal government ____________________ the country should double its coal use in ten years.
3. The speaker ____________________ the United States had the largest coal reserves in the world.
4. Environmentalists ____________________ new ways to burn coal cleanly must be found.
5. The Federal Energy Administration ____________________ only about 20 percent of energy used in the United States was from coal.
6. The Federal Energy Administration ____________________ technological advances would make converting coal into a synthetic natural gas more economical.

SENTENCE PRACTICE

Write six original sentences containing included that-clauses about a current news event. Use a different introductory clause verb in each sentence, and remember the sequence of tenses rule.

Subjunctive Noun Clauses

The verb in a dependent that-clause is in the simple form after certain introductory clause verbs indicating urgency, advisability, and desirability:

The following is a list of common verbs used in the introductory clause:

advise	demand	move	recommend[1]
ask	direct	propose	suggest[1]
command	insist	urge	

Example:

The company president demanded that the sales department increase its sales volume.

He has insisted that their foreign competitors be pushed out of the domestic market.

He directed that the sales force not be increased at this time.

[1]The verbs in the *that* noun clause following the verbs *suggest* and *recommend* can be used with the modal *should.*

Example:

Did the president suggest that the sales manager (should) increase sales?

The accountant recommended that the sales figures (should) be reduced to reflect merchandise returned.

The simple form of the verb is also used in the noun clause after certain adjectives:

advisable	necessary	important
essential	urgent	vital

Example:

It is essential that this country export more of its products.
It is vital that our country's imports not exceed its exports.

PRACTICE 21: Subjunctive Noun Clauses

Rewrite the following questions as statements to introduce subjunctive noun clauses.

Situation: Many areas of the United States are suffering from a serious drought.* As a result, each district's water department is proposing water usage restrictions.

Example:

What did the Marin Water Department order?
a. Residents must not waste water.
b. Residents have to decrease their water usage.

a. *The Marin Water Department ordered that residents not waste water.*
b. *The Marin Water Department ordered that residents decrease water usage.*

1. What did the Marin Water Department demand?
People must reduce their water usage by 35 percent.

____

____

2. What is necessary?
All residents comply* with the Water Department's regulations.

____

____

3. What did the Water Department propose?
a. Everyone must take five-minute showers.
b. Car owners shouldn't use a hose while washing their cars.

____

____

____

____

drought: lack of rainfall
comply: follow a request or rule

4. What is advisable?
Restaurants do not serve water except upon request.

5. What are water conservationists recommending?
Homeowners should not water their gardens frequently.

6. What is urgent?
People must realize the seriousness of the drought.

7. What do most homeowners demand?
The Water Department should increase their water allotment.*

8. What did the Water Department urge?
Everyone had to cooperate in order to conserve water.

9. What is essential?
Each person should reduce water consumption* to approximately 85 gallons per day.

SENTENCE PRACTICE

Write six sentences with subjunctive noun clauses. Write three sentences using introductory clause verbs of urgency, advisability, or desirability and three sentences using adjectives.

Wh-Question Clauses

A wh-question clause is a dependent noun clause formed from a direct wh-question that is first changed into a statement and then joined to an introductory clause to form a complex sentence.

A wh-question clause can follow two patterns: the *subject pattern* or the *object pattern.* In the subject pattern, the wh-word is the subject of its own clause. In the object pattern the wh-word is only a subordinator; it is not the subject.

Subject Pattern

In the subject pattern, a direct wh-question becomes a dependent noun clause without any change in word order. The following is a short list of direct wh-questions.

Who started the space race?
What happened in 1965?

allotment: allowance
consumption: usage

How many astronauts have walked on the moon?
Which achievement was the most significant?
How much money was spent to put a man on the moon?

In the following table, these questions have been transformed into dependent noun clauses. Notice that there is no change in word order.

Wh-Question Clause Word Order—Subject Pattern

	Wh-Question Clause		
Introductory Clause	Wh-question word	Verb	Complement
Do you know	who	started	the space race?
Can you tell us	what	happened	in 1965?
Does he remember	how many astronauts	have walked	on the moon?
The professor asked us	which achievement	was	the most significant.
Some people complain about	how much money	was spent	to put a man on the moon.

PRACTICE 22: *Wh-Question Clauses—Subject Pattern*

Add the direct wh-question to the introductory clause to form a complex sentence.

Example:

Which companies offer the best opportunities in your field?

The job center can tell you *which companies offer the best opportunities in your field*

1. Who is responsible for creating pollution and wasting resources?
   The ecologist* will explain ______________________________

2. How many big cities have antipollution laws?
   The Environmental Protection Agency will tell you ______________________________

3. Who is in charge of the Environmental Protection Agency?
   Does anyone know ______________________________

4. What is required to solve the problem of air pollution?
   I would like to know ______________________________

5. Which state has the most stringent* antipollution laws for automobiles?
   The E.P.A. has statistics showing ______________________________

---

ecologist: a scientist who studies the relationship between living things and their environments
stringent: strict

SENTENCE PRACTICE

Write six complex sentences containing wh-question clauses in the subject pattern.

STEP 1 Write six direct wh-questions in the subject pattern.

STEP 2 Connect each to an introductory clause. Remember the sequence of tenses rule, and punctuate your sentences correctly.

Object Pattern

In the object pattern, the word order changes when you transform a direct wh-question into a wh-question clause. This pattern occurs when the wh-word is *not* the subject of the noun clause, and when you have questions containing the verb *to be* plus a subject complement. Study the following direct wh-questions.

Who are the hijackers?	(with *to be* and a subject complement)
How can we end airplane hijackings?	(with modal verbs)
Where have they taken the hostages?	(with the auxiliaries *has/have/had*)
What do the hijackers want?	(with the auxiliaries *do/does/did*)

Notice what happens to the word order when you transform wh-questions into wh-question clauses:

Wh-Question Clause Word Order—Object Pattern

	Included Wh-Question Clause			
Introductory Clause	Wh-word	Subject	Verb	Complement
No one knows	who	the hijackers	are.	
It's difficult to determine	how	we	can end	airplane hijackings.
The police won't reveal	where	they	have taken	the hostages.
The government wouldn't say	what	the hijackers	wanted.	

In the object pattern, wh-question clauses use the statement word order, and the auxiliaries *do/does/did* are deleted.

PRACTICE 23: *Wh-Question Clauses—Object Pattern*

A. Change the direct wh-questions below into wh-question clauses and connect them to the introductory clauses to form complex sentences. Remember the sequence of tenses rule on page 182, and punctuate your sentences correctly.

Example:

How many marine mammals die each year?

The magazine hasn't reported *how many marine animals die each year.*

1. When did polluters start infesting* the seas?
   U.S. News & World Report clearly states ______________________
   ____
2. Why is plastic pollution hazardous* to birds and sea mammals?
   It is obvious ______________________
   ____
3. What are the major kinds of plastic pollutants dumped into the seas?
   Does anyone know ______________________
   ____
4. How do drifting plastic nets endanger diving sea birds?
   The writer clearly explains ______________________
   ____
5. When will the U.S. Congress pass anti-dumping legislation?
   The government hasn't stated ______________________
   ____

B. Change these direct wh-questions into wh-question clauses and connect them to an introductory clause to form complex sentences.

Example:

At which university did Albert Einstein teach?

I can't remember at which university Albert Einstein taught.

1. When did he receive the Nobel Prize?
   ____
   ____
2. For which theory did Einstein win the Nobel Prize?
   ____
   ____
3. What is Einstein's quantum explanation of the photoelectric effect?
   ____
   ____
4. How long has Einstein been dead?
   ____
   ____
5. How long will he be remembered?
   ____
   ____

---

infesting: being spread in a troublesome manner
hazardous: dangerous

SENTENCE PRACTICE

Write six sentences containing wh-question clauses in the object pattern. Use each of the four verb combinations given in the examples in the table on page 188 at least once.

STEP 1 Write six direct wh-questions in the object pattern.

STEP 2 Change them into wh-question clauses and connect them to introductory clauses. Remember the sequence of tenses rule.

Yes/No Question Clauses

Yes/no question clauses are dependent noun clauses that are formed from yes/no questions. A yes/no question is changed into a statement by adding the subordinator *whether, whether or not,* or *if.*

Here are some direct yes/no questions:

Do final examinations begin next month?
Will the university accept late registration?
Was the notice posted on the bulletin board?
Has the quiz been postponed?

Notice how the word order of these direct yes/no questions changes when they are transformed into yes/no question clauses:

Yes/No Question Clause Word Order

	Yes/No Question Clause	
Introductory Clause	Subordinator	Subject + Verb + Complement
Do you know	if	final examinations begin next month?
We would like to inquire	whether (or not)	the university will accept late registration.
The professor didn't know	if	the notice had been posted on the bulletin board.
Ask the teacher	whether	the exam has been postponed.

A yes/no question clause is formed by:

1. changing the word order to statement form;
2. deleting the auxiliaries *do, does,* and *did;*
3. adding *if, whether (or not)* or *whether . . . or not.*

Whether is formal; *if* is informal. *Whether* and *if* may both occur alone.
Whether and *if* may both occur alone.

I don't know whether he is coming.
I don't know if he is coming.

Whether or not may be written together at the beginning of the clause or may be separated.

I don't know whether or not he is coming. ("If or not" is not possible.)
I don't know whether he is coming or not.

PRACTICE 24: *Yes/No Question Clauses*

A. Change the following direct yes/no questions into yes/no question clauses, and connect them to the introductory clause given to form a complex sentence. Use any of the possible variations shown in the table on page 190.

Remember the sequence of tenses rule, and punctuate your sentence correctly.

Example:

Are food additives safe?

a. Does the public know whether food additives are safe?

b. Does the public know whether or not food additives are safe?

c. Does the public know whether food additives are safe or not?

d. Does the public know if food additives are safe?

1. Is the food industry concerned about the health of the people?
The American public would like to know ______________________

2. Do food additives present health hazards?
Will the Federal Drug Administration reveal ______________________

3. Has the safety of MSG,* which is frequently used in Chinese cooking, been thoroughly tested?
Have you read ______________________

4. Does MSG cause cancer in humans?
Will the FDA determine ______________________

5. Can food additives approved by the FDA be considered safe to eat?
We need to ascertain ______________________

B. Add an introductory clause and the subordinator: *whether, whether or not, whether . . . or not,* or *if* to introduce the dependent clause. Make sure your introductory clause is a question if there is a question mark at the end of the sentence.

Example:

Do you know whether or not all food additives are fat soluble?*

1. ______________________ toxicological* phenomena* can always be predicted with accuracy?

MSG: monosodium glutamate, a chemical compound used to enhance the flavor of food
soluble: able to be dissolved
toxicological: related to the science of poisons
phenomena: (plural of *phenomenon*) unusual and/or scientific facts or events

2. ______________________ toxicological phenomena can be explained on the basis of physical or chemical laws.
3. ______________________ this unpredictability of accurate results on additives establishes the need to perform tests on animals?
4. ______________________ the animals were fed different concentrations of the chemical and examined for signs of disease.
5. ______________________ the definition of food includes chewing gum and candy.

SENTENCE PRACTICE

Write six sentences with yes/no question clauses. Use the subordinators *whether, whether or not, whether . . . or not,* or *if.*

WRITING PRACTICE: *Noun Clauses*

Pretend you are going to graduate from the university and are now looking for a position in your field (business, accounting, engineering, medical technology, etc.). You could look in your local newspaper to see what job opportunities are available. The following are examples of help-wanted ads that you might find:

HELP WANTED

Do you have a BA or BS in accounting? No experience necessary. Training program in national firm. Inquiries welcomed. Write: Billings, Goodwill and Rush Accountancy Corp., 354 Waterfront Center, San Francisco, CA 94117.

Affirmative Action Employer

ENGINEERING GRADUATES

Must possess degree in electrical or mechanical engineering, physics or computer science. Job opportunities on West or East Coasts and in Middle East. Submit letters of inquiry to:
Frank Memry, Computech Corp., 475 Evanston Drive
Santa Clara, CA 94301.

An Equal Opportunity Employer

If you are planning to become an accountant or engineer, you might answer one of the ads above. If you are going into another field, however, look in your local newspaper for a help-wanted ad that answers your specific needs. Attach your ad to your assignment.

Write a letter of inquiry using noun clauses. Use that-clauses to state information which you already know. ("Your ad stated that your company was seeking . . ."); use wh-question and yes/no question clauses to ask for information. You might want to inquire about:

size of company	salary	vacation
number of employees	advancement	housing
training program	insurance program	recreational facilities

For example, if you are applying for a position in a foreign country, you would be interested in available housing, recreational facilities, etc. You are the applicant. Ask questions that you want answered by using noun clauses. Your letter should contain at least five complete sentences with noun clauses.

MODEL: *Letter of Inquiry*

Heading (your address) (date)

777 Oak Avenue Apt. 2-C
San Francisco, CA 94116
May 10, 19 ____

Inside Address

Mr. Frank Memry
Computech Corporation
475 Evanston Drive
Santa Clara, CA 94301

Salutation

Dear Mr. Memry:

Body

I am writing to inquire about the positions for engineering graduates that were advertised in the **Metropolitan Tribune** on April 30, 19____. I will graduate this coming June from the Massachusetts Institute of Technology with a B.A. in electrical engineering.

I would like to have some information about your company and its employment policies. Would you please tell me how long your company has been in business? I would also like to know whether your company has a training program and how long the training program lasts. Your ad mentioned that you offer positions in the Middle East. Please tell me if you send only single employees there, or if you also send families.

Kindly send this information, along with an application form, to me at the address above.

Thank you very much for your attention.

Closing

Very truly yours,

Signature (handwritten and typed)

Marvin Lemos

Marvin Lemos

Review

These are the main points you should have learned from this chapter:

The noun clause is a dependent clause that can function like a noun as a subject, a subject complement, and an object. The noun clause in object position is placed after the introductory (independent) clause.

When writing a complex sentence with a noun clause, you must observe the sequence of tenses rules. When the introductory verb is in:

- Present tense—the verb in the noun clause can be in any tense.
- Past tense—the verb in the noun clause must be in a past tense form. If the noun clause states a general truth, use simple present tense.

The three types of noun clauses are as follows:

1. A **that-clause** is introduced with the subordinator *that* and is formed from statements.

   President Gorbachev and his wife told the press (that) San Francisco was a beautiful city.

   Note: The subordinator *that* can be omitted.

   A **subjunctive noun clause** occurs with verbs of urgency, advisability, and desirability, such as *advise, ask, demand, insist, recommend,* and *suggest,* in the introductory clause. The verb in the subjective noun clause that follows is in simple form.

   The president suggested that San Francisco residents pay higher taxes.

2. A **wh-question clause** is introduced with a wh-question subordinator and has two patterns:

   - Subject pattern: the wh-question word can be the subject or a part of the subject of the noun clause.

     Do you know who interpreted for the Russian leader?
     The reporter asked him which companies planned to do business in the Soviet Union.

   - Object pattern: the wh-question word is *not* the subject of the noun clause. The noun clause is written in statement form after the introductory clause:

     . . . + wh-word + subject + verb + complement.

     Examples:

     to be and a subject complement:

     The question is what American businessmen think about their proposal.

     modals:

     The State Department wouldn't reveal where the visiting Russians would stay.

     has/have/had:

     The public wasn't told where the motorcade had gone after leaving the St. Francis Hotel.

     do/does/did (Leave out in noun clauses.)

     The governor doesn't know what the visiting dignitaries* want to see.

3. A **yes/no question clause** is introduced with a subordinator: *whether, whether or not,* or *if.*

   The reporter wanted to know whether/whether or not/if the Russians enjoyed their visit.

---

dignitaries: important officials

CHAPTER 13

Adverbial Clauses

An **adverbial clause** is a dependent clause introduced by an adverbial subordinator. It is used to modify the verb of the independent clause and tells when (time), where (place), why (reason), for what purpose, how, how long, and how far. It is also used to show contrast and concession. The adverbial clause pattern is formed with:

Subordinator + Subject + Verb + Complement

Because scientists are interested in the planets . . .
. . . so that man can learn more about the universe.

Since the adverbial clause is a dependent clause, it cannot stand alone. It must be combined with an independent clause to form a complex sentence. An adverbial clause can come either before or after the independent clause. If it comes at the beginning of the sentence, a comma is placed after it:

Because scientists are interested in the planets, they send spacecraft to orbit them.

If the adverbial clause comes after the independent clause, no comma is necessary:

Scientists send spacecraft to orbit the planets because they are interested in them.

Man will explore the universe as far as spaceships can travel.

Types of Adverbial Clauses

There are several different kinds of adverbial clauses. The chart on the next page lists the different kinds along with the subordinators that introduce them. In the pages that follow, you will study and practice each kind in detail.

Adverbial Subordinators

	Subordinator	Meaning
Time	when whenever while as soon as after since as before until	a point in time/short duration at anytime longer duration of time immediately at or instantly after the time that following the time that from that time/moment while when earlier than the time when up to the time of
Place	where anywhere wherever everywhere	a definite place anyplace
Distance/Frequency	as + adverb + as	make a comparison
Manner	as as if/as though	in the way or manner that/like
Reason	because as since	for the reason that
Result	so + adj. + that so + adv. + that such a(n) + noun phrase + that	with the result that
Purpose	so that in order that (in order to + verb)	for the good of
Contrast/Concession	although even though though	in spite of the fact that
Strong contrast	while whereas	direct opposition

Time Clauses

An adverbial time clause tells when the action described by the independent clause verb took place. The action or situation in a time clause can occur at the same time, or it can happen in a sequence of events.

A time clause is introduced by such subordinators as *when(ever), while, as soon as, after, since,* and *before.*

When people had to hunt for food, they had continuous moderate exercise.
People were eating a lot of protein while they were living on farms.
After people moved to urban areas, they had less protein in their diet.
Our eating habits changed as soon as food processing methods improved.

PRACTICE 25: ***Time Clauses***

STEP 1 Add a time subordinator to the appropriate sentence to form an adverbial clause.

STEP 2 Write a new sentence by combining the adverbial clause with the independent clause.

STEP 3 Circle the subordinator, and punctuate the sentence if necessary.

Example:

The United States is in the process of changing to the metric system.
Both the metric and English systems will be used.

(While) the United States is in the process of changing to the metric system, both the metric and English systems will be used.

1. American industries are slowly converting to the metric system.
Many food products will indicate contents by ounces and kilograms.

2. It showed that more women were opposed to the metric system than men.
A recent survey was taken.

3. U.S. soft drink companies have been using the 2-liter no-return bottle.
Conversion to the metric system began in the 1970s.

4. The chemical industry converts from ounces to grams.
All package chemicals to consumers will also be changed.

5. The United States converts to the metric system.
Cooking recipes using the English system will have to be changed.

Place Clauses

An adverbial clause of place tells where the action described by the main verb took place. A place clause is introduced by the subordinator *where* (a definite place), *wherever* (any place), *everywhere* (every place), and *anywhere* (any place).

> Most people prefer to shop where they can be sure of quality.
> Consumers usually prefer to do business wherever credit cards are accepted.
> Everywhere I shop, I use my credit cards.
> I usually stop for lunch anywhere that is handy.*

handy: conveniently located

PRACTICE 26: *Place Clauses*

STEP 1 Add a place subordinator to the appropriate sentence to form an adverbial clause.

STEP 2 Write a new sentence by combining the adverbial clause with the independent clause.

STEP 3 Circle the subordinator and punctuate the sentence if necessary.

Example:

People prefer to shop.
Credit cards are accepted.

People prefer to shop (where) credit cards are accepted.

1. Consumers have a tendency* to buy more.
Credit cards are accepted for payment of the merchandise.

____

____

2. You cannot use credit cards.
You shop.

____

____

3. There is hardly a place of business.
A credit card is not accepted.

____

____

4. They are accepted.
Travelers can use credit cards in foreign countries.

____

____

Manner, Distance, and Frequency Clauses

Adverbial clauses of manner, distance, and frequency are introduced by:

as
as if/as though[1]

Adverbial clauses of manner answer the question: How?
Adverbial clauses of distance answer the question: How far?
Adverbial clauses of frequency answer the question: How often?

The demonstrators left as the police had ordered. (manner)
The students completed the experiment as quickly as they could. (manner)
Pat jogs on the beach as far as she can. (distance)

---

tendency: acting in a particular way, an inclination

[1]*As if/as though* introduces a clause that expresses a non-fact and uses a subjunctive verb form. (Use *were*, not *was*, with both singular and plural nouns.)

She jogs on the beach as often as she can. (frequency)
Kathleen spoke as if (as though) she were an authority on the subject. (manner)

PRACTICE 27: *Manner, Distance, and Frequency Clauses*

STEP 1 Add a manner, distance, or frequency subordinator in the blank to form an adverbial clause. In some sentences, an adverb is suggested.

STEP 2 Form a new sentence by combining the adverbial clause with the independent clause.

Example:

The American people should try to conserve energy.

as often as they can (frequency)
The American people should try to conserve energy as often as they can.

1. The public must conserve energy.
   ____________ the President has requested (manner)
   ____
   ____

2. Many Americans want to move.
   ____________ they can from polluted cities (distance)
   ____
   ____

3. We should not consume our natural resources.
   ____________ we have in the past (manner—wastefully)
   ____
   ____

4. Citizens should make a strong effort to conserve all natural resources.
   ____________ the government has advised (manner)
   ____
   ____

5. The Environmental Protection Agency must remind people.
   ____________ they can about the dangers of pollution (frequency)
   ____
   ____

6. No nation in the world can afford to act
   ____________ pollution were not its problem. (manner—use *as if* or *as though*)
   ____
   ____

Reason Clauses

An adverbial reason clause answers the question "Why?" A reason clause is introduced by the subordinators *because*, *since*, and *as*.

> Some women are choosing coal mining as a job because modern technology has improved working conditions.
> Since coal production will more than double by the end of the 1990s, the work force will also have to increase.
> As a tremendous quantity of coal deposits is deep underground, miners must bring it up.

PRACTICE 28: *Reason Clauses*

STEP 1 Add a reason subordinator to the appropriate sentence to form an adverbial clause.

STEP 2 Write a new sentence by combining the adverbial clause with the independent clause.

STEP 3 Circle the subordinator and punctuate the sentence if necessary.

Example:

They need them to fight the crops' natural enemies.
Farmers rely on chemicals for their crops.

Farmers rely on chemicals for their crops (because) they need them to fight the crops' natural enemies.

1. Chemical preservatives for crops are necessary.
   They help to protect against spoilage, disease, and pests.

   ___

   ___

2. Chemicals improve nutrition and quality.
   They are used in agriculture.

   ___

   ___

3. Many drugs are synthesized* in the laboratory.
   Natural materials are scarce.*

   ___

   ___

4. Chemicals have become an important part of our lives.
   The chemical industry has grown tremendously.

   ___

   ___

5. Millions of people work in the chemical industry.
   It has grown rapidly.

   ___

   ___

synthesized: produced by artificial (especially chemical) means
scarce: insufficient

Result Clauses

An adverbial result clause expresses the result of the independent clause statement. The result clause is introduced by:

so + adjective/adverb + that, or by
such a(an) + adjective + noun + that

New textbooks are so expensive that many students buy used ones.
The cost of education is rising so rapidly that students are looking for ways to cut expenses.
The library is such a big place that I could not find the book I needed.

PRACTICE 29: *Result Clauses*

STEP 1 Add a result subordinator to the first sentence in the following pairs to form an adverbial clause.

STEP 2 Write a new sentence by combining the adverbial clause with the second sentence.

STEP 3 Circle the subordinator.

Example:

Oil plays an important part in engine protection.
It must be changed regularly.

Oil plays such an important part in engine protection that it must be be changed regularly.

1. Changing the oil and filter in a car is easy.
Anyone can do the job.

____

____

2. Changing the oil is an easy job.
An understanding of automotive mechanics is not necessary.

____

____

3. The oil can be changed with little effort.
The job can be completed in about twenty minutes.

____

____

4. Oil contamination* occurs rapidly.
It is important to change the oil every 2,000 to 3,000 miles.

____

____

5. The viscosity* of the oil is critical.*
Using the right weight of oil is important for proper engine performance.

____

____

contamination: impurity **viscosity:** thickness **critical:** extremely important

Purpose Clauses

An adverbial purpose clause states the purpose of the action in the independent clause. The purpose clause is introduced by *so that* or *in order that*. *In order that* is formal and is usually used with *may* or *might*.

The purpose clause action is generally in the future of the time stated in the independent (main) clause. The modals *may/might, can/could,* or *will/would* usually occur in the purpose clause.

> Farmers use chemical pesticides so that they can grow bigger harvests.
> Farmers also spray their fields in order that consumers might enjoy unblemished* fruits and vegetables.

PRACTICE 30: *Purpose Clauses*

STEP 1 Add a purpose subordinator—either *so that* or *in order that*—to the appropriate sentence in order to form an adverbial clause.

STEP 2 Write a new sentence by combining the adverbial clause with the independent clause.

STEP 3 Circle the subordinator.

Example:

Chemists are constantly creating new products in the laboratory.
People can have substitutes for scarce or unavailable products.

Chemists are constantly creating new products in the laboratory (so that) people can have substitutes for scarce or unavailable products.

1. Chemicals are used in many food products.
   They will stay fresh longer.

   ____

   ____

2. Farmers use chemical fertilizers and pesticides.
   They can increase food crops.

   ____

   ____

3. The Clean Air Act was adopted.
   Public health would be protected.

   ____

   ____

4. Environmentalists endorse the Clean Air Act.
   Air quality in the United States will improve.

   ____

   ____

---

unblemished: free of imperfections

5. Environmentalists* want strong antipollution laws.
Less damage to lakes and fish will occur.

____

____

Concession Clauses

Adverbial clauses of concession are used to express ideas or actions that are not expected. The information in the independent clause indicates a concession or unexpected result of information in the dependent clause. The adverbial clauses of concession are introduced with the subordinators *although, even though,* and *though.*

Although most students dislike English courses, they must take them in order to graduate.
Andrew is going to sail his boat in the race although a storm is due.

Notice the difference in meaning between *because* and *even though.*

Because the weather was cold, I didn't go swimming. (Expected result)
Even though the weather was cold, I went swimming. (Unexpected result)

PRACTICE 31: *Concession Adverbial Clauses*

STEP 1 Add a concession subordinator to the appropriate sentence.
STEP 2 Rewrite the sentence by combining the adverbial clause with the independent clause.
STEP 3 Circle the subordinator, and punctuate the sentence as necessary.

Example:

Chemicals are beneficial to man.
They also cause risks.

Although chemicals are beneficial to man, they also cause risks.

1. Scientists do not agree about the safe levels of chemical exposure.
They do agree that everyone must be protected from unnecessary risks.

____

____

2. Government regulations are strict.
All risks cannot be eliminated entirely.

____

____

3. Chemicals may not be 100 percent safe.
Their benefits are significant.

____

____

environmentalists: people who work to solve air and pollution problems, to save natural resources, and to check uncontrolled population growth.

4. The insecticide DDT was once considered an important aid to pest control.
It was later considered dangerous.

5. Natural vitamins are preferable.
Artificial ones are almost as good for you.

6. A new law requires that consumers be given warnings about harmful products.
Not all products pose* risks.

Strong Contrast Adverbial Clauses

In adverbial contrast clauses, the information in the first clause of the sentence is in strong contrast to or is the direct opposite of the information in the second clause of the sentence. In such a sentence, either clause can be introduced by the subordinators *while* or *whereas*. Place a comma between the strong contrast clauses.

> San Francisco is very cool during the summer, whereas San Juan is extremely hot.
>
> While San Juan is extremely hot during the summer, San Francisco is very cool.

PRACTICE 32: *Strong Contrast Adverbial Clauses*

A. STEP 1 Add a strong contrast subordinator to either sentence.
STEP 2 Rewrite the sentence by combining the two clauses.
STEP 3 Circle the subordinator, and add a comma.

1. The West Coast suffered a severe drought.
The East Coast had heavy rainfall.

2. The Northwest rainfall averages hundreds of inches annually.
The Southwest averages less than twelve inches annually.

3. The air is polluted in industrial areas.
The air is clean in many rural areas.

4. Smokers claim the right to smoke in public places.
Nonsmokers claim the right to clean air.

pose: present

5. College graduates with engineering and business degrees are in demand. Graduates with liberal arts degrees are not.

____

____

6. The space shuttle Columbia landed in the desert. The Apollo spacecrafts splashed down in the ocean.

____

____

B. STEP 1 Complete the following sentences with a strong contrasting idea.
STEP 2 Circle the subordinator, and add a comma.

1. While Americans usually drink coffee for breakfast ____
2. My English professor is witty and stimulating ____
3. While Helen understands calculus ____
4. San Francisco has many hilly streets ____
5. My uncle is wealthy ____
6. Living in a metropolitan area is expensive ____
7. Eating at home is economical ____

Review

These are the main points you should have learned from this chapter:

The adverbial clause is a dependent clause that modifies the verb of the main clause or an adjective or adverb. It answers such questions as Where? When? Why? How? For what purpose?

Most adverbial clauses can come either before or after the independent clause. If it comes before the independent clause, it is followed by a comma.

There are several types of adverbial clauses, each with its own subordinating conjunctions. They are

1. Time Clause—*while, when, since, as soon as, after,* etc.
   While the drought was going on, many people took fewer showers and baths.
2. Place Clause—*where, wherever, everywhere, anywhere*
   Everywhere people went to dine, they drank beer, wine and soft drinks instead of water.
3. Manner, Distance, Frequency Clauses—*as, as* + adverb + *as, as if, as though*
   People conserved water as often as they could.
4. Reason Clause—*because, since, as*
   Californians still practice conservation because they remember the distressful years of the water shortage.

5. Result Clause—*so* + adjective/adverb + *that*
such (a) + adjective + noun + *that*

Rainfall was so plentiful that streams, lakes, and reservoirs* were filled at the end of the rainy season.
The drought was such a depressing experience that Californians will remember it for a long time.

6. Purpose Clause—*so that, in order that*

Concerned citizens are still conserving water, however, so that they will not have to suffer so extremely again.

7. Concession Clause—*although, even though, though*

Although the farmers needed the rain, the sudden downpour ruined their crops.
The people were delighted with the change in the weather pattern even though the rain was excessive.

8. Strong Contrast Clause—*while, whereas*

While Californians were having a severe drought, Easterners were having record snowfalls.
Easterners were having record snowfalls, whereas Californians were having a severe drought.

PRACTICE 33: *Adverbial Clauses*

A. Complete the following sentences by adding adverbial clauses as indicated in the parentheses. Circle the subordinator, and punctuate the sentence if necessary.

Example:

I reviewed my class notes (before) I took the final exam. (time)

1. I bought all of my textbooks ______ (time)
2. Tom rode on the subway ______ (distance)
3. ______ the company hired me. (reason)
4. I study in the library ______ (purpose)
5. ______ I will study for a master's degree. (time)
6. I registered for my classes early ______ (purpose)
7. A serious student spends time studying ______ (reason)
8. Tom wanted to become a doctor ______ (concession)

---

reservoirs: places for water storage

9. ____
______________ many young couples prefer living together. (concession)

10. Many people drove big gas-consuming cars ______________
____ (time)

11. Pollution becomes a problem ______________________
____ (place)

12. City living is stressful ______________________
______________________________________ (strong contrast)

13. A single person leads a carefree life ______________
______________________________________ (strong contrast)

B. Fill in the blanks with the correct adverbial subordinators, and punctuate the sentences correctly.

Several years ago ______________ (time) I was driving toward Miami from Tampa a tire on my old Volkswagen blew out. ______________ (time phrase) I realized my problem I brought my car to a stop on the side of the highway. ______________ (time) I was checking the damaged tire a man stopped his car. ______________ (concession) he could not help me I was glad he was there. ______________ (time) he left he told me that he would notify the highway patrol. ______________ (time) he left I felt nervous again ______________ (reason) it was dark foggy and windy. ______________ (at any time) I saw a car approaching I thought it was someone coming to help me. ______________ (time) an hour had passed I saw the flashing lights of a tow truck and my heart sang songs of joy. ______________ (time) the driver would tow my car to Miami I had to pay him ______________ (reason) I didn't carry insurance. Now ______________ (any place) I decide to go I doublecheck my car ______________ (time) I leave. ______________ (concession) I carry insurance I still don't want to have such a frightening experience again.

WRITING PRACTICE

Using the above paragraph as a model, write an original description of a personal experience, such as an accident, a concert, a fire, or a wedding. Use as many adverbial clauses as you can and circle the subordinators.

CHAPTER 14

Relative Clauses

A **relative,** or **adjective, clause** is a dependent clause introduced by a relative pronoun or relative adverb. It functions as an adjective; that is, it modifies or describes a noun or pronoun in the independent clause.

Relative Pronouns and Adverbs

A **relative pronoun** replaces a noun phrase or pronoun in the dependent clause. The relative pronouns are *who, whom, which, that,* and *whose* + noun.

. . . the attorney who ran for mayor of our city last year. . . .

. . . the pianist whom I told you about. . . .

. . . Hawaiian Islands, which are located in the Pacific Ocean, . . .

. . . product that is causing a major problem in the auto industry. . . .

. . . Sunlight Corporation, whose main office is in Chicago, . . .

Who refers only to people and is a subject pronoun.
Whom refers only to people and is an object pronoun.
Which refers to things and is a subject or object pronoun.
That refers to things or people and is a subject or object pronoun in restrictive clauses only.
Whose + noun refers to things or people and is a possessive.

A **relative adverb** replaces a prepositional phrase in the dependent clause. The relative adverbs are *where, when,* and *why.*

The supermarket where I shop. . . .	(*where* has the same meaning as *in which.*)
July 4 is the day when I was born.	(*when* has the same meaning as *on which.*)
The reason why I was late. . . .	(*why* has the same meaning as *for which.*)

Where refers to a place.
When refers to a time.
Why refers to a reason.

A reference chart of the relative clause subordinators follows.

Relative Clause Subordinators

	Subordinator	Meaning
Relative Pronouns	who	person/people (subject)
	whom	person/people (object)
	whose + noun	person/people, thing(s)—possessive
	that	person/people, thing(s)—restrictive clauses only
	which	thing(s)
Relative Adverbs	when	time
	where	place
	why	reason

Position of Relative Clauses

Since the relative clause is a dependent clause, it must be combined with an independent clause to form a complex sentence. The relative clause comes right after the noun phrase it modifies (the antecedent).[1]

Guam Island, which is located in the Pacific Ocean, was an important military base during World War II.
A situation that is causing a major problem in the auto industry is the popularity of Japanese cars in the U.S.
Tom Brown, who ran for mayor of our city last year, is a friend of my brother.
He went to work for Computer Corporation, whose main offices are in Chicago.
She is the wonderful counselor whom I told you about.
The store where we shop for groceries is closed for remodeling.

Punctuation of Relative Clauses

Relative clauses are either restrictive (necessary) or nonrestrictive (unnecessary). The information in a restrictive clause is necessary to identify the noun phrase it modifies. Do not use a comma to separate the restrictive clause.

The information in a nonrestrictive clause is not necessary to identify the noun phrase it modifies; it merely provides additional information. Use a comma to separate the nonrestrictive clause from the independent clause.

[1]Sometimes a prepositional phrase may come between the noun phrase and the relative clause.
Peggy visited her friend from Germany, who graduated from Yale University.

Restrictive (necessary):

The attorney who represented Mrs. Gaines in her medical lawsuit received a fee of $550,000.

A body of land that[1] is surrounded on three sides by water is called a peninsula.

Nonrestrictive (unnecessary):

Mr. Walter Winter, who represented Mrs. Gaines in her medical lawsuit, received a fee of $550,000.

San Francisco, which is surrounded on three sides by water, is a peninsula.

PRACTICE 34: *Restrictive and Nonrestrictive Clauses*

STEP 1 Underline the relative clause or clauses. (Some sentences have two.)

STEP 2 Write R for a restrictive and NR for a nonrestrictive clause in the parentheses.

STEP 3 Add commas to the nonrestrictive clauses.

Example:

(R) The senator whose family is politically active in Massachusetts visited China.

(NR) Senator Kennedy, whose family is politically active in Massachusetts, visited China.

( ) **1.** The sun which in forty minutes can produce enough solar energy to meet man's needs for a year is one of the Earth's potential sources of power.

( ) **2.** All tobacco companies whose goal is to get the public to buy their cigarettes claim that their particular brands have the lowest nicotine and tar content.

( ) **3.** We are at the door of the medical computer revolution according to an article which the professor cited*.

( ) **4.** The machine that analyzes and delivers laboratory test and electrocardiogram results is a medical computer.

( ) **5.** Laser beams which are useful in both medicine and industry were first predicted in science fiction stories fifty years ago.

( ) **6.** Physicians who feed patient symptoms into the computer receive a list of diseases that fit the symptoms of their patients.

( ) **7.** The country that has the highest per capita* income is not the United States which is only in third place.

( ) **8.** Kuwait which is a small country in the Middle East is in first place.

( ) **9.** It was a thrilling experience to meet the author of the book that we had been reading all semester.

( ) **10.** The public is highly suspicious of the oil industry whose profits have been increasing in spite of the energy crisis.

---

cited: quoted
per capita: per person (literally, "per head" in Latin)

[1]Use the subordinator *that* in restrictive clauses only.

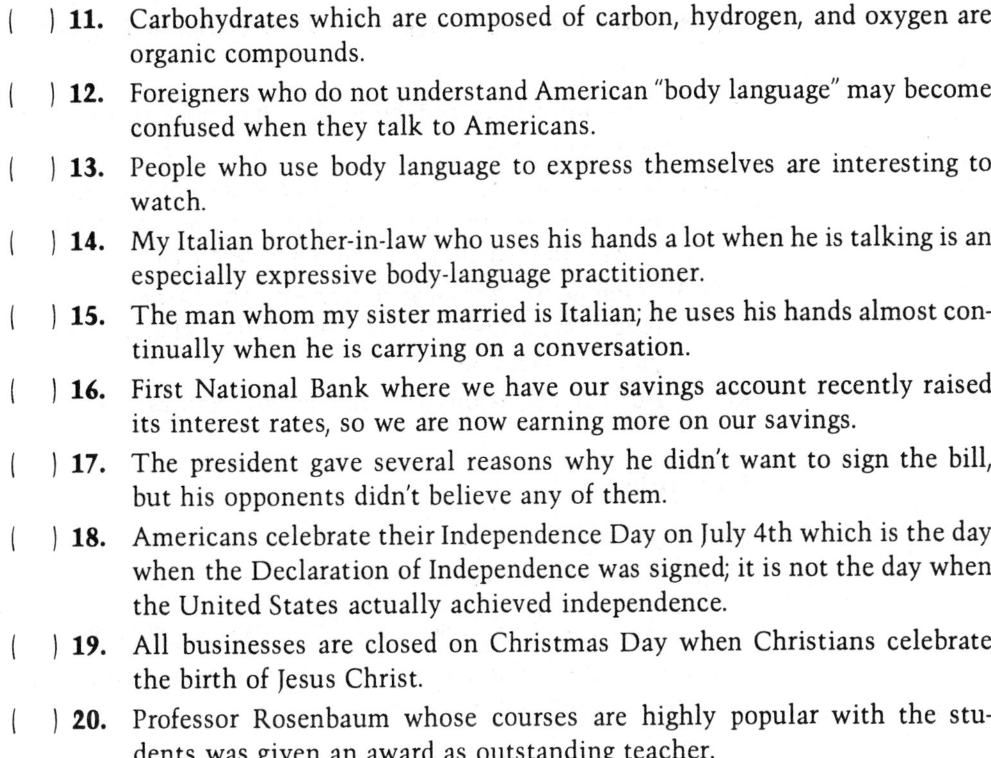

( ) **11.** Carbohydrates which are composed of carbon, hydrogen, and oxygen are organic compounds.

( ) **12.** Foreigners who do not understand American "body language" may become confused when they talk to Americans.

( ) **13.** People who use body language to express themselves are interesting to watch.

( ) **14.** My Italian brother-in-law who uses his hands a lot when he is talking is an especially expressive body-language practitioner.

( ) **15.** The man whom my sister married is Italian; he uses his hands almost continually when he is carrying on a conversation.

( ) **16.** First National Bank where we have our savings account recently raised its interest rates, so we are now earning more on our savings.

( ) **17.** The president gave several reasons why he didn't want to sign the bill, but his opponents didn't believe any of them.

( ) **18.** Americans celebrate their Independence Day on July 4th which is the day when the Declaration of Independence was signed; it is not the day when the United States actually achieved independence.

( ) **19.** All businesses are closed on Christmas Day when Christians celebrate the birth of Jesus Christ.

( ) **20.** Professor Rosenbaum whose courses are highly popular with the students was given an award as outstanding teacher.

Relative Pronouns as Subjects

The relative pronoun may be the subject of its own clause. A relative clause in the subject pattern is formed with

Who
Which + verb + complement
That

In the examples below, notice how sentences a and b are combined to form a new sentence c, which contains a relative clause:

1. **a.** People want to save time and energy.
b. They use microwave ovens.
c. People who use microwave ovens want to save time and energy.

2. **a.** Ovens use microwave energy.
b. They are capable of cooking foods quickly.
c. Ovens that are capable of cooking foods quickly use microwave energy.

3. **a.** An electron tube produces microwaves.
b. Microwaves cook foods quickly.
c. An electron tube produces microwaves, which cook foods quickly.

4. **a.** Microwave ovens have push-button controls.
b. They defrost and cook food automatically.
c. Microwave ovens, which defrost and cook foods automatically, have push-button controls.

PRACTICE 35: *Relative Pronouns as Subjects*

STEP 1 Look for nouns and pronouns that refer to the same person or thing in both sentences.

STEP 2 Change the noun or pronoun in the second sentence to a relative pronoun to make a relative clause. Use *that* to introduce a restrictive clause. Use *which* or *who* to introduce a nonrestrictive clause.

STEP 3 Combine the second sentence with the first sentence to make a complex sentence. Remember to put the relative clause immediately after the noun phrase it modifies.

STEP 4 Add commas if the relative clause is nonrestrictive.

Example:

Mr. Lawson passed the bar examination.*
Mr. Lawson teaches political science.

Mr. Lawson, who teaches political science, passed the bar examination.

1. John Fish explained the tapeworm's complex structure.
He is a research biologist.

____

____

2. While he lectured, he showed us a slide.
The slide diagrammed the various parts of the tapeworm's structure.

____

____

3. Words in English are often difficult for foreigners to pronounce.
They begin with the consonants *th*.

____

____

4. Foreigners also have difficulty with English spelling.
English spelling is not always logical.

____

____

5. The drugs have the same effects on human beings.
They are used on experimental animals.

____

____

6. A person must be able to work logically.
A person wants to be a computer programmer.

____

____

7. The thyroid is an endocrine gland.
The thyroid controls our growth.

____

____

bar examination: the examination that law students must pass in order to practice law

SENTENCE PRACTICE

Write six sentences about your major subject or future career. Three should contain restrictive relative clauses, and three should contain nonrestrictive relative clauses. In the relative clauses, use *who, which,* or *that* in the subject position.

Relative Pronouns as Objects

The relative pronoun may be the object of its own clause. A relative clause in the object pattern is formed with:

Whom
Which + subject + verb + complement
(That)

Note: The relative pronoun may be omitted in object pattern restrictive clauses.

In the examples that follow, notice how sentences a and b are combined to form a new sentence c, which contains a relative clause.

Restrictive:

1. **a.** The science magazine is published in England.
   b. The professor discussed the science magazine.
   c. The science magazine that the professor discussed is published in England.
   The science magazine the professor discussed is published in England.
2. **a.** The professor is Dr. White.
   b. You should see Dr. White.
   c. The professor whom you should see is Dr. White.
   The professor that you should see is Dr. White.
   The professor you should see is Dr. White.

Nonrestrictive:

1. **a.** Dr. White is an ecologist.
   b. You met Dr. White in my office.
   c. Dr. White, whom you met in my office, is an ecologist.
2. **a.** The Space Museum in Washington, D.C. has many fascinating displays.
   b. Our science class visited the Space Museum during Easter vacation.
   c. The Space Museum in Washington, D.C., which our science class visited during Easter vacation, has many fascinating displays.

PRACTICE 36: *Relative Pronouns as Objects*

STEP 1 Change the second sentence into a relative clause, as in the preceding examples.

STEP 2 Combine it with the first sentence and add punctuation if it is nonrestrictive. Write restrictive clauses both with and without a relative pronoun.

1. This is the geology book.
The professor recommended it.

____

____

____

2. Geologists are searching for uranium.
Our nation needs uranium.

____

____

____

3. Uranium is an important source of energy.
Nuclear power plants use uranium.

____

____

____

4. Albert Einstein was a high school dropout.
The world recognizes him as a genius.

____

____

____

5. Einstein is famous for his theory of relativity.
He developed this theory while he lived in Switzerland.

____

____

____

6. As a young boy, Einstein had trouble in elementary and high school.
He attended these schools in Germany.

____

____

____

7. He did poorly in subjects.
He disliked them.

____

____

____

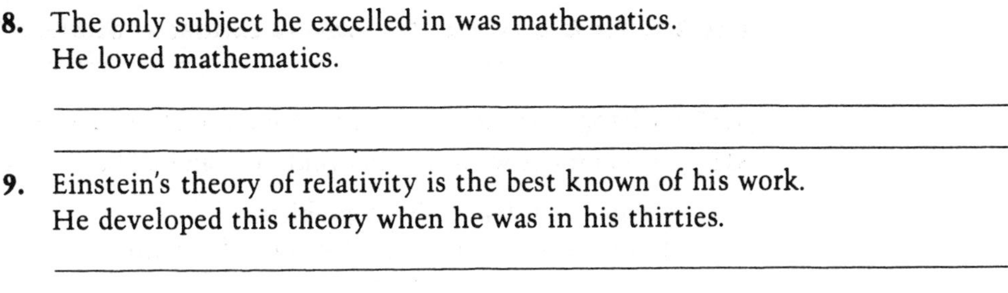

8. The only subject he excelled in was mathematics.
   He loved mathematics.

9. Einstein's theory of relativity is the best known of his work.
   He developed this theory when he was in his thirties.

SENTENCE PRACTICE

Write six sentences using relative clauses in the object pattern. (Remember your two choices with restrictive clauses in object pattern: using *that, whom,* or *which* or dropping the relative pronoun.)

Possessive Relative Clauses

These clauses are used to show possession. As with other relative clauses, they may be used as subjects or as objects. When used as a subject, the *whose* + noun phrase is the subject of its clause.

A relative clause in the subject pattern is formed with:

Whose + noun + verb + complement

The relative pronoun *whose* replaces a possessive word.

Possessive—Subject Pattern

In the sentences below, notice how sentences a and b are combined to form a new sentence c, which contains a relative possessive clause in the subject pattern:

1. **a.** Opportunities for college graduates may be on the upswing.*
   b. College graduates' degrees are in business and engineering.
   c. Opportunities for college graduates whose degrees are in business and engineering may be on the upswing.
2. **a.** A meteorologist cannot forecast conditions a month in advance.
   b. A meteorologist's job is to make weather predictions.
   c. A meteorologist, whose job is to make weather predictions, cannot forecast conditions a month in advance.
3. **a.** A population of between 252 and 373 million people for the year 2025 is predicted by the U.S. Census Bureau.
   b. The U.S. Census Bureau's figures take into consideration projected births, deaths, and immigration.
   c. A population of between 252 and 373 million people for the year 2025 is predicted by the U.S. Census Bureau, whose figures take into consideration projected births, deaths, and immigration.

---

on the upswing: increasing

PRACTICE 37: *Possessive Clauses—Subject Pattern*

STEP 1 Change the second sentence into a relative clause.

STEP 2 Combine it with the first sentence, and add commas if it is nonrestrictive.

1. Denver still has dirty air problems.
   Denver's pollution is not considered serious.

2. Securities Corporation's president is Mr. Mann.
   His expertise* on financial investments is well known.

3. Large corporations can afford costly research and development.
   Large corporations' investments lead to new manufacturing techniques.

4. Companies that manufacture products usually spend large sums of money for advertising to attract consumers.
   Consumers' business is necessary for profits.

5. A manufacturer can sell to consumers at lower prices.
   A manufacturer's costs are lower because of mass production.

6. Stockholders are not responsible for a corporation's debts.
   Stockholders' financial liability is limited.

7. First Space Bank publishes a brochure for women investors.
   The bank's president is a woman.

Possessive—Object Pattern

Possessive relative clauses can also be in the object pattern. In that case, the relative pronoun phrase (*whose* + a noun) is the object of the verb or main statement of the relative clause.

A possessive relative clause in the object pattern is formed with:

Whose + noun + subject + verb + complement

Again, notice how sentences a and b are combined to form a new sentence c, which contains a relative possessive clause.

---

expertise: skill, knowledge

1. **a.** Farmers depend on meteorologists.
   b. They need meteorologists' accurate forecasts for successful agricultural planning.
   c. Farmers depend on meteorologists, whose accurate forecasts they need for successful agricultural planning.
2. **a.** Independent research laboratories test many new products on the market.
   b. Consumers trust their evaluations.
   c. Independent research laboratories, whose evaluations consumers trust, test many new products on the market.
3. **a.** The young woman traveled 1700 miles across Australia's western wilderness.
   b. I read her article in *National Geographic.*
   c. The young woman whose article I read in *National Geographic* traveled 1700 miles across Australia's western wilderness.

PRACTICE 38: *Possessive Clauses—Object Pattern*

STEP 1 Change the possessive noun into *whose* + noun and make the sentence into a relative clause.

STEP 2 Combine it with the first sentence, and punctuate it if it is nonrestrictive.

1. The community college offers vocational training.
   I received the ~~college's~~ whose bulletin in the mail.
   The community college, whose bulletin I received in the mail, offers vocational training.
2. Bay View City College is popular with many students in the city.
   My brother took the college's computer programming class last summer.
   ____
   ____
3. The King of Xanadu was deposed by a revolution.
   The United States had supported his government.
   ____
   ____
4. The author of this poem died penniless and heartbroken.
   The world never recognized his talent.
   ____
   ____
5. Mr. French is the state's budget director.
   The newspaper published his report yesterday.
   ____
   ____
6. There are several women claiming to be Princess Anastasia of Russia.
   The revolutionaries executed her entire family in 1918.
   ____
   ____

7. The actress has played in several successful films.
I can't remember her name right now.

____

____

SENTENCE PRACTICE

Write six sentences containing possessive relative clauses introduced with the relative pronoun *whose* + noun. Try to write three sentences in the subject pattern and three in the object pattern.

Relative Pronouns as Objects of Prepositions

A relative pronoun can be the object of a preposition in its own clause. A relative clause in the object of preposition pattern is formed in two ways:

Formal:

Preposition + Whom / Which / Whose + Noun + subject + verb + complement

Informal:

Whom / Which / That / Whose + noun + subject + verb + complement + preposition

The first pattern is more formal than the second pattern. In the formal pattern, the preposition comes before the relative pronoun. The relative pronoun *that* can only be used in the informal pattern (preposition at the end of the clause) in restrictive clauses.

In the following sentences, notice how sentences a and b are combined to form a new sentence c, which contains a relative clause.

1. **a.** The total environment includes the geosphere, the biosphere, and the sociosphere.
   b. Scientists are interested in the total environment.
   c. The total environment, in which scientists are interested, includes the geosphere, the biosphere, and the sociosphere. (formal)
   The total environment, which scientists are interested in, includes the geosphere, the biosphere, and the sociosphere. (informal)
2. **a.** The candidate didn't win the election.
   b. I voted for the candidate.
   c. The candidate for whom I voted didn't win the election. (formal)
   The candidate whom I voted for didn't win the election. (informal)
   The candidate that I voted for didn't win the election. (informal)
   The candidate I voted for didn't win the election. (informal)
3. **a.** The names of the victims are unknown.
   b. This monument was built in the victims' memory.
   c. The names of the victims in whose memory this monument was built are unknown. (formal)

PRACTICE 39: *Relative Pronouns as Objects of Prepositions*

STEP 1 Change the underlined preposition + noun phrase into preposition + relative pronoun to make the second sentence into a relative clause.

STEP 2 Combine it with the first sentence, and punctuate it if it is nonrestrictive.

STEP 3 Write each new sentence twice: once in the formal pattern and once in the informal pattern.

1. Finding reasonably priced housing is becoming a problem.
Many young couples are concerned about the problem.

Formal:

Finding reasonably priced housing is becoming a problem about which many young couples are concerned.

Informal:

Finding reasonably priced housing is becoming a problem which many young couples are concerned about.

2. Single-family homes are becoming harder to find.
Buyers must pay high prices for single-family homes.

____

____

____

____

3. There are many young people.
Such homes would be ideal for many young people, yet they can't afford them.

____

____

____

____

4. One solution may be condominiums.
Many families occupy single units in condominiums.

____

____

____

____

5. Many former apartment buildings are being converted into "condos."
Buyers must still pay high prices in addition to monthly maintenance fees for them.

____

____

____

____

6. Another type of housing is the two-master-bedroom dwelling.
Two couples live in this dwelling.

7. One problem with this type of housing is choosing the people.
You are going to share living space with these people.

8. You must get along well with the people.
You are going to live with these people.

9. Since you will be sharing a kitchen and a living room, a strict time schedule will have to be observed.
Both couples must work around this time schedule.

SENTENCE PRACTICE

Write six sentences about your house or apartment, or about your family. Each should contain a relative clause in the object of preposition pattern.

Relative Pronouns in Phrases of Quantity

A relative pronoun can also occur in a phrase of quantity: *some of which, one of whom, each of whom, all of whom,* etc. A relative clause in this pattern is formed with:

. . . some of which . . . one of which . . . all of whom . . . each of whom etc.	}	+ subject + verb + complement + verb + complement

All such clauses are nonrestrictive.

In the following sets, notice how sentences a and b are combined to form a new sentence c, which contains a relative clause:

1. **a.** The members of the special commission on crime meet weekly.
   b. Some of them were appointed by the mayor.
   c. The members of the special commission on crime, some of whom were appointed by the mayor, meet weekly.
2. **a.** A witness to the crime has to identify the suspect by viewing a line-up of people.
   b. One of those people is the accused person.
   c. A witness to the crime has to identify the suspect by viewing a line-up of people, one of whom is the accused person.
3. **a.** As an experiment, the television station decided to show only movies.
   b. I had already seen most of the movies.
   c. As an experiment, the television station decided to show only movies, most of which I had already seen.

PRACTICE 40: *Relative Pronouns in Phrases of Quantity*

STEP 1 Change the second sentence to a relative clause.

STEP 2 Combine it with the first sentence and punctuate it, following the examples above.

1. The students wrote a letter of protest to the Dean.
   Half of the students had received a failing grade in chemistry.

   ____

   ____

2. The State of Nevada has very little agriculture.
   Most of the state is desert land.

   ____

   ____

3. My three older sisters are living abroad.
   Each of them attends a different university.

   ____

   ____

4. At our school's annual international fair, I ate a lot of native foods.
   I had not tasted some of the foods before.

   ____

   ____

5. Medical researchers have tested thousands of cancer-fighting drugs.
   Most of the drugs prove to be useless.

   ____

   ____

6. Humphrey Bogart made many films.
   One of the films was *Casablanca.*

   ____

   ____

7. She has seven brothers and two sisters.
   One of her brothers is the head of the family.

   ____

   ____

SENTENCE PRACTICE

Write six sentences of your own that contain relative pronouns in prepositional phrases of quantity.

Relative Pronouns in Phrases of Quality

A relative pronoun can also occur in a phrase of quality: *the best of which, the least expensive of which, the most important of which, the most intelligent of whom,* etc. A relative clause in the prepositional phrase of quality pattern is formed with:

$$\text{The}\left\{\begin{array}{l}\text{more}\\ \text{most}\\ \text{least}\\ \text{less}\\ \text{etc.}\end{array}\right\}\underset{\text{(adjective)}}{\underline{\hspace{3em}}}\text{ of which/whom + verb + complement}$$

These clauses are nonrestrictive.

In the following sets, notice how sentences a and b are combined to form a new sentence c, which contains a relative clause.

1. **a.** Ten sports cars were rated in *Auto Journal.*
   b. The Super X was the most expensive.
   c. Ten sports cars, the most expensive of which was the Super X, were rated in *Auto Journal.*
2. **a.** I looked at three imported cars.
   b. The Jaguar was the most beautiful.
   c. I looked at three imported cars, the most beautiful of which was the Jaguar.
3. **a.** I talked to three salesmen.
   b. Mr. Carr was the least helpful.
   c. I talked to three salesmen, the least helpful of whom was Mr. Carr.

PRACTICE 41: *Relative Pronouns in Phrases of Quality*

STEP 1 Change the second sentence into a relative clause.

STEP 2 Combine it with the first sentence and punctuate it. Follow the examples above.

1. There is a chain of islands in the Caribbean Sea.
The most beautiful and charming island is Puerto Rico, "the land of enchantment."

____

____

____

2. The original inhabitants of Puerto Rico were hardworking farmers.
The best farmers were Indians.

____

____

3. Puerto Ricans speak two languages.
The most popular language is Spanish.

____

____

4. On our last trip, we met many Puerto Ricans.
The friendliest people live in the small towns.

____

____

5. Puerto Rico's economy is basically agricultural products.
The most important product is sugar cane.

____

____

6. Puerto Rico has many resources.
The most important resources are its water and fertile soil.

____

____

7. Puerto Rico has many lovely beaches.
The best beach is Luquillo Beach, lying about 30 miles east of San Juan, the capital.

____

____

____

8. Many restaurants are located outside of San Juan in the heart of the island's exotic rain forest.
El Yunque is the best restaurant.

____

____

9. Many tourist attractions are found in San Juan.
The most historical tourist attraction is Old San Juan.

____

____

SENTENCE PRACTICE

Write six sentences that contain relative pronouns in prepositional phrases of quality. You may write about a country, city, or other place you are familiar with.

Relative Adverbial Clauses

Relative clauses may also be introduced by the relative adverbs *where, when,* and *why* and follow the nouns that they modify.

Where replaces a prepositional phrase of place.
When replaces a prepositional phrase of time.
Where and *when* relative clauses may be restrictive or nonrestrictive.
Why introduces a reason and is always restrictive. (*That* may be used in place of *why.*)

Notice how sentences a and b can be combined to form a new sentence c, which contains a relative clause.

1. **a.** The village was destroyed by an earthquake.
   b. My mother was born in the village.
   c. The village where my mother was born was destroyed by an earthquake.
2. **a.** Kyoto is famous for its many beautiful temples and shrines.
   b. My mother was born in Kyoto.
   c. Kyoto, where my mother was born, is famous for its many beautiful temples and shrines.
3. **a.** December 25 is the day.
   b. Christians celebrate the birth of Jesus Christ on that day.
   c. December 25 is the day when Christians celebrate the birth of Jesus Christ.
4. **a.** Many people exchange gifts on December 25.
   b. Christians celebrate the birth of Jesus Christ on December 25.
   c. Many people exchange gifts on December 25, when Christians celebrate the birth of Jesus Christ.
5. **a.** The slavery issue was only one reason.
   b. The northern and southern states fought against each other during the U.S. Civil War for a reason.
   c. The slavery issue was only one reason why (that) the northern and southern states fought against each other during the U.S. Civil War.

PRACTICE 42: *Relative Adverbial Clauses*

STEP 1 Change the second sentence to a relative clause introduced by *where, when,* or *why.*

STEP 2 Combine it with the first sentence and punctuate it if it is nonrestrictive.

1. 1849 was the year.
   Gold was discovered in California in that year.

   ____

   ____

2. By 1850, thousands of people had joined the "California Gold Rush."
   California became a state in 1850.

   ____

   ____

3. Many large cities contain ethnic neighborhoods.
   Members of the different ethnic groups live in those neighborhoods.

   ____

   ____

4. San Francisco, for example, has a very large "Chinatown."
Thousands of Chinese people live in Chinatown.

____

____

5. One reason may be that they can find familiar food.
People like to live together with their own people for a reason.

____

____

6. Another reason may be that people can communicate more easily in their native language.
Ethnic neighborhoods develop in large cities for a reason.

____

____

7. No one can predict the day.
A strong earthquake will strike California on a day.

____

____

8. Most people remember what they were doing on the day.
President Kennedy was assassinated on that day.

____

____

9. Most people remember what they were doing on November 22, 1963.
President Kennedy was assassinated on that day.

____

____

10. We may never know the real reason.
President Kennedy was assassinated for a reason.

____

____

SENTENCE PRACTICE

Write six sentences of your own. Use each of the relative adverbs *where, when,* and *why* twice.

Review

Relative Pronouns

Subject pattern
Who refers only to people, both singular and plural.

The instructor who teaches intermediate accounting is a senior analyst with Banking Investments, Inc.
Instructors who teach only night classes do not usually hold regular office hours.

Object pattern
Whom refers only to people, both singular and plural.

My physics professor, whom the students respect, is retiring at the end of this semester.
My mother and father, whom I haven't seen in a year, are coming to visit me during vacation.
The person whom I look up to the most is my father.
The English teachers, most of whom have Ph.D. degrees, are on strike for higher salaries and smaller classes.

Subject and object pattern
Which refers to things, both singular and plural. *Which* is used in nonrestrictive clauses.

Electrical Engineering 455, which is a review course, is offered during the summer session.
Electrical Engineering 455, which I signed up for last summer, was very helpful.
You must maintain at least a B average in your major courses, all of which must be taken at this college.

Subject and object pattern
That refers to things or people, both singular and plural. *That* can be substituted for *who, whom,* and *which* in restrictive clauses only. *That* can be omitted in the subject pattern.

The course that reviews mechanical engineering is Engineering 456.
The course that I signed up for has been cancelled.
The person that I look up to the most is my father.

Subject and object pattern
Whose + noun shows possession and refers to people or things, both singular and plural.

College students, whose incomes are usually fixed,* may have a hard time in an inflationary period.
I don't remember the name of the music teacher whose course I took last semester.

Relative Adverbs

Where refers to a place.

The city where I live is the capital of my country.
Riyadh, where I live, is the capital of my country.

When refers to a time.

I can't remember a night when I didn't have a mountain of homework to do.
Last night, when I couldn't sleep, I read an entire novel.

Why refers to a reason.

There are several reasons why I didn't call you last night.

The Relative Clause

1. A relative clause is a dependent clause introduced by a relative pronoun (*who, whom, which, that, whose*) or a relative adverb (*where, when, why*).

---

fixed: unchanging

2. The relative clause is used as an adjective and modifies a noun or noun phrase in the independent clause.

   The woman who is giving the lecture tomorrow is a meteorologist.
   Ms. Brown, whom we will hear tomorrow, is a meteorologist.
   The city where I was born had a big earthquake recently.

3. When a relative clause gives necessary identifying information about the noun phrase it modifies, it is *restrictive* and is not set off with commas.

   The experts who predict future global climate are called climatologists.

4. When a relative clause gives additional but unnecessary information about the noun phrase it modifies, it is *nonrestrictive* and is set off with commas.

   Earthquakes, which are among the most destructive natural disasters, cannot be predicted with any accuracy.

PRACTICE 43: *Reviewing Relative Clauses*

Insert relative clauses into the following short story.

STEP 1 Change the sentences in parentheses into relative clauses and write them in the blanks provided.

STEP 2 Add commas if necessary.

A Day in Central Park

Yesterday was a beautiful spring day, so Mei-Ling ____________________ (Mei-Ling is from China) and Maryam ____________________ (Maryam is from Iran) decided to go sightseeing. The subway train ____________________ (They rode in a subway) made several stops before they arrived at their destination. The Central Park Station ____________________ (They got off at the Central Park Station) was crowded with people ____________________ (The people were waiting for their trains). Unfortunately, Mei-Ling and Maryam lost each other in the crowd, but after some anxious moments, they saw each other on the escalator ____________________ (They rode on the escalator up to the street level). Arriving at the park, they decided to stroll around for a while. They strolled on the paths ____________________ (The paths were bordered by beautiful flowers) and watched the people ____________________ (Some of the people were relaxing on the grass and some of the people were playing games). An hour later, Mei-Ling and Maryam decided to leave. As they were crossing the street, they saw a crowd of people ____________________ (The people were laughing and applauding). Squeezing themselves through the crowd, they saw a funny man dressed in a black tuxedo,*

tuxedo: formal suit worn by men.

a top hat, and white gloves. He had an unusual face ____________________. He also had
(The face was painted white)

brightly painted red lips and black makeup around his eyes ____________________
(The black makeup around his eyes

____________________. Maryam asked a bystander* who this odd-looking fellow was.
made him look like a clown)

The woman said that he was a mime. She further explained that a mime is an actor ________
(A mime

____________________. He makes only body movements and gestures
acts out situations without speaking)

____________________. While Mei-Ling and Maryam
(The body movements and gestures are stiff and mechanical)

were listening to the woman, the mime began to mimic a woman ____________________.
(A woman was walking by)

The mime followed stiffly behind the unsuspecting woman to the entrance of a nearby store

____________________. The audience laughed as he returned to the center of his
(She disappeared into the store)

sidewalk stage ____________________ much to the delight of the
(He continued his act on the sidewalk stage)

crowd. He continued to do other clownish acts such as walking up an imaginary ladder and walking on a tightrope. After the mime had completed his performance, he passed around his

top hat ____________________. Mei-Ling and Maryam really enjoyed
(The audience dropped money into his top hat)

seeing a different form of entertainment ____________________
(They decided to tell their classmates about the dif-

____________________.
ferent form of entertainment in their next conversation class)

WRITING PRACTICE

Using the above paragraph as a model, choose one of the following topics and write a description of an amusement park, city, or other interesting place you have visited. Use as many relative clauses as you can, and underline the subordinators.

bystander: person standing nearby

CHAPTER 15

Participles and Gerunds

Participles

A **participle** is a word formed from a verb that is used as an adjective to modify nouns.

Notice how an active voice verb is changed to a present participle by adding the suffix *-ing* to the verb. An active voice verb (present, past, or future tense) becomes a present participle.

Changing Active Verbs to Participles

Verbs	Present Participles
The custom *fascinates* me.	The *fascinating* custom interests me.
The woman *jogged* in the park	The *jogging* woman ran through the park.
The hostages *will return* soon.	The *returning* hostages were treated like heroes.

Now notice how a passive voice verb (present or past tense) becomes a past participle.

Changing Passive Verbs to Participles

Verbs	Past Participles
The movie *is rated* "X."	The *X-rated* movie was banned.*
The steak *was burned.*	The *burned* steak tasted terrible.
My heart *was broken.*	My *broken* heart will never heal.

Note: The terms *present* and *past participle* are misleading because these forms have nothing to do with present tense or past tense. Rather, they are based on active or

banned: forbidden

passive voice. The present participle comes from an active voice verb, and the past participle comes from a passive voice verb.

There are also perfect and continuous forms of participles, as shown on the following chart.

Summary of Participle Forms[1]

Forms	Active	Passive
The *general forms* do not indicate time: time is determined by the main clause verb	*Verb + ing* opening	*Verb + ed, en, t, d* opened bought taken sold
The *continuous form* emphasizes action going on *right now*; may also express future time		*Being + Past Participle* being opened
The *perfect form* emphasizes that the action happened before the time of the main clause verb	*Having + Past Participle* having opened	*Having Been + Past Participle* having been opened

Participial Phrases

A **participial phrase** is a reduction of a subject pattern relative (adjective) clause or an adverbial clause. A participial phrase is:

participle + modifiers + noun

... the fascinating Chinese custom
... an extremely well-written paragraph
... not knowing the correct answer
... being too young to get married
... wounded in his right hand

Participial Phrases from Relative Clauses

Participial phrases may be formed by reducing subject-pattern relative clauses. To do this, delete the relative pronouns (*who, which,* or *that*) and change the verb to a present or past participle form.

Just like relative clauses, participial phrases can be restrictive or nonrestrictive. If the original relative clause was restrictive, the participial phrase formed from it will be also. Conversely,* if the original clause was nonrestrictive, the phrase will be also. Participial phrases are made negative by placing the word *not* in front of the participle.

conversely: oppositely

[1]There is a sixth participle form, the perfect continuous active:

Having been opening jars all morning, my hand has become cramped.

It is not included here because it is not commonly used.

General Forms in the Active Voice

In the following sets of sentences, the relative clause in the first sentence has been changed to a participial phrase in the second. Notice that the general form in the active voice can be made from a present, past, or future tense verb. Also notice the similar punctuation of restrictive and nonrestrictive clauses and phrases.

1. **a.** Many students who study in this university are from foreign countries.
   b. Many students studying at this university are from foreign countries.
2. **a.** Many students who are studying at this university are from foreign countries.
   b. Many students studying at this university are from foreign countries.
3. **a.** The president's wife, who looked tired after the long trip, could hardly smile at the cheering crowd.
   b. The president's wife, looking tired after the long trip, could hardly smile at the cheering crowd.
4. **a.** Commercial airliners that were arriving at the same time as the president's plane couldn't land immediately.
   b. Commercial airliners arriving at the same time as the president's plane couldn't land immediately.
5. **a.** Everyone who will go on our field trip next weekend must sign up now.
   b. Everyone going on our field trip next weekend must sign up now.
6. **a.** Linda, who did not understand physics, failed the course.
   b. Linda, not understanding physics, failed the course.

PRACTICE 44: *Participial Phrases: Active Voice*

STEP 1 Rewrite each sentence, changing the relative clause to a participial phrase.

STEP 2 Use the same punctuation as in the original sentence.

1. Robotics is a complex field which combines electronics, computer science, and mechanical engineering.

   ____

   ____

2. The number of scientists who are working in the field of artificial intelligence is relatively small.

   ____

   ____

3. In the future, robots that will work in assembly plants will be equipped with visual and tactile* senses.

   ____

   ____

4. Robots, which have the ability to withstand extreme temperatures and radiation levels, can perform jobs that are too dangerous for humans.

   ____

   ____

tactile: related to the sense of touch

5. Robots, which do not need to eat or sleep, can work nonstop.

General Forms in the Passive Voice

The next sets of sentences show the general participial forms in the passive voice. Again, the relative clause in sentence a has been changed to a participial phase in sentence b.

Notice that the general form in the passive can be formed from present or past tense verbs.

1. **a.** Children under the age of sixteen may not be admitted to movies that are rated X by the Film Censorship Board.
   b. Children under the age of sixteen may not be admitted to movies rated X by the Film Censorship Board.
2. **a.** The president, who was surrounded by bodyguards, was only slightly wounded in the assassination* attempt.
   b. The president, surrounded by bodyguards, was only slightly wounded in the assassination attempt.

The Continuous Form

The continuous form emphasizes that the action is happening now (and, less frequently, in the future). It uses only one form of the verb *to be* as an auxiliary: *being.* Notice in these sentences how relative clauses have been changed to the passive continuous form of the participial phrase.

1. **a.** The law that is currently being debated is about abortion.
   b. The law currently being debated is about abortion.
2. **a.** The circulars that were being distributed on campus support a woman's right to have an abortion.
   b. The circulars being distributed on campus support a woman's right to have an abortion.
3. **a.** The movie that will be shown tomorrow was made by an anti-abortion group.
   b. The movie being shown tomorrow was made by an anti-abortion group.

PRACTICE 45: *Participial Phrases: Passive Voice*

STEP 1 Rewrite each sentence, changing the relative clause to a participial phrase.

STEP 2 Use the same punctuation as in the original sentence.

STEP 3 Use the continuous form to express action in the participle that is occurring *right now;* otherwise, use the general form.

1. Computers that are known as "expert systems" will combine textbook knowledge and rules of experience to make decisions.

assassination: murder by sudden or secret attack

2. Computers that are programmed to diagnose* diseases accurately are an important development for doctors.

3. The use of artificial intelligence that is now being developed has created excitement in the field of robotics.

4. Robots that are currently being designed will do many dangerous jobs in the American workplace.

5. There are a variety of robots that are equipped with sensors to see, read, touch, hear, and smell.

Perfect Forms

Perfect forms, whether active or passive, emphasize the completion of that action before the action of the main verb.

1. **a.** The secrets of the universe, which have fascinated men for centuries, are slowly being revealed. (present perfect, active)
   b. The secrets of the universe, having fascinated men for centuries, are slowly being revealed.
2. **a.** The film, which had been shown too often in movie theaters, did not attract a large audience when it was aired* on television. (past perfect, passive)
   b. The film, having been shown too often in movie theaters, did not attract a large audience when it was aired on television.

PRACTICE 46: *Participial Phrases—The Perfect Forms*

STEP 1 Rewrite each sentence, changing the relative clause to a perfect participial phrase, as in the examples above.

STEP 2 Use the same punctuation as in the original sentence.

1. American blacks, who for 200 years have had little political power, saw hope in Jesse Jackson.

2. Jesse Jackson, who received over seven million votes in the 1988 primary elections,* almost became the candidate of the Democratic Party.

diagnose: identify **aired:** broadcast
primary elections: elections at which voters elect political party candidates for the main elections

3. Jackson, who has always been a spokesman for poor and working class people, won many white as well as black votes.

____

____

4. This remarkable man, who had never been elected to public office before, at first had difficulty getting financial support for his campaign.

____

____

5. By the end of the primary election period, however, Jackson, who had won primary elections in several states, began to receive large donations.

____

____

Punctuating Participial Phrases

Punctuating participial phrases is the same as for relative clauses; that is, it depends on whether the participial phrase is restrictive or nonrestrictive.

A *restrictive* participial phrase is not set off with commas because it is necessary to correctly identify the noun phrase it modifies:

A person belonging to the Sierra Club can participate in many outdoor activities.

Students hoping to graduate next semester must file petitions for graduation now.

A *nonrestrictive* participial phrase is set off by commas because it gives unnecessary additional information about the noun it modifies:

The Browns, belonging to the Sierra Club, participate in many outdoor activities.

Bob, hoping to graduate next semester, filed his petition for graduation today.

The position of the participial phrase depends on whether it is restrictive or nonrestrictive. A restrictive participial phrase follows the word it modifies:

The computer science course offered this semester is COBOL.
The instructor teaching the course is a systems specialist.

A nonrestrictive participial phrase may be in the following positions.

1. At the beginning of a sentence, before the noun it modifies:

   Working on computers for cars, the American car industry will soon put electronic controls into every new automobile.

2. In the middle of a sentence, after the noun it modifies:

   These future cars, using safer fuels, will pollute the air less.

3. At the end of a sentence if it modifies the entire sentence:

   The jury's verdict* was guilty, shocking the defendant.*

---

verdict: decision, especially in a trial **defendant:** a person on trial

PRACTICE 47: *Participial Phrases—Mixed Forms*

STEP 1 Rewrite the following sentences, changing the relative clauses to participial phrases.

STEP 2 Use the same punctuation (commas or no commas) as in the original sentence.

STEP 3 Use the appropriate participle form (active or passive—general, continuous, or perfect).

STEP 4 If it is possible, write each sentence twice: once with the participial phrase after the noun it modifies and once with the participial phrase at the beginning of the sentence.

Example:

Alaska, which was purchased from Russia in 1867, became the 49th state of the United States in 1959.

a. *Alaska, purchased from Russia in 1867, became the 49th state of the United States in 1959.*

b. *Purchased from Russia in 1867, Alaska became the 49th state of the United States in 1959.*

1. The purchase of Alaska, which was negotiated by Secretary of State Seward, became a good investment.

a. ____________________

b. ____________________

2. The people of the United States, who did not understand the value of the purchase, called it "Seward's Folly."*

a. ____________________

b. ____________________

3. The state, which was once connected to Russia by a land bridge, is now separated from it by only a few miles of water.

a. ____________________

b. ____________________

4. The native inhabitants of Alaska, who had migrated across this land bridge from Asia, can be considered distant cousins of modern Asians.

a. ____________________

b. ____________________

---

folly: silly act, foolishness

5. The Eskimos, who have lived in Alaska for millions of years, have adapted well to their harsh environment.

 a. ____

 ____

 b. ____

 ____

6. The Eskimos have to live in cold and darkness most of the year, which causes them to develop a lively sense of humor and a hospitable* attitude.

 a. ____

 ____

 b. ____

 ____

7. The Eskimos, who had been hunters and fishermen before the arrival of the white man, are experiencing a difficult time adapting to modern ways.

 a. ____

 ____

 b. ____

 ____

8. A problem that is being discussed by the Alaskan government concerns the rights of Alaska's natives.

 a. ____

 ____

 b. ____

 ____

9. Those Eskimos who want to preserve their traditional way of life do not care about the modern world.

 a. ____

 ____

 b. ____

 ____

10. On the other hand, Eskimos who want to improve their standard of living hope that they can combine both worlds—old and new.

 a. ____

 ____

 b. ____

 ____

PRACTICE 48: *Participial Phrases—Mixed Forms*

Rewrite the following sentences, using participial phrases.

STEP 1 Change the relative clause into a participial phrase.

STEP 2 Combine the participial phrase with the independent clause. Use different positions for the nonrestrictive participial phrases.

STEP 3 Punctuate the participial phrase if necessary.

---

hospitable: welcoming, friendly toward strangers

Example:

Thousands of people work with everyday issues and problems.
(who are currently employed as computer programmers)

Thousands of people currently employed as computer programmers work with everyday issues and problems.

1. A new computer is for household use.
(that is being advertised)

2. A home computer can perform many time-consuming tasks.
(which will free individuals to do other things)

3. Some people do not want one in their homes.
(who are frightened by the complexity of the computer)

4. They may be afraid that the computer will take control of their lives.
(who have seen the movie *2001*)

5. They may be right, for computerized robots are already being used in many factories. (which are programmed to perform complex functions)

6. In addition, many aspects of business can be computerized.
(which include accounting systems, inventory control, and statistics)

7. In the schools, computers can teach students many subjects.
(which will replace the need for personal contact with a tutor)

8. A big breakthrough in computer technology was the microprocessor, or "computer chip." (that was developed in the 1970s)

9. Information can now be put into a piece of silicon* no larger than the head of a nail. (which formerly required miles of computer tape)

10. Furthermore, the price of computers will be even less in the future. (which has fallen for a number of years)

SENTENCE PRACTICE

Write ten sentences containing participial phrases. First, write ten sentences that contain relative clauses. Then, change the relative clause to a participial phrase and rewrite your sentence. You should have a total of twenty sentences.

Participial Phrases from Adverbial Clauses

Participial phrases can also be formed from certain adverbial clauses, but only from those dealing with time and reason. (See Chapter 13.)

Participial Phrases from Time Clauses

Adverbial clauses introduced by the time subordinators *after, while, when, before, since,* and *as* may be reduced to participial phrases if the subjects of the adverbial clause and the independent clause are the same. One of those subordinators must be removed from the phrase; others must be removed in certain situations.

To change a time adverbial clause into a participial phrase:

1. Make sure that the subjects of the adverbial clause and the independent clause are the same.

> While high technology is creating new production methods, it is also causing unemployment.

The subject the time clause, *high technology*, and the subject of the independent clause, *it*, refer to the same thing.

2. Move the subject of the time clause and move it to the subject position in the independent clause.

> While high technology is creating new production methods, ~~it~~ is also causing unemployment.

3. Change the verb to the appropriate participle.

> While creating new production methods, high technology is also causing unemployment.

silicon: nonmetallic element

4. Delete or retain the time subordinator according to the following rules:
   a. *Before* and *since* must be retained.
   b. *As* must be deleted.
   c. *After, while,* and *when* must be retained if the participial phrase follows the independent clause; otherwise, they may be omitted.

A participial phrase reduced from an adverbial clause may occupy several positions in a sentence. If it precedes the independent clause, it must be followed by a comma. If it follows the independent clause, no comma is necessary. Also, the subordinator is usually retained.

It is also possible to place a participial phrase formed from an adverbial clause immediately after the subject noun phrase. In this position, it acts as a participial phrase formed from an adjective clause. It is separated from the independent clause by commas, and it follows the rules given above for deletion or retention of the subordinator.

The samples below show how a time adverbial clause can be changed into a participial phrase.

1. While the president was traveling in Europe, he met many important political leaders.
   a. While traveling in Europe, the president met many important political leaders.
   b. Traveling in Europe, the president met many important political leaders.
   c. The president met many important political leaders while traveling in Europe.
   d. The president, while traveling in Europe, met many important political leaders.
   e. The president, traveling in Europe, met many important political leaders.
2. After the president had visited Europe, he flew on to the Middle East.
   a. After having visited Europe, the president flew on to the Middle East. (Also possible: After visiting Europe, the president flew on to the Middle East. The general form of the participle is possible here as long as the time subordinator *after* is retained. Because *after* already indicates the correct time relationship, the perfect participle form is not needed.)
   b. Having visited Europe, the president flew on to the Middle East.
   c. The president flew on to the Middle East after having visited Europe.
3. When the president's plane landed in Cairo, it lost a wheel and almost crashed.
   a. When landing in Cairo, the president's plane lost a wheel and almost crashed.
   b. Landing in Cairo, the president's plane lost a wheel and almost crashed.
   c. The president's plane lost a wheel and almost crashed when landing in Cairo.
4. As the First Lady was stepping off the plane, she stumbled and almost fell.
   a. Stepping off the plane, the First Lady stumbled and almost fell.
   b. The First Lady stumbled and almost fell stepping off the plane.

   (***Note:*** The subordinator *as* must be deleted even when the participial phrase follows the independent clause.)

5. Before they were driven away in a limousine, the president and his wife were greeted by a group of government officials.
   a. Before being driven away in a limousine, the president and his wife were greeted by a group of government officials.

   (***Note:*** The continuous form of the participle seems to be preferred when it is derived from a passive verb in time clauses. Additional examples: after I was asked = after being asked; before they were served = before being served; after they are born = after being born.)

   b. The president and his wife were greeted by a group of government officials before being driven away in a limousine.
6. Since the president left Washington, he has traveled more than 50,000 miles.
   a. Since leaving Washington, the president has traveled more than 50,000 miles.
   b. The president has traveled more than 50,000 miles since leaving Washington.

PRACTICE 49: *Participial Phrases from Time Clauses*

STEP 1 Rewrite the following sentences, changing the adverbial time clauses to participial phrases.

STEP 2 Write each new sentence in as many ways as possible, following the examples above, and punctuate them correctly.

1. While people were watching the launch of the space shuttle Columbia on television, they felt as tense and excited as the spectators at Cape Canaveral.
   a. ______________________________
   b. ______________________________
   c. ______________________________
2. Since the Americans landed on the moon in 1969, they have been steadily losing the "space race" to the Russians.
   a. ______________________________
   b. ______________________________
   c. ______________________________

3. As the space shuttle Columbia orbited the globe every 90 minutes, it followed an almost circular path.

a. __________

b. __________

c. __________

4. Before the astronauts returned to Earth, they had been busy testing fire control rockets at regular intervals.*

a. __________

b. __________

c. __________

5. After many world leaders had witnessed America's success in space, they sent messages of congratulations.

a. __________

b. __________

c. __________

6. When we saw the Columbia coming in for a landing in the California desert, we celebrated with a bottle of champagne.

a. __________

b. __________

c. __________

---

intervals: periods of time

SENTENCE PRACTICE

STEP 1 Write six sentences containing adverbial clauses of time. Use each of the following time subordinators once: *before, after, while, when, since,* and *as.*

STEP 2 Change the adverbial clause into a participial phrase and rewrite each sentence in at least two ways.

Participial Phrases from Reason Clauses

Reason adverbial clauses introduced by the subordinators *because, since,* and *as* may also be reduced to participial phrases. Here, however, the subordinator *must* be deleted. To change an adverbial clause of reason to a participial phrase:

1. Make sure that the subjects of the adverbial clause and the independent clause are the same.

   Because American industry is competing with high quality foreign imports, it must raise its standards of quality.

   The subject of the reason clause *American industry* and the subject of the independent clause *it* refer to the same thing.

2. Move the subject of the reason clause to the subject position in the independent clause.

   Because American industry is competing with high-quality foreign imports, it must raise its standards of quality.

3. Always delete the reason subordinator.
4. Change the verb to the appropriate participle.

   Competing with high-quality foreign imports, American industry must raise its standards of quality.

A reason participial phrase may come before or after the independent clause. However, putting the phrase *before* the independent clause is preferred. In both positions, it is separated by a comma. See how this is done in the examples below.

1. Because Carlos had only recently arrived in this country, he didn't speak English fluently.
   - **a.** Having only recently arrived in this country, Carlos didn't speak English fluently.
   - **b.** Carlos didn't speak English fluently, having only recently arrived in this country.
2. As he had never been away from home before, he was a little homesick at first.
   - **a.** Never having been away from home before, he was a little homesick at first.
   - **b.** He was a little homesick at first, never having been away from home before.
3. Since he didn't know anything about the area, he decided to live in a college dormitory for a while.
   - **a.** Not knowing anything about the area, he decided to live in a college dormitory for a while.
   - **b.** He decided to live in a college dormitory for a while, not knowing anything about the area.

PRACTICE 50: *Participial Phrases from Reason Clauses*

Rewrite the following sentences, changing the adverbial reason clauses to participial phrases. Write each sentence only once, with the participial phrase in front of the independent clause.

1. Because Carlos came from a very conservative family, he was shocked at the American system of coed* dormitories.

____

____

____

2. As he ~~had~~ having lived never shared living space with people outside his family, he felt very strange at first.

____

____

____

3. Carlos didn't understand the American students' attitude toward coed living since he came from a different culture.

____

____

____

SENTENCE PRACTICE

STEP 1 Write three sentences with reason adverbial clauses on a topic of your choice, using each of the reason subordinators once.

STEP 2 Change the adverbial clause to a participial phrase and rewrite each sentence. Place the participial phrase in front of the adverbial clause.

PRACTICE 51: *Time and Reason Participial Phrases*

Rewrite the following sentences using participial phrases of time or reason.

STEP 1 Change the adverbial clause into a participial phrase.

STEP 2 Move the noun phrase in the adverbial clause to the subject position in the independent clause.

STEP 3 Combine the participial phrase with the independent clause, deleting the subordinator and adding commas if necessary.

Example:

As the students were listening intently to the professor's lecture, they took notes rapidly.

Listening intently to the professor's lecture, the students took notes rapidly.

____

coed: men and women

1. While the scientist spoke about solar power satellites of the future, he showed many slides.

2. Since the federal government disclosed* the hazards of an energy shortage, it has been working closely with industry.

3. As the people are excited about new space technology, they enjoy seeing spectacular movies about adventures in space.

4. As we are approaching the twenty-first century, we are facing many more exciting technological challenges.

5. People wasted a tremendous amount of natural resources because they did not realize that a serious shortage would result.

6. Since the public realized the problems of the gas shortage, it has made every effort to stop unnecessary waste.

PRACTICE 52: *Participial Phrases from Relative and Adverbial Clauses*

Read the following sentences and underline the participial phrases. In the blank space, name the origin of the participial phrase—adverbial clause or relative (adjective) clause. Some could be either.

Example:
Although NASA engineers have spent ten years on the development of the tiles used on the Columbia space shuttle, they must still work out some imperfections.
Relative clause

1. Having waited for hours for the launching of the Columbia, the spectators screamed with joy as the space shuttle blasted off into space. ________
2. After traveling through space for two and one half days, the Columbia ended its flight in the California desert. ________
3. While crossing the California coast and coming in for a landing, the Columbia's course was being watched by the flight controllers on video display screens. ________
4. After watching the landing of the Columbia on television, the president sent a congratulatory message to the astronauts. ________

disclosed: revealed

5. The space shuttle Columbia, launched from Florida's Cape Canaveral on April 12 and November 12, 1981, was termed a 100 percent success.
   ____

6. Having returned safely, the spaceplane is going to be prepared for several more missions. ____________________

Participial Phrases from Simple Sentences

You have learned that participial phrases can be formed from relative clauses and adverbial clauses. Participial phrases can also be used to combine simple sentences that have the same subject. Here are some examples.

1. **a.** Laser-light shows were shown at many concerts. They produced exciting designs with colored lights.
   b. Laser-light shows, producing exciting designs with colored lights, were shown at many concerts.
2. **a.** Lasers can blister and burn the retina* of the eyes. They produce intense beams of light.
   b. Lasers, producing intense beams of light, can blister and burn the retina of the eyes.
3. **a.** Laser beams can cause instant and permanent damage. They are directed or reflected into the human eye.
   b. Laser beams directed or reflected into the human eye can cause instant and permanent damage.

P R A C T I C E 5 3 : *Participial Phrases from Simple Sentences*

Combine the sentences in each set into one sentence by using participial phrases.

Example:

Robots are able to think and perform tedious* tasks. They will become more widely used in the 21st century.

Robots, being able to think and perform tedious tasks, will become more widely used in the 21st century.

or

Being able to think and perform tedious tasks, robots will become more widely used in the 21st century.

1. Engineers are working on a robot.
   It is designed to be a lifeguard in space.

   ____

   ____

2. EVA Retriever Robot is programmed as a lifeguard.
   It can save an astronaut. The astronaut is drifting in space.

   ____

   ____

---

retina: back of the eyeball **tedious:** repetitive

3. EVA is a large metallic robot.
It is equipped with two mechanical arms.

____

____

4. A robot is programmed to understand human speech.
It will be operated by voice command.

____

____

5. Engineers are working on a prototype* of EVA.
They have an intense interest in retriever-type robots.

____

____

PRACTICE 54: *Writing Participial Phrases*

STEP 1 Rewrite the statements in parentheses as participial phrases; add subordinators where possible.

STEP 2 Punctuate the sentences correctly.

I had an extraordinary dream last week. In my dream, I was a flight attendant on a plane ______________________ (that was flying over the Pacific Ocean to Hawaii). The flight attendants and I were going up and down the aisle ______________________ (We were making sure the passengers were comfortable.) ______________ . Suddenly, two gunmen appeared out of nowhere. One of them went to the back of the plane while the other one ______________ (who rushed up to the front) ordered everyone to freeze.* ______________________ (Because some of the passengers were terrified and shaken by the gunmen's sudden appearance) ______________________ some of the passengers began screaming. ______________________ (While I tried to calm them down) I waited for a chance to grab one of the gunmen's weapons. ______________ (Because I saw one gunman go into the pilot's cabin) ______________ I decided to bring the other one a cup of coffee. ______________ (While I was approaching him with the coffee) ______________ I was smiling. ______________ (He thought that I had brought the coffee for him) ______________ he smiled back. At that moment, I threw the hot coffee in his

____

prototype: the first model of an invention **freeze:** slang expression for "Don't move!"

face. ____________ (When the flight attendants saw what I had done) the flight attendants quickly jumped on him ____________ (They grabbed his gun.).

Then, I quickly ran into the pilot's cabin with the gun in my hand. ____________ (When I opened the door) I saw the gunman ____________ (who was holding his weapon to the pilot's head). "Drop your gun!" I demanded. ____________ (He was surprised.) he quickly turned around. ____________ (Before he dropped his gun) the gunman shot me in the arm and tried to shoot me again. But I returned his fire* first, and he dropped his gun to the floor. ____________ (Because we were wounded by the gunfire) both the gunman and I were bleeding. The gunman ____________ (who was quickly overtaken by the co-pilot), gave up without a struggle.

While the plane was landing at the Honolulu airport, I heard Hawaiian music. Just then, I woke up. I heard my clock radio ____________ (which was playing the same song) I had heard in my exciting dream.

PRACTICE 55: *Using Participial Phrases*

The following paragraphs contain simple sentences and complex sentences with relative clauses and adverbial clauses; however, they do not contain any participial phrases. Your task is to rewrite the paragraphs, adding participial phrases. See how many participial phrase sentences you can create.

(1) The Soviet Union has an outstanding manned space flight program. (2) The Soviet space ship Soyuz TM-3 was launched into orbit on February 6, 1987. (3) It returned to Earth on December 30, 1987, after it had been in space for 326 days. (4) The space ship was destined for a long life. (5) It carried three cosmonauts, Yuri Romanenko, a flight engineer, and a test pilot. Romanenko and his colleagues,* who set an endurance* record in space, felt well after their record space voyage. (6) During his flight, Romanenko, who conducted more than 1,000 experiments in biology, medicine, materials processing, and geology, gathered data about the remote areas of the universe. (7) The endurance tests that were conducted on this voyage have produced an abundance of evidence about weightlessness on the human body.

(8) Soviet scientists are studying the development of irritability and "cabin fever"* among cosmonauts who are forced to live in the close quarters of a space ship for months. (9) These problems must be solved before the Soviets' goal of a manned flight to Mars can be met. (10) It is

---

returned fire: shot back
colleagues: co-workers
endurance: the power to withstand hardship or stress
cabin fever: a condition of increased anxiety and boredom caused by living in confined space for a period of time

planned for early in the 21st century. (11) Scientists, who are excited about the trip to Mars, estimate the round trip will take about three years. (12) Because Soviet scientists are aware of the physical effects of a long space mission, they must solve these problems before the Mars mission.

WRITING PRACTICE

Write one or two paragraphs, using as many participial phrases as you can. Choose your topic from the selection below.

1. Write your autobiography. Include some interesting comments about yourself; don't just state the basic facts.

   Being an only child, I became very spoiled at an early age.
   Having finished high school with excellent grades, I was sent to continue my studies abroad.

2. Write about a frightening or exciting experience, real or imaginary.

   Suddenly realizing that a burglar was in my apartment, I started screaming, hoping that the neighbors would hear me.

Gerunds

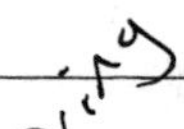

A gerund is a word formed from a verb that ends in *-ing*: *studying, working, speaking.* It is always used as a noun in both subject and object positions.

> Studying English is difficult. (subject position)
> The students enjoy studying. (object position)
> I am interested in applying for a job. (object of preposition)

If the gerund has a definite subject before it, the possessive form is used in both subject and object positions.

> John's winning the scholarship to Oxford University didn't really surprise us.
> His winning the scholarship to Oxford University didn't really surprise us.
> We just heard about John's winning a scholarship to Oxford University.

Gerunds Used as Subjects

A gerund phrase can be used as a subject of a sentence.

> Drinking too much beer is unwise.
> Drinking and smoking are harmful to your health.

PRACTICE 56: *Gerunds in Subject Position*

Combine the following sentences into one sentence.

STEP 1 Change the first sentence into a subject gerund phrase. If it has a definite subject, change it to a possessive.

STEP 2 Combine it with the verb in the second sentence and rewrite it as one sentence.

Example:

I am taking financial accounting. It requires a lot of studying.

Taking financial accounting requires a lot of studying.

1. The company promotes beer sales on college campuses.
   It encourages students to drink.

2. It encourages students to drink. It isn't a good idea.

3. They post flyers on safe drinking in the student union.
   That will hopefully lessen overdrinking.

4. The students drink in dormitories. It shouldn't be allowed

5. However, they find ways to break the rules. That is never a problem for students.

SENTENCE PRACTICE

Write six sentences using gerund phrases in subject position.

Gerunds Used as Objects

In addition to being used as subjects, gerunds can also be used as objects when they follow certain verbs. Common verbs that can be followed by gerunds include:

admit	deny	keep (on)	quit
appreciate	discuss	miss	recall
avoid	enjoy	plan	stop
consider	finish	practice	take up
delay	give up	put off	understand

Don't avoid taking responsibility for your actions.
Tony enjoys jogging around the lake every day.
He should quit smoking immediately.

PRACTICE 57: *Gerunds in Object Position*

Complete the following sentences with a gerund (phrase) in object position. Choose a word from the list below.

go	work	choose	earn	relocate
look	make	study	move	interview

1. John graduated from college last semester. He discussed ______________________ for a job with Professor Thompson.
2. The professor advised him to consider ______________________ a company with international branches.
3. John thought he would enjoy ______________________ with such a company.
4. But he delayed ______________________ a decision until he had thought it over for a while.
5. Because John enjoyed ______________________ Japanese at the university, he decided ______________________ to go to Japan.

SENTENCE PRACTICE

Choosing verbs from the list on page 249, write six sentences using gerund phrases in object position.

Gerunds as Objects of Prepositions

Gerunds are also used as objects of prepositions in the same way that nouns are used. Gerunds occur frequently after certain verb + preposition combinations, including:

be aware of	be concerned about	insist on
be fond of	think about	put off
be interested in	think of	call on
be accustomed to	talk about	be capable of
be capable of	look forward to	

John is thinking about looking for a job this summer.
He is interested in going to a foreign country.

PRACTICE 58: *Gerunds as Objects of Prepositions*

STEP 1 Add the correct preposition in the blank.

STEP 2 Choose an appropriate word from the list below and add its gerund form after the preposition.

drink	reform	overdrink	permit	allow	stop
see	halt	change	watch	ban	prohibit
advertise					

Example:

The U.S. Surgeon General is aware _of_ _drinking_ by young people.

1. He talked ______ ______ the way alcohol is promoted in the United States.
2. Young people are accustomed ______ ______ beer commercials on TV.
3. Consumer and public health activists are thinking ______ ______ the sale of alcoholic beverages on campus.
5. They have insisted ______ ______ campus marketing of alcohol to reduce alcohol abuse.
6. My roommates are accustomed ______ ______ a few beers every day.

SENTENCE PRACTICE

Write six sentences using gerunds after prepositions.

Review

These are the important points you should have learned from this chapter.

Participles

1. Participles are adjectives formed from verbs. Some participles are from active voice verbs:

   The baby cried. ... the crying baby
   The speaker bored the audience. ... the boring speaker

   Some participle forms are from passive voice verbs:

   The soldier was wounded. ... the wounded soldier
   The audience was bored by the speaker. ... the bored audience

   The five commonly used participle forms and the times they indicate are shown in the chart below:

Participle Forms

Forms	Active	Passive
General—no time indicated	speaking	spoken
Continuous—current time (right now) and future		being spoken
Perfect—time before that of the main verb	having spoken	having been spoken

2. Participial phrases may be formed by reducing relative clauses.

   The audience, which was listening intently to the music, failed to notice the fire that started to smolder* in the back of the auditorium.
   The audience, listening intently to the music, failed to notice the fire starting to smolder in the back of the auditorium.
   (also)
   Listening intently to the music, the audience . . .

   A nonrestrictive participial phrase ("listening intently to the music") may precede or follow the noun it modifies and is set off by commas. A nonrestrictive participial phrase may also modify an entire sentence, in which case it comes at the end of the sentence and is set off by a comma.

   A restrictive participial phrase ("starting to smolder") must follow the noun it modifies and is not set off by commas.

3. Participial phrases may also be reduced from time and reason adverbial clauses.

   a. Time clauses:

Time clauses:	Participial phrases:
While we were waiting . . .	While waiting . . .
Before he came . . .	Before coming . . .
After they had finished . . .	After finishing . . .
(also)	Having finished . . .
Since I arrived . . .	Since arriving . . .

   Participial phrases reduced from time clauses may occupy various positions in a sentence, and the time coordinators are sometimes deleted and sometimes retained.

   b. Reason clauses:

Reason clauses:	Participial phrases:
Because I wanted . . .	Wanting . . .
Since I had arrived . . .	Having arrived . . .
As he had been killed . . .	Having been killed . . .

   Participial phrases reduced from reason clauses may come before or after the independent clause in a sentence and must be set off by commas. Reason subordinators are always deleted.

Gerunds

Gerunds are nouns formed from *-ing* verbs. Like nouns, gerunds may be subjects or objects.

Writing is a learnable skill. (subject)
Not many students enjoy writing. (direct object)
Americans are accustomed to eating their main meal in the evening, whereas Europeans are used to eating it at noon. (object of preposition)

---

smolder: burn without flame

APPENDIX A
Punctuation

Commas

Commas function in four ways:

1. as *introducers,*
2. as *coordinators* in compound sentences,
3. as *inserters,* and
4. as *linkers.*

Let's start by analyzing how commas relate to the main (or independent) clauses of a sentence. Notice below how the additional words, phrases, or clauses modify the main clause.

Introducer:

_______, [MAIN CLAUSE]

Recently, the legislature banned smoking in public places.

Coordinator:

[MAIN CLAUSE], (COORDINATING CONJUNCTION) [MAIN CLAUSE]

Many people opposed the new law, but it finally passed.

Our thanks to Anne Katz of ARC Associates, Oakland, California for permission to adapt her presentation of comma rules.

Inserter:

MAIN , ______________ , CLAUSE

Smallpox, once a widespread disease, is under control.

Linker:

1. MAIN CLAUSE , ______

The word *color* is spelled *colour* in British English, for example.

2. ______ [ ], [ ], [ ], ______.

Cecile speaks English, French, Spanish, and Italian.

Introducers

A comma is used after introductory words, phrases and clauses.

Words: However, the new law was largely ignored by the public.
Phrases: As a result, an even stricter law was proposed.
After a long vacation, he returned to work.
Having studied very hard, she passed the exam easily.
Clauses: Because he had missed so many classes, he had to drop the course.
Appositives: An old man, my grandfather can barely walk.

Coordinators

A comma is used between two independent clauses joined by the FAN BOYS coordinating conjunctions *for, and, nor, but, or, yet,* and *so* to form compound sentences.

for Your decision is important, for our future plans depend on it.
and The exam was quite easy, and most students passed.
nor He didn't come to class during the last three weeks, nor did he take the final exam.
but The exam was quite easy, but most students failed.
or Will you write your thesis this semester, or will you wait until next semester?
yet The experiment was considered successful, yet the results were disappointing.
so He didn't study, so he didn't pass the course.

Note: *Nor* is a troublemaker. It is a negative word, and it signals inverted word order. The verb must come before the subject. Also, do not confuse compound sentences with simple sentences that have two verbs. A compound sentence has two subjects and two verbs:

She asked the question, and she answered it in the same breath. (comma necessary)

A simple sentence can also have two verbs, but it has only one subject:

She asked the question and answered it in the same breath. (no comma)

Inserters

A comma is used before and after words, phrases and clauses that are inserted into the middle of a main clause.

Transitions:	The new law, however, was largely ignored by the public.
	The students, on the other hand, felt that the test was unfair.
	The computer, for example, has positive and negative uses.
Appositives:	My grandfather, an old man, can barely walk.
	Dr. Danielson, a professor in the English Department, has written several books.
	Dr. William Porter, a professor at Boston University, suggested in his article, "The Effects of Marijuana on Motor Responses," that pot-smokers'* reactions are slower.
Nonrestrictive Clauses:	Income taxes, which all people who receive an income must pay, are due on April 15 every year.
	My husband, who used to smoke three packs of cigarettes a day, has stopped smoking.

Linkers

A comma is used (a) when adding words and phrases at the end of a sentence and (b) when linking items in a series.

Transitions:	The new law was largely ignored by the public, however.
	I do, too.
Items in a series	Cholera, smallpox, yellow fever, and diphtheria are some of the diseases that have been conquered in this century.
	A nurse has to be willing to work at night, on weekends, and on holidays.
	We ran into the airport, checked our luggage, raced to the boarding area, gave the attendant our tickets, and collapsed* in our seats.

PRACTICE 1: *Using Commas*

STEP 1 Add commas wherever they are necessary. (Not all sentences need them.)

STEP 2 Name the function of each comma (introducer, coordinator, inserter, or linker).

FUNCTION

_____ **1.** The advertising industry which is one of the largest industries in the United States employs millions of people and spends billions of dollars.

_____ **2.** A company that wants to be successful must spend a great deal of money to advertise its products.

_____ **3.** Advertising is essential to the free enterprise system yet it can sometimes be very annoying.

_____ **4.** Every minute of the day and night people are exposed to ads on television on billboards in the newspapers and in magazines.

_____ **5.** You can't even avoid advertising in the privacy of your own car or your own home for advertisers have begun selling their products in those places too.

_____ **6.** In the last few years advertising agencies have started to hire young people to hand out circulars on street-corners and in parking lots.

---

pot-smoker: marijuana smoker **collapsed:** fell down

____ 7. You can often find these circulars stuck on your windshield thrust* through the open windows of your car stuffed in your mailbox or simply scattered on your front doorstep.

____ 8. Because Americans are exposed to so much advertising they have become immune* to it.

____ 9. As a result advertisers have to make louder commercials use brighter colors and hire sexier models to catch the public's attention.

____ 10. Many people object especially to commercials that use sex as a sales strategy.

____ 11. Sexy commercials that sell everything from toothpaste to automobiles seem to imply that you will become sexier if you buy the product.

____ 12. Sex is used in many cigarette and liquor ads for example.

____ 13. The women in such ads are often dressed in revealing clothes and are surrounded by handsome men and the men in such ads are always extremely handsome and virile.

____ 14. As everyone knows smoking and drinking do not make you sexy or virile.

____ 15. On the contrary drinking makes you fat and smoking makes you sick.

____ 16. The government is considering a ban on sex in cigarette and liquor ads because of their potentially harmful effect on teenagers.

____ 17. The government is considering a ban but no action has been taken yet.

____ 18. If such action is taken my boyfriend the Marlboro man will be out of a job.

____ 19. Catherine Deneuve who sells automobiles and perfume would lose some work too.

Semicolons

Using **semicolons** is not difficult if you remember that a semicolon (;) is more like a period than a comma. It is a very strong punctuation mark. Semicolons are used in three places:

1. Between two sentences that are closely connected in idea.
2. Before conjunctive adverbs and some transitional phrases.
3. Between items in a series if the items already contain commas.

Between Sentences

Use a semicolon at the end of a sentence when the following sentence is closely connected in meaning. You could also use a period, but when the sentences are connected in meaning, it is better to use a semicolon.

INDEPENDENT CLAUSE	;	INDEPENDENT CLAUSE
Alice is going to Harvard;		she isn't going to M.I.T.
Computer use is increasing;		computer crime is, too.
The meeting adjourned* at dawn;		nothing had been accomplished.

thrust: pushed forcefully **adjourned:** ended
immune: cannot be affected

Before Connectors

Use a semicolon before conjunctive adverbs such as *however, therefore, nevertheless, moreover,* and *furthermore.* You may also use a semicolon before some transitional phrases such as *for example, as a result, that is, in fact,* etc.

		CONJUNCTIVE ADVERB		
INDEPENDENT CLAUSE	;	TRANSITION PHRASE	,	INDEPENDENT CLAUSE

Skiing is dangerous; nevertheless, hundreds of people ski.
Stefi Graf is a great tennis player; moreover, she is attractive.
Boris Becker played well; however, he lost the match.
He had smoked all his life; as a result, he died of lung cancer.
I have never been to Europe; in fact, I have never been outside my country.

Between Items in a Series

Semicolons may be used as well to separate items in a series when some of the items already contain commas.

I cannot decide which car I like best: the Ferrari, with its quick acceleration and ease of handling; the small, conventional Ford, with its reclining bucket seats; or the uncomfortable Volkswagen, with its economical fuel consumption.

PRACTICE 2: *Using Semicolons and Commas*

A. STEP 1 The following sentences need semicolons and commas; add the correct punctuation in the appropriate places.

STEP 2 In the space provided at left, state whether the semicolon is

1. between two closely connected sentences,
2. before a conjunctive adverb or a transition expression, or
3. between items in a series if the items already contain commas.

Example:

__2__ Professor Smith is at a conference; however, Dr. Jones, who is the department chairman, will be glad to see you.

_____ **1.** Grace works for a prestigious law firm she is their top criminal lawyer.

_____ **2.** My favorite leisure-time activities are going to movies especially musicals reading novels* especially stories of love and adventure listening to music both rock and classical and participating in sports particularly tennis and volleyball.

_____ **3.** The future of our wild animals is uncertain for example illegal shooting and chemical poisoning threaten the bald eagle.*

_____ **4.** Homework is boring therefore I never do it.

---

novels: fiction books **bald eagle:** a large bird of prey, symbol of the United States

_____ **5.** The freeways are always crowded during the busy rush hours nevertheless people refuse to take public transportation.

_____ **6.** I like the following foods: ice cream sundaes with lots of hot fudge pizza with garlic and mushrooms and waffles with lots of melted butter and syrup.

_____ **7.** The Smiths' marriage should succeed they share the same interests.

_____ **8.** Hoping that he would pass the course he stayed up all night studying for the final exam unfortunately he overslept and missed the test.

_____ **9.** In general I enjoy my English class the amount of homework our teacher assigns is definitely not enjoyable however.

_____ **10.** If you are a college student, an average day is filled with challenges: you have to avoid running into Professor Jones whose class you missed because you overslept you have to race across the campus at high speed to reach your next class which is always at the other side of the campus and you have to secretly prepare your homework assignment during class hoping all the time that the teacher won't catch you.

B. Punctuate the following sentences by adding semicolons and commas. Use semicolons wherever possible.

1. My bus was late therefore I missed my first class.
2. The politician was discovered accepting bribes as a result his political career was ruined.
3. My father never cries in fact he never shows any emotion at all.
4. The restaurant was closed consequently we went home to eat.
5. Some people feel that grades are unnecessary on the other hand, some people feel that grades motivate students.
6. Technology is changing our lives in insidious* ways for example the computer is replacing human contact.
7. The computer dehumanizes business nevertheless it has some real advantages.
8. Writing essays is easy it just takes a little practice.
9. Americans love pets every family seems to have at least one dog or cat.
10. The life expectancy of Americans is increasing for example the life expectancy of a man born today is 77.2 years which is an increase of 26.12 years since 1900.
11. Your proposal is a good one however I do not completely agree with your final suggestion.
12. Efficiency is a highly prized quality among Americans it has almost attained the status of a moral attribute.*

C. Write three original sentences for each of the three rules for using semicolons:

1. Between closely connected sentences.
2. Before conjunctive adverbs and some transitional phrases.
3. Between items in a series.

---

insidious: secretly harmful **attribute:** characteristic, quality

Colons

A **colon** (:) can be used in five ways:

Lists

Use a colon to introduce a list.

> Libraries have two kinds of periodicals: bound periodicals and current periodicals.
> I need the following groceries: eggs, milk, and coffee.
> The causes of the U.S. Civil War were as follows: the economic domination of the North, the slavery issue, and the issue of states' rights versus federal intervention.

Note: Do *not* use a colon to introduce a list after the verb *to be* unless you add *the following* or *as follows.*

> To me, the most important things in life *are* health, happiness, good friends and a lot of money.
> To me, the most important things in life *are the following:* health, happiness, good friends, and a lot of money.

Long Quotations

Use a colon to introduce a quotation longer than three lines. This type of quote is indented on both sides, and no quotation marks are used.

> As Albert C. Baugh and Thomas Cable state in their book, *The History of the English Language:*
>
> > There is no such thing as uniformity in language. Not only does the speech of one community differ from that of another, but the speech of different individuals of a single community, even different members of the same family, is marked by individual peculiarities.*

Subtitles

Use a colon between the main title and the subtitle of a book, article or play.

> A popular book on nonverbal communication is Samovar and Porter's *Intercultural Communication: A Reader.*
> The name of an article from *The New York Times* is "Space Stations: Dream or Reality?"

Time

Use a colon between the numbers for hours and minutes when indicating the time of day.

> Helen left the class at 12:30.
> Our plane arrived at 1:40, six hours late.

---

peculiarities: strange characteristics

Formal Salutations

Use a colon after the salutation of a formal letter.

Dear Professor Danielson:
Dear Sir:
Gentlemen:
Dear Mrs. Smith:
To Whom It May Concern:

In informal letters, a comma is more appropriate.

Dear Mom,
Darling,
Dear Mark,

PRACTICE 3: ***Using Punctuation Marks***

A. Add commas, semicolons, and colons to the following.

1. The library offers many special services the Student Learning Center where students can receive special tutoring the phonorecord library where you can listen to records and tapes and group study rooms.
2. Dear Dr. Patterson
   Dear Alice
   Dear Mr. Carter
3. To check a book out of the library you should follow this procedure write down the call number of the book find the book bring it to the circulation desk fill out the card and show your student I.D.
4. The principal sources of air pollution in our cities are factories airplanes and automobiles.
5. I have a dental appointment at 330 today. Please pick me up at 300.

B. Write a sentence in which you list two pieces of advice that you have received from your parents. Use a colon to direct attention to them.

____

____

C. Write the title and subtitle of the following book correctly. Remember to underline the full title.

(Title) Paris (Subtitle) A Visitor's Guide to Restaurants

____

____

Quotation Marks

Quotation marks ["..."] have three basic functions:

Direct Quote

Use quotation marks to enclose a direct quotation that is shorter than three lines. A direct quotation states the *exact* words of a speaker.

Punctuation with quotation marks can be a little tricky. Here are some rules to follow:

1. Periods and commas go inside quotation marks.
   "I thought he was responsible," he said, "but he isn't."
2. Colons and semicolons go outside quotation marks.
   "Give me liberty or give me death": these are immortal* words.
3. Exclamation points (!) and question marks (?) go inside quotation marks if they are a part of the quotation; otherwise, they go outside.
   "Is it eight o'clock?" she asked.
   Did she say, "It's eight o'clock"?
4. When a quoted sentence is divided into two parts, the second part begins with a small letter unless it is a new sentence.
   "I thought he was responsible," he said, "but he isn't."
   "I think he is responsible," he said. "Look at his fine work."
5. Use single quotation marks ('. . .') to enclose a quotation within a quotation.
   As John F. Kennedy reminded us in his inaugural address, "We should never forget the words of Martin Luther King, Jr., who said, 'I have a dream.'"

Unusual Words

Use quotation marks to enclose foreign words or words that are used in a special or uncommon way.

A lot of people talk about "machismo" these days, but few people really know what it means.

The "banquet" turned out to be no more than hot dogs and soft drinks.

Titles

Use quotation marks to enclose the titles of (a) articles from periodical journals, magazines, and newspapers; (b) chapters of books; (c) short stories; (d) poems; and (e) songs.

In the article "The Future of Space," published in the July 19, 1974 issue of Scientific American, the authors explore the possibility of manned space stations.

The New York Times recently published an article entitled "Space Stations: Dream or Reality?" in which the potential of space cities in orbit was discussed.

Note: The titles of books, journals, magazines, newspapers, and movies should be underlined or italicized.

PRACTICE 4: *Using Quotation Marks*

Get a copy of any newspaper and write a paragraph about any article. Copy five quotations from the article. Mention the name of the newspaper and the article in your sentence and include the name of the speaker.

---

immortal: long-remembered

APPENDIX B

Chart of Transition Signals

Meaning/ Function	Sentence Connectors[1]	Clause Connectors: Coordinators	Clause Connectors: Subordinators	Others
To introduce an **additional** idea	also, too besides furthermore moreover in addition	and		another (+ noun) an additional (+ noun)
To introduce an **opposite** idea	on the other hand however in contrast instead nevertheless nonetheless	but yet	although though even though whereas while	in spite of (+ noun) despite (+ noun)
To introduce an **example**	for example for instance			an example of (+ noun) such as (+ noun) e.g.
To introduce a **restatement** or **explanation**	indeed			i.e. that is
To introduce a **conclusion** or **summary**	in conclusion in summary to conclude to summarize			

[1]includes conjunctive adverbs

To clarify **chronological order**	first (second, third, fourth, etc.) next, last, finally first of all meanwhile after that since then		before after while until as soon as	the first (+ noun) the second (+ noun) before the (+ noun) in the year since the (+ noun)
To indicate **order of importance**	more important(ly), most important(ly) above all			the most important (+ noun)
To introduce an **alternative**	otherwise	or	if unless	
To introduce a **cause** or **reason**		for	because since as	because of as a result of as a consequence of due to to result from the result of the effect of X on Y the consequence of
To introduce an **effect** or **result**	accordingly as a result as a consequence therefore thus consequently hence	so		the cause of the reason for to result in to cause to have an effect on to affect
To introduce a **comparison**	similarly likewise also too	and	as just as	like just like alike similar (to) the same as both . . . and not only . . . but also to compare to/with
To introduce a **concession**	however nonetheless	but yet	although though even though	despite + noun in spite of + noun
To introduce strong **contrast**	however in contrast in (by) comparison on the other hand on the contrary	but		different from dissimilar unlike to differ from to compare to to compare with

APPENDIX C

Summary of Verb Forms

When you are deciding which verb form, or tense, to use, you should make certain that you do not confuse the words *tense* and *time.* Tense refers to the *form* of a verb, such as eating, has eaten, will eat. *Time* is not a grammatical form; it is a concept existing in the mind of the speaker or writer. There are only three "times"—past, present, and future—but there are many tenses in English. These tenses express the relationships between time and other factors, such as whether the action is completed or still in progress and whether the sentence states a true fact or only a wish.

For example, the verb forms (or tenses) in the four sentences below all express different relationships to present time:

Present Continuous:

He is working for his brother while his brother is in the hospital.

By using the present continuous form, the writer is emphasizing that the action is taking place *now*—during the time that his brother is unable to work—and that it is only a temporary activity.

Simple Present:

He studies during the day and works at night.

By using the simple present form, the writer is telling us that this is a habitual activity which has happened in the past, is happening in the present, and will probably continue to happen in the future.

Present Perfect:

He has lived in the apartment for ten years.

By using the present perfect form, the writer is indicating that the person still lives there now. If the person no longer lived there, the writer would have used the simple past form.

Simple Past:

He lived in the same apartment for ten years.

From these examples, you can see that verb tense and time are not the same thing. Many factors determine the correct verb tense.

The Present Tenses

Simple Present:	SIMPLE FORM	I go.
	SIMPLE FORM + S	He goes.

Simple present states general truths. The time is unimportant.

Heavy rainfall accompanies a hurricane except in the eye,* which remains relatively calm.
The sun rises in the east and sets in the west.

Simple present tense also describes repeated or habitual actions. In this case, an adverb of frequency (*always, often, sometimes, occasionally, seldom, never,* etc.) or other time expressions (*every day, every weekend, daily,* etc.) are often added to indicate the frequency of repetition.

John attends classes three times a week.
Businessmen usually fly to save time.

In addition, the simple present is used with certain non-activity verbs to describe feelings, perceptions, and conditions at the moment of speaking. These verbs are not normally used in the present continuous:

I love you.	Do you believe in God?
I don't understand you.	They need a loan.
He knows the answer.	They want to get married.

Present Continuous:	AM		I am going.
	IS	+ VERB + ING	He is going.
	ARE		We are going.

Present continuous describes a temporary action or condition that is actually taking place at the moment of speaking:

The students are taking a grammar quiz now.
They are writing as fast as they can.

The present continous also describes an action or condition that is currently in progress even if not actually at the moment of speaking:

Scientists are investigating the ocean for new sources of food.
The cost of living is still climbing.

---

eye: the center of a hurricane

Present Perfect: HAS / HAVE + PAST PARTICIPLE — I have gone. He has gone.

Present perfect links the present and the past. It *must* be used for actions and conditions that began in the past and still exist in the present.

I have lived in the same apartment for two years.
They have been married since 1975.

In addition, it *may* be used when the action began in the past and (1) is somehow still important in the present (in the mind of the speaker), (2) happened in the very recent past, or (3) is a recurring action in the past. The simple past may also be used in these three cases.

You have worked very hard this semester.
He has just finished his term paper.
We have moved three times in the past year.

Present Perfect Continuous: HAS / HAVE BEEN + VERB + ING — I have been going. He has been going.

This tense *must* be used to combine a point-in-time action with a period-of-time time expression:

He has been writing this book for a year.
(Not: He has written this book for a year.)
I have been catching a cold for several days.
(Not: I have caught a cold for several days.)

The present perfect continuous *may* be used instead of the present perfect to emphasize the continuous or incomplete nature of an action.

Continuous action:

The price of gas has been rising steadily since the Arab oil embargo precipitated* the energy crisis.
It has been raining all morning.

Incomplete activity:

I have been reading *War and Peace* for several weeks.
(but I haven't finished it yet)
He has been smoking my cigarettes.
(but there are still some left in the package)

The Past Tenses

Simple Past: SIMPLE FORM + ED — He worked.
IRREGULAR PAST FORMS — He went.

The simple past describes an action or event that took place *and was completed* at a definite time in the past. Expression of past time, such as *a week/month/year ago, yesterday,* and *last year,* etc., indicate the simple past:

precipitated: caused to happen suddenly

I saw the opera "Othello" on television last night.
The store installed a small XYZ computer a month ago.
The company doubled its profits in 1990.

Past Continuous: WAS / WERE + VERB + ING He was going. We were going.

This tense describes an incomplete or temporary past action:

The president was talking on the way to the White House.
The little girl was dancing.

In two-clause sentences, past continous also describes a temporary action that was in progress when a second action took place. The second action can either happen at the same time, or it can interrupt the first action:

Use *while* + past continous for the action in progress.
Use *when* + simple past for the interrupting action.

His wife was working to support him while he was attending medical school.
The president was smiling and waving to the crowd when the band struck up.*
While the president was smiling and waving to the crowd, the band struck up.
We were driving across the bridge when it collapsed.
While we were driving across the bridge, it collapsed.

Past Perfect: HAD + PAST PARTICIPLE He had gone.

Past perfect expresses one past time before another past time. Use past perfect when you want to emphasize that one action occurred earlier than another action. The more recent action usually is in the simple past tense.

He drove his car to school because he had missed the bus.
The president did not begin the news conference until the room had become quiet.

Sometimes the more recent action is not expressed.

Until last year, the government had not concerned itself with the problem of illegal aliens.

Past Perfect Continuous: HAD + BEEN + VERB + ING He had been going.

Like the past perfect, past perfect continuous expresses one past time before another past time. However, the continuous tense emphasizes the duration of the earlier action:

We had been waiting for an hour before we were told that the concert had been cancelled.
The president had been speaking for almost two hours when the protesters arrived.
Because he had been working too hard, he was nervous and irritable.

The Future Tenses

Will: WILL + SIMPLE FORM He will go.

This is the most neutral way to express future time:

The government will raise income taxes next year.
The sun will set at exactly 6:48 p.m. tomorrow.

---

struck up: began playing

Going to: IS / ARE + GOING TO + VERB He is going to go.

This form is also used to express future time, especially when the idea of intention or inevitability is involved:

I am going to change my major. (intention)
She is going to have a baby next month. (inevitably)

Present Continuous Future Time: AM / IS / ARE VERB + ING He is going (tomorrow).

The present continuous tense is also used to express future time. Normally, a future time expression (*"tomorrow," "next week," "this evening"*) is necessary to convey the future meaning.

We are leaving on our vacation tomorrow.
I am meeting my advisor at 2:15 this afternoon.

Simple Present Future Time: SIMPLE FORM / SIMPLE FORM + S He leaves (tomorrow).

The simple present tense may also be used to describe future actions in the following three situations:

(a) with verbs like *come, go, arrive, depart, leave* and a future time expression:

The president leaves on his goodwill trip to South America tomorrow.

(b) in time clauses introduced by a time subordinator (*after, before, until,* etc.):

After the president delivers his speech, he will leave for the airport.
I will not receive my degree until I complete my master's thesis.

Note: The present perfect tense may also be used in these time clauses to express future time.

After the president has delivered his speech, he will leave for the airport.
I will not receive my degree until I have completed my master's thesis.

(c) in conditional clauses:

If we finish the project before the end of the term, we won't have to work on it

Future Continuous: WILL + BE + VERB + ING He will be going.

Future continuous describes a future action that will be in progress at a specific time or times in the future.

I will be working on my term paper for the next several weekends.
The children will be sleeping by the time we get home.

Future Perfect: WILL + HAVE + PAST PARTICIPLE He will have gone.

Future perfect describes a future action that precedes another future action.

He will have become a millionaire by the time he is twenty.
The movie will have already started before we get to the theater.

Future Perfect Continuous:	WILL + HAVE + BEEN + VERB + ING	He will have been working.

Future perfect continuous is used to emphasize the *duration* of a future action that occurs before another future action. This tense usually occurs with a "for + period of time" expression.

The movie will have been playing for thirty minutes by the time we get to the theater.

Index

Abbreviations in library references, 148
Academic writing, 2-15, 128
  audience, 2-3
  purpose, 2-3
  review of, 15
  revising drafts, 12-15
  tone, 2-3
  writing process, *see* Processes of writing
Adjective clauses, *see* Relative clauses
Adverbial clauses, 195-207, *see also* Relative clauses
  of concession, 203-204
  definition of, 195
  of distance, 198-199
  of frequency, 198-199
  of manner, 198-199
  of place, 197-198
  punctuation of, 195
  of purpose, 202-203
  of reason, 200
  of result, 201
  review of, 205-207
  of strong contrast, 204-205
  subordinators, chart of, 196
  of time, 196-197
Appositive, use of comma with, 254, 255
Assignment format, 18
Audience, 2-3

Block organization
  cause and effect, 104-106
  comparison and contrast, 122-124
Body, of essay, 76-77
Brackets, use in quotations, 131
Brainstorming, 4-9
Business letter format, 193

Card catalog, 145-147
Cause and effect essay, 104-113
  organization of, 104-107
  structure words for, 108-112
Chain organization, 104, 106-107
Checklist
  essay, 125
  paragraph, 73
Choosing and narrowing a topic, 4
Choppy sentences, 173-174
Chronological order, 53-58
  in essays, 95-100
  organization, 98
  in paragraphs, 53-58
  thesis statements for, 99-100
  topic sentences for, 55-56
  transition signals, chart of, 56
Chronological process essay, 95-100
Citations within text, 141-143
Clauses, 154-156, *see also* Sentences
  adverbial, 195-207
  definition of, 154
  dependent, 45, 155, 162
  independent, 44, 154, 157, 159, 256-257
  noun, 180-194
  relative, 208-228
Clause connectors, 44-45, 155-156
  charts of, 43, 262-263
  coordinating conjunctions (coordinators), 44
  subordinating conjunctions (subordinators), 45
Clustering, 8-9
Coherence, 17, 39-52
  consistent pronouns and, 41
  logical order and, 48-50, 53-64
  repetition of key nouns and, 39-40
  review of, 50
  transition signals and, 41-48; chart of, 43
Colon, 259-260
  in thesis statements, 103
  in topic sentences, 62
Comma, 253-256
  in adverbial clauses, 162, 195
  in compound sentences, 157
  with end-of-paragraph signals, 26
  with nonrestrictive participial phrases, 234
  with nonrestrictive relative clauses, 209-211
  with participial phrases from reason clauses, 242
  with participial phrases from time clauses, 238
  with strong contrast clauses, 204
  with transition words, 43, 254, 255, 257
Comma splice sentences, 175-177
Comparison and contrast essay, 49, 113-125
  comparison structure vocabulary, 115-118
  contrast structure vocabulary, 119-122
  organization of, 122-124

Complex sentences, 161-164
Compound sentences, 157-161, 254
Compound-complex sentences, 164
Computer data banks, 150
Concession clauses, 203-204
Conclusion
  concluding paragraph, 76, 82-83
  concluding sentence, 17, 25-27
  end-of-paragraph, 26
Concrete support, 65-73
  details for, 67-68
  examples and illustrative incidents, 68-70
  facts vs. opinions, 65-66
  figures and statistics, 70-72
  quotations, paraphrases, and summaries, 128-140
  review of, 73
Conjunctions
  coordinating, 44, 156, 157-159, 168, 253-254
  correlative, 62, 103, 168-171
  subordinating, 43, 45, 156, 262-263
Conjunctive adverbs, 42-44, 156, 159-161, 256-257
  chart of, 159
Contrast, 48, 119-125
  concessive structure words, chart of, 119
  strong opposition structure words, chart of, 119
  structure vocabulary, 119-122
Contrast clause, strong, 204-205
Controlling idea, 17, 22-25
Coordinating conjunctions, *see* Conjunctions
Coordination vs. subordination, 165-166
  overcoordination, 165
Coordinators, *see* Coordinating conjunctions
Correlative conjunctions, *see* Conjunctions

Dependent clauses, 45, 155, 162, 164
  adjective (relative), 162
  adverbial, 162, 195-207
  noun, 162, 180-194
  relative, 208-228
Documenting sources, 140-143
  citations within text, 141
  works cited, list of, 141-143
Drafts, writing and revising, 12-15, 89-93

Ellipsis, use in quotations, 131
"Equivalent value" rule, 35-36
Essay, 76-94
  checklist, 94, 125
  concluding paragraph, 82
  definition of, 76
  final copy, 92
  introductory paragraph, 78-81
  outlining, 83-86
  paragraph, correspondence to, 77
  parts of, 76
  review of, 93
  transition signals, 86-89
  writing and revising of, 89-93
Essay patterns of organization, 95-126
  block, 104-106, 122-124
  cause and effect, 104-113
  chain organization, 104, 106-107
  chronological order, 95-100, *see also* Chronological process
  comparison and contrast, 113-115
  logical division, 100-103
  organization of, 98, 104, 122-124
  point-by-point, 122-124
  process, 98
  review of, 125
  structure vocabulary, 106, 115-122
  thesis statement for, 99
  transition paragraph, 104-105
  transition signals and thesis statements, 102
Examination questions, 126
Examples, as support, 67-70

Facts vs. opinions, 65-66
Figures and statistics, 70-72
Final copy, writing of, 13-15, 92-93
Fragments, *see* Sentence fragments
Freewriting, 6-8
Future verb tenses, 267-269

Gerunds, 248-252
  definition of, 248
  as objects, 249-250
  as objects of preposition, 250-251
  review of, 251-252
  as subjects, 248-249

Illustrative incidents as support, 67-70
Importance, order of, 60-62
  topic sentences for, 61-62
  transition signals for, 60-61
Independent clauses, *see* Clauses
Inserters, comma used with, 254-255
Introducers, comma used after, 254
Introduction, *see* Introductory paragraph
Introductory clause, 180-181
  chart of verbs, 183
Introductory paragraph, 76, 78-80

Key nouns, repetition of, 39-40

Letter of inquiry, 193
Library, using, 145-152
  card catalog, 145-147
  other sources of information, 150-152
  periodical indexes, 147-149
  review of, 152
Linkers, comma used with, 255
Linking expressions, *see* Transitions between paragraphs
Listing, 5-6
Logical division organization
  essay, 100-103
  paragraph, 49, 58-62
  thesis statements for, 102-103
  topic sentences for, 61-62
  transition signals, chart of, 59
Logical order, 48-50, 53-64
  of cause and effect, 104-113
  chronological, 53-58, 95-100
  of comparison and contrast, 113-125
  division of, 58-62, 100-103
  of order of importance, 60-62
  review of, 63
  transition signals for, 59

Manner, distance, and frequency clause, 198-199
Microfilm, 150

Narrowing a topic, 4
Nonrestrictive participial phrases, 234
Nonrestrictive relative clauses, 209-211, 255
Noun clauses, 180-194
  chart of, 181
  definition of, 180
  in object pattern, 188-189
  punctuation of, 182
  review of, 193-194
  sequence of tenses in, 182
  in subject pattern, 186-188
  of subjunctive, 184-186
  of that-clauses, 182-184
  types of, 180-181
  of wh-question clauses, 186-190
  of yes/no question clauses, 190-192

Object of preposition, relative clause as, 218-220
Opinions vs. facts, 65-66
Order of importance paragraph, 60-62
  transition signals, chart of, 61
Outlining
  essay, 83-86, 89
  paragraph, 9-11, 33-36
Overcoordination, 165

Paired conjunctions, *see* Correlative conjunctions
Paragraph, 16-28
  assignment format, 18
  chronological order, 53-58
  coherence, 17
  concluding sentence, 25-27
  correspondence to essay, 77
  definition of, 16

logical division of ideas, 58-63
logical order, 48-50
order of importance, 60-63
parts of, 17
review of, 27
title, 19
topic sentences, 19-25
transition, 104-105
transition signals, 56, 59, 60-61
unity, 17
"Parallel form" rule, 34-35
Parallelism, 168-171, *see also* Conjunctions
definition of, 168
Paraphrases and paraphrasing, 133-137
review of, 144
Participial phrases, 230-248
from adverbial clauses, 238-245
definition of, 230
position of, 234, 239, 242
punctuation of, 234, 239, 242
from relative clauses, 230-238
review of, 251-252
from simple sentences, 245-246
Participles, 229-252
active voice, 231-232
chart of, 230
continuous form, 232-233
definition of, 229
passive voice, 232
perfect, 233-234
Past verb tenses, 266-267
Patterns of essay organization, *see* Essay patterns of organization
Periodical index, 147-149
Place adverbial clauses, 197-198
Plagiarism, 128, 140
Planning stage, 9-11
Point-by-point organization, 122-124
comparison/contrast, 122-124
Possessive relative clauses, 215-218
Present verb tenses, 265-266
Prewriting, 3-9
Processes of writing, 3-15, 89-93
stage I: prewriting, 3-9
stage II: planning (outlining), 9-11
stage III: writing and revising drafts, 12-15
writing and revising the essay, 89-93
Pronouns
as adverbs, 208-209
consistent use of, 41
as objects, 213-215
as objects of preposition, 218-220
in phrases of quality, 222-223
in phrases of quantity, 220-222
relative, 211-215
as subjects, 211-213
Proofreading, 13, 90-91
Punctuation, 182, 253-261
of adverbial clauses, 195
with connectors, 257
colon, 259-260
comma, 162, 253-256
of compound sentences, 157
with coordinators, 175, 253, 254-256
with end-of-paragraph signals, 26
of formal salutations, 260
with inserters, 255
between items in series, 257
with introducers, 254
with linkers, 253, 254, 255
lists of, 259
of long quotations, 259
of participial phrases, 234, 239, 242
of relative (adjective) clauses, 209-211
semicolon, 256-258
between sentences, 175, 256
of strong contrast clauses, 204
of subtitles, 259
of thesis statements, 103
with time notations, 259
of topic sentences, 62
of work cited lists, 142
Purpose, of writing, 2-3
Purpose clauses, 202-203

Quotations, 67, 128-133
punctuation of, 129-131, 259, 260-261
review of, 144
Quotation marks, 260-261

Reason clauses, 200
Reference books, 146, 150
References, using outside, *see* Documenting sources
Relative adverbial clauses, 224-225
Relative adverbs, 208-209, 224-225
Relative clauses, 208-228
and adverbs, 208-209
definition of, 208
as objects, 213-215
as objects of preposition, 218-220
in phrases of quality, 222-223
in phrases of quantity, 220-222
positions of, 209
possessive relative clause, 215-218
punctuation of, 209-211
relative adverbial clauses, 224-225
relative pronouns, *see* Pronouns
review of, 225-227
as subject of clause, 211-213
Reptition of key nouns, 39-40
Reporting verbs and phrases, 130
Restrictive clauses and phrases, 209-211, 234
Result clauses, 201
Revising, *see* Drafts, writing and revising
Run-on sentences, 175-177
Semicolon, 256-258
in compound sentences, 159, 161
with conjunctive adverbs, 44, 159-161
Sentence connectors, 42-44
charts of, 43, 262-263
Sentence problems, 171-179
choppy sentences, 173-174
comma splices, 174-177
fragments, 171-173
review of, 179
run-on, 175
stringy, 177-178
Sentences, kinds of, 156-164
complex, 45, 161-164
compound, 44, 157-161, 254
compound-complex, 164
simple, 156
Sequence of tenses, 182
Simple sentences, 156
Stringy sentences, 177-178
Structure vocabulary
cause and effect, 108-112
comparison, 115-118
contrast, 119-122
Subjunctive noun clauses, 184-186
Subordinating conjunctions, 43, 45, 156, 262-263
adverbial, 196
noun clauses, 181
relative clauses, 208-209
subordination vs. coordination, 165-167
Subordinator, *see* Subordinating conjunctions
Summarizing, 137-140
review of, 144
Supporting sentences, 17, 29

That-clauses, 182-186
subjunctive, 184-186
Thesis statements, 78-82, 99-100
Time clauses, 196-197
Titles, how to write, 19
Tone, 2-3
Topic sentences, 11, 17, 19-25, 55
for chronological order, 55-56
controlling idea in, 22-24
for logical division and order of importance, 61-62
position of, 20
tips for logical division/order of importance, 62
two parts of, 22-24
Transition between paragraphs, 77, 86-89
Transition paragraphs, 104-105
Transition signals, 17, 41-48, *see also* Structure vocabulary
charts of, for general use, 43, 262-263
for chronological order, 56-57
of clause connectors, 44-45
for logical division, 59

for order of importance, 60-61
of others, 42, 43, 45
punctuation of, 254-255, 257
of sentence connectors, 43-44

Unity, 17, 29-33
Urgency verbs and adjectives, 184-185
Using the library, *see* Library

Verb forms, summary of, 264-269
future, 267-269
past, 266, 267
present, 265-266
Verb tenses, *see* Verb forms
Verbs of urgency, advisability, and desirability, 184

Wh-question clauses, 186-190
Works cited, list of, 141-143
Writing an essay, *see* Essay
Writing and revising
essay, 89-93
paragraph, 12-15
Writing process, *see* Processes of writing

Yes/no question clauses, 190-192